KALEIDOSCOPE

SHAPING LANGUAGE, SHAPING IDENTITY

Second Edition

D0222744

Kendall Hunt
publishing company

DEBORAH SCAGGS

Cover image © Shutterstock, Inc. Used under license.

www.kendallhunt.com
Send all inquiries to:
4050 Westmark Drive
Dubuque, IA 52004-1840

Copyright © 2016, 2019 by Kendall Hunt Publishing Company

ISBN 978-1-5249-6028-5

All rights reserved. No part of this publication may be reproduced,
stored in a retrieval system, or transmitted, in any form or by any means,
electronic, mechanical, photocopying, recording, or otherwise,
without the prior written permission of the copyright owner.

Published in the United States of America

CONTENTS

CHAPTER 11: ARGUMENT-SYNTHESIS   255

PART 4: APPENDICES 289

APPENDIX A: CITATION KNOW-HOW   291

APPENDIX B: ANNOTATING RESEARCH MATERIALS   325

APPENDIX C: COLLABORATIVE PROJECTS AND TEAMWORK   329

PART 1

Getting Oriented to Writing and Why It Matters

1

CHAPTER 1

Introduction

In this chapter, we will cover:

1. key principles to keep in mind as you write;

2. what being an effective communicator means, especially at university or college; and

3. how this text is structured to help you become a stronger writer.

A kaleidoscope is a useful metaphor for how to see yourself as a writer and to see writing in general. If you have never seen one, a kaleidoscope is a long, enclosed cylinder with mirrors that contains colored

FIGURE 1.1 A Kaleidoscope

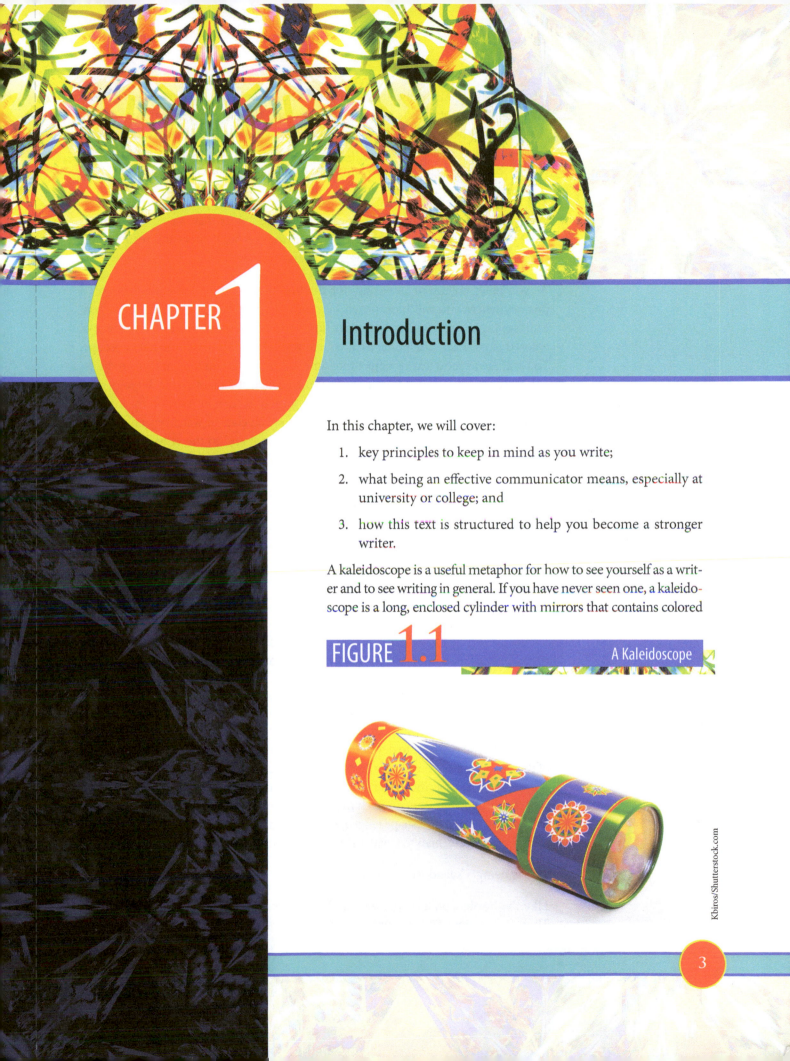

Kbiros/Shutterstock.com

pieces of glass, plastic, or beads. As you peer into it from one end, light enters in from the other. The light reflects off of the mirrors, and the pieces form patterns. As you shake the cylinder (or, in some cases, turn a knob at the one end), these colored pieces move and change shape, creating new patterns. You will never see the same pattern twice because every shake or turn moves the colored pieces and creates something new.

The image on the cover of this text is an example of what you might see in a kaleidoscope, and its collection of lines, shapes, and colors that is ever-changing is what makes it a useful metaphor for what writing can be. Writers and readers shift perspectives, shape understanding, and change minds.

As you enter college or university for the first time, you will be embarking on a journey where you will be exposed to a number of different disciplines: English, Philosophy, History, Biology, and Arts (just to name a few), each a different piece of colored glass. Each discipline, each course you take, is a turn of the kaleidoscope. You will never see a text or object the same way twice as you look at it from different perspectives. Imagine peering into a microscope at a plant cell in Biology class and then peering through a telescope at the rings of Saturn in Astronomy. Imagine reading a poem about the family bonds in an English class or watching a film about World War I in a History class. From the very close and to the very far, from the everyday and familiar to the historic and unfamiliar, your experience in academia creates a shift (a turn of the knob) that shapes how you will view the world.

Part of that change comes from reading and writing. As you encounter a writing situation, you may need to shift your perspective to take into consideration what others might also say. You have to shift your perspective so that you can communicate your ideas with others, thereby shifting *their* perspective. As you learn to write for different purposes, different readers, and on different topics, you shape your writing style to accommodate the new situation. Writers need to adjust the way they communicate to meet these circumstances. Although this may seem quite obvious, the ways in which a writer makes those adjustments are not so easily accomplished, and it takes time and practice to make writing strong and effective.

At university, writers also must adjust their writing for the different kinds of writing that there are. Sometimes you will write reports on scientific experimentation in Biology or Anatomy class; sometimes you will have to interpret a poem or short story; other times you will have to develop an argument for a position on public policy. Each of these require that you adopt a "writerly self" who is writing for a specific reason in a specific form to a specific reader. You are shifting and shaping your language, your assumptions, and your stance, which means you are also shaping an identity as a writer. Your ability to shift and shape language means you can take on different perspectives and communicate them to a wider range and multiplicity of readers.

This is being a kaleidoscopic writer.

Like the borders on a map, there are boundaries that seem to exist in academia. There are majors and minors and certificates; there are colleges of Education,

Nursing and Health Sciences, Arts and Sciences, and Business; there are departments and disciplines, yet all of these are parts of a whole. They are interlocking elements that can be shifted through or into one another. As you shake or turn a kaleidoscope's knob, the image changes, perhaps in color or shape, yet it is still an image that is made up of parts that create the whole. As you move from English into Mathematics or from Art into Business, think of the kaleidoscope and how each experience is contributing to the whole of your experience, providing you with a rich array of perspectives that will help you to understand the complexities of the world. In other words, although they may appear disparate, these various disciplines contribute to a larger view of the world. Each discipline, each course, each class, each writing/reading assignment contributes to the end product: an educated individual who can see the complexities of the world, make sense out of it, and make informed decisions about how to engage in it.

The goal for you—and this text—is to understand when to change perspective or your "writerly self," why, and how. As you move through this text, you will be exposed to the expectations of university, why these expectations matter, and how to make adjustments to not only what you are writing about but also how to best communicate to an audience. Let us begin this exploration of your writerly self, focusing on the writer you are now and build up to the kind of writer you want to be and will become at university as you learn more about the world in its kaleidoscopic nature.

A NEW WAY OF SEEING

Writers are always shifting, changing, and altering the ways they see their subject matter as well as themselves as writers. As you move through your studies at university, you are seeing a new pattern, a new way of *seeing*. Like every turn of a kaleidoscope, writers shape and are shaped by every experience they have with reading, writing, and thinking, allowing for new ideas to emerge. One of the goals of this textbook is to help you, the student-writer, to learn to see the complexities of writing as you work through your writing process and engage in the world—from its politics to science, from literature to laboratory experimentation, from local to international concerns—and to see that with every turn of the page or movement from one course into another, your kaleidoscopic view changes.

Foxy's Forest Manufacture/Shutterstock.com

To be an effective communicator, which is what writing and reading are all about, you need to have something to say, something you are passionate about, believe in, or something that you want others to know. You have to keep an open mind, however, that your readers may not know much about your topic or have a different view of it, be as passionate about it as you are, or believe it is important. The readers have their own perspective, experience, and beliefs, and if you want them to hear you, you have to imagine what they know, what that knowledge might suggest about how they view their world around them, what they might not believe or will have a hard time accepting, and how they might best be persuaded to listen or reconsider and adopt your perspective.

You, the writer, are in control of the focus and shape of what you write and what the reader will read. You control the kaleidoscopic view that your reader will see. Hence, you need to understand the best way to express yourself to meet the needs of your readers without compromising your own perspective. You shape the message to shape your readers' response to it.

This is kaleidoscopic writing.

There are boundaries and lines in the world. On a map, one state, one country, one city is defined by lines on a page that indicate "here is where I live; there is where you live." These lines were drawn for a number of reasons: geography, politics, land ownership, etc. However, those lines are imagined. There is no "real" or physical boundary that lies along a border. In fact, you could stand in two states at the same time placing one foot on either side of a state line. You could swim in the ocean where the Gulf of Mexico and the Caribbean Sea meet, and the only way you would know you were in one or the other would be because of a GPS system. These kinds of boundaries function to show "here" and "there," to allow us to move between places and directions and to help us make sense of the world around us, yet they are still manufactured, created. Thus, they can be traversed.

Each course you take at university helps to shape you as a person who is well rounded—that is, experienced in many disciplines. As you adopt new ways of seeing the world, you learn to choose which way is the best for a given situation. Each new experience (in this case, each new reading, thinking, and writing activity about ideas/texts/subject matter) alters ever so slightly the way you see a situation. As your learning shifts, so does how you explain the world around you. You are coming into your own and shaping your own kaleidoscopic version of the world, in all of its complexity and wonder. With time and practice, these various experiences become explorations into how different views contribute to a more comprehensive understanding of the world from which you will harness the power of what it means to be a writer.

As most Americans would argue, there is a gulf between high school and university with regard to what is actually done in secondary (high school) and postsecondary (college or university) education. This text does not aim to explain the reasons how this gulf was created. Rather, this text aims to bridge the gap with explanations, exercises, and writing assignments that make explicit what is expected and why. This will help you—the writer—understand how to make your writing more effective and meet the university-level standards that your instructors want. In order for this transition to occur, writers must understand a few fundamental principles of writing that inform how this book is structured, why the chapters are what they are, and why the exercises and assignments will help you to become more effective and persuasive writers.

KEY PRINCIPLES FOR WRITING

1. There is an effective method for writing called the "process of writing" or the "writing process."

2. There are techniques or strategies for how to work through that process.

3. There are strategies for identifying the important elements of any writing situation: the writer, the reader, and the subject.

4. There is a kind of writing at university called "academic writing," and it has special features and imbedded expectations that you learn to control over time.

5. There are different kinds of writing that you will do at university, and each discipline (major) has its own features. There are commonalities between them, yet there are differences that make them unique and discipline specific.

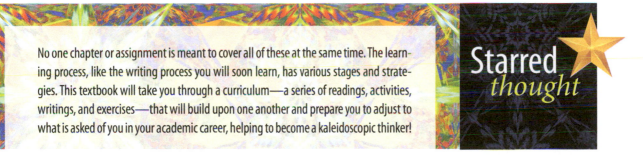

No one chapter or assignment is meant to cover all of these at the same time. The learning process, like the writing process you will soon learn, has various stages and strategies. This textbook will take you through a curriculum—a series of readings, activities, writings, and exercises—that will build upon one another and prepare you to adjust to what is asked of you in your academic career, helping to become a kaleidoscopic thinker!

Starred *thought*

The intention of this text is to help you understand what differences there are between high school writing expectations and university or college-level writing expectations so that you, the writer, can make the transition into higher education more smoothly. This textbook is unlike others in that it will reveal what kind of writing you are being asked to do; why you are being asked to do it; and how, in very explicit terms, to go about writing. You will come to control your writing, directing it to say what it is you want to say, and you will learn how powerful the written language can be.

The first few chapters are set up to orientate you to the ways universities or colleges expect students to approach writing and reading in general and why. They will take you through a journey of examining what your own writing practices are, what works and what does not work, and will offer you opportunities to try new strategies that have proven to many writers to be helpful. As the textbook progresses, you will begin to write in specific genres, using a variety of readings as a place of departure or a place from which you can develop what you want to write about, and the kinds of writing you will be introduced to will become more "academic" versions of writing, the kinds that you might typically encounter in your studies.

Before we get started, complete the following survey. This will raise your awareness about your relationship to reading, writing, and thinking that we will compare to what you think when you have finished the work in this textbook.

Name: _____ Course: _____ Date: _____

PRE-SURVEY

How much do you agree to the following statements? Circle the appropriate number following each statement.

5	4	3	2	1
Strongly Agree	**Agree**	**Not sure**	**Disagree**	**Strongly Disagree**

1	I am able to express my ideas clearly.	5	4	3	2	1
2	When I write, I am able to identify my purpose for writing.	5	4	3	2	1
3	When I write, I am able to identify the needs of my audience.	5	4	3	2	1
4	I am an active reader.	5	4	3	2	1
5	I can identify and use appropriate sources.	5	4	3	2	1
6	I give good, effective feedback to my peers.	5	4	3	2	1
7	I am a confident writer.	5	4	3	2	1
8	I understand the concept of genre.	5	4	3	2	1
9	I want to write.	5	4	3	2	1
10	"Writing is a process" is a concept that I appreciate	5	4	3	2	1
11	Writing is easy for me.	5	4	3	2	1
12	I am able to help my peers with their writing.	5	4	3	2	1
13	I can apply the rhetorical triangle to any writing situation.	5	4	3	2	1
14	I understand the "features of the form" concept.	5	4	3	2	1
15	I am a writer.	5	4	3	2	1
16	I use active reading strategies often.	5	4	3	2	1
17	I know how to do academic research.	5	4	3	2	1
18	I can identify errors in my writing.	5	4	3	2	1
19	I can correct errors in my writing.	5	4	3	2	1
20	I use several writing strategies.	5	4	3	2	1

CHAPTER 2

How Writing Works

In this chapter, you will learn to:

1. describe three ways this text approaches writing;

2. identify key terms about writing that will appear throughout this text;

3. define the components of the "rhetorical triangle";

4. use active reading strategies to critically read texts; and

5. evaluate the use of active reading strategies.

WRITING APPROACH TRIFECTA

There are many ways that instructors teach writing, and this textbook approaches writing from a blended perspective. There are three approaches to writing—the trifecta—that we will use to improve your writing.

1. *Rhetorical Approach to Writing*: This approach to writing focuses on three major rhetorical components: the reader, the writer, and the subject matter. The writer (you) is writing about a topic (the subject matter) to someone who is reading it (the reader). There is a dynamic between these three components that, once fully realized, will help a writer determine how much background information to provide, what kind of examples are needed to illustrate a point, what kind of sources should be used, and how informal or formal the style should be.

2. *Discourse Communities Approach to Writing*: Depending upon to whom you are writing to and why, you will need to adjust the language and style that you use to meet the expectations of your reader and of the subject matter. For example, when you share adventures from a weekend outing with your friends, you might include details that you would not share with your parents. If your listeners are close friends, ones that you know very well and speak with often, you might provide more details than you would to someone you just met. Another example is when you discuss literature in the classroom with your fellow peers and your instructor that might be quite different than how you would talk about the literature with your non-English major friends. You make decisions about what to say and how to say it based upon who is listening and the relationship you have with them.

3. *Genre-based Approach to Writing*: "*Genre*" is a French word that means "kind." Every piece of writing, from a diary entry to a research paper, has particular features that make it what it is. Like genres of movies—action, drama, comedy, documentary, and all the different kinds within those—there are *genres of writing*. Each discipline has its own set of expectations for writing. Hence, when you are writing at university, you are also writing in particular *genres*. In Science classes, you might have to conduct an experience or lab activity that requires you to document what you did and what the results were. You would be asked to write a report that follows a very specific structure, omits "flowery" language, and provides the facts or the observations as they occurred. In a Literature class, on the other hand, you might read a poem and have to interpret its meaning. The meaning may not be obvious, so you have to explain how you are reading the lines and words and how they, together, create an idea. Your literary analysis will not have "facts" as much as it will have claims that you will support with evidence from the text.

Altogether, then, we are going to look at the complexity of writing using the rhetorical situation, the discourse community, and the genre to determine the best method for you to communicate your message to someone.

KEY TERMS AND DEFINITIONS FOR WORK AHEAD

Because we are learning to write at university, we need to have some working vocabulary that will help us to analyze texts (yours and others) and create texts that will meet the desired outcome. The following are key terms, followed by a brief explanation of what they mean for us as writers, that we will use throughout the textbook. As we move through the chapters, we will learn more about each of these and how they function as you write and read.

ACADEMIA (OR THE ACADEMY): These words are intended to mean the environment of higher education, whether a two-year junior college or a four-year university. There are particular kinds of thinking, writing, and reading expected in academia. Sometimes these activities are focused on the specific learning in a particular class, but more generally, there is a particular way of seeing the world—critically, analytically, and reflectively—that make "academic" reading, writing, and thinking unique.

STANDARD ACADEMIC AMERICAN ENGLISH (SAAE): This is a term meant to convey a specific style or register that is valued in academia. Most students know that when they write in their classes, they are supposed to be formal and correct, yet what does "formal" and "correct" look like? We will learn the differences between grammar (what rules govern English as a distinct language), usage (what expectations there are in a particular community), and style (what values exist in ways writers combine sentences and ideas). In other words, we will focus on American university language use.

STRATEGIES: Some instructors may use the word "skills" as a way to describe discrete steps or actions that writers and readers follow or take to read and write. However, this text will use the word "strategies" to indicate *possible methods or tools* for accomplishing a task or doing some activity. Depending upon the text and context, readers and writers must determine what kinds of strategies are best suited for the desired outcome. Sometimes we will need to combine different reading and writing strategies to get the most effective and thorough understanding of the text. Then, depending upon what we are going to do with that text (whether we are responding to it or analyzing or synthesizing it with other texts), we will be able to determine what strategies are the best for meeting that goal.

This text has a number of suggested strategies along the way, all intended to build your repertoire of possible methods for accomplishing what you are trying to do. You might think of these strategies as tools in the toolbox that you carry with you from course to course, from one writing situation to another. What works in one situation may not work in another, so it is best to have several different tools that can be tried. Not all of the strategies will work for everyone or for every situation, yet having options to help you overcome trouble spots or challenges in your academic work is what these are intended to do. You may find that a combination of these strategies is the most helpful or that certain strategies are most helpful only in specific circumstances that you discover for yourself. The idea is to keep an open mind and try them out to see what works best for you.

TEXTS: This is a term used to indicate the general idea of something we examine at university. Some texts are written, some are oral, and some are visual. Some are a combination of these. The word "text" will mean different things as we work with different kinds of reading and writing. A "text" might be a work of art, a short story, or a nonfiction essay. It might be an advertisement or an object, such as the layout of a park or room in a house. "Text," then, is the "thing" we are examining. How we examine it depends on the kind of "thing" it is and why we are looking at it.

INTERTEXTUALITY: This is a term used to describe the relationship between texts. Often, writers will include explicit or implicit references to other texts in their own writing. These references are a kind of intellectual engagement that occurs when writers explore the ideas, concepts, and texts of others and incorporate them in their own writing. You can think of intertextuality as one text shaping how we read another, which is what academic writing allows writers to do: engage in an ongoing conversation.

CONTEXT: This term is used in conjunction with the word "text" and is used to indicate the particular surroundings the "text" in question is in. We might look at the historical context, for example, of a painting or advertisement and ask what was going on at the time this text was made that would help us to understand its meaning. We might look at the cultural context, for example, of a novel by Tim O'Brien to determine how his novel *The Things They Carried* spoke to a particular American experience of Vietnam. The surrounding time period, the events, the ideas, and the beliefs of a particular place all shape how we might read and interpret texts, so we must be ready to ask questions and investigate the nature of a text's context.

SUBJECT (OR TOPIC): Every text is focused on some subject matter—a topic. Magazines like *Vogue* focus on fashion; *Muscle and Fitness* focuses on health and body building; *Home and Garden* focuses on domestic life. In academia, the subject matter is tied to the discipline you are studying, so you might be looking at plant cells in one class and then switch to business economics in the next. The subject matter, therefore, will determine what *can be said* and *how it should be said* in the *context* it is found.

WRITERS (OR AUTHORS): There are as many kinds of writers as there are readers, each with their own process. Some writers, like Stephen King, typically write for an adult audience; other writers, like Suzanne Collins, write for young adults. These kinds of authors typically write fiction, yet there are other kinds of writers who write nonfiction. Nonfiction writers might write narratives about their personal experiences, memos about new safety measures for their employer, or reports about experiments in a laboratory. Each one of these writers has a different purpose, a different set of readers, and different subject matter. They all must understand their role as an author and the relationship they have with their readers.

READERS (OR AUDIENCE): Consider the different kinds of texts you read. These may include online blogs, emails, text messages, newspapers, sports stats, graphic novels, textbooks, maps, menus, assignments, and academic articles. Each of these is a different kind of text with features that make them what they are. We do not read text messages the same way we do our textbooks, and that is because these texts have different functions. Hence, we have to change our method for reading to meet the needs of the given text and reason for reading it. For our purposes, then, consider yourself not just a writer but a reader who is engaged in communication with other writers who are also readers.

CONTROLLING IDEA (OR THESIS): Your experience with writing has imprinted the idea that a "thesis statement" is needed at the beginning of an essay to establish your essay's focus. This is true, in part. Establishing foci for your essays is needed, but how a focus is stated and where it is located will shift according to the genre in which you are writing, your purpose, and the audience you imagine is reading your work. "Thesis" is also a word adopted from the sciences and suggests a rigid understanding of what is true. "Controlling idea" suggests its function for writing: It controls what you say about the main topic or subject matter and how you say it. Whether you "prove" it to your reader is contingent upon how convincing you are to your reader. What is "true" is what you can prove or persuade your reader to consider as "true." Hence, instead of thesis, we will use "controlling idea" or "argument" for what you have previously called "thesis."

Now that we have established a few key terms that we will be using throughout this text, let us now turn to some fundamental content that every writer needs to know and practice.

THE RHETORICAL SITUATION

Every writing is *situated*, placed in a specific time and place where the writer must communicate with someone about something. There are three components that inform that situation: the writer, the reader, and the subject. This is referred to as the rhetorical situation or the rhetorical triangle, a concept we learn from Lloyd Bitzer.[1]

FIGURE 2.1　　　　　　　　An equilateral triangle representing the rhetorical triangle.

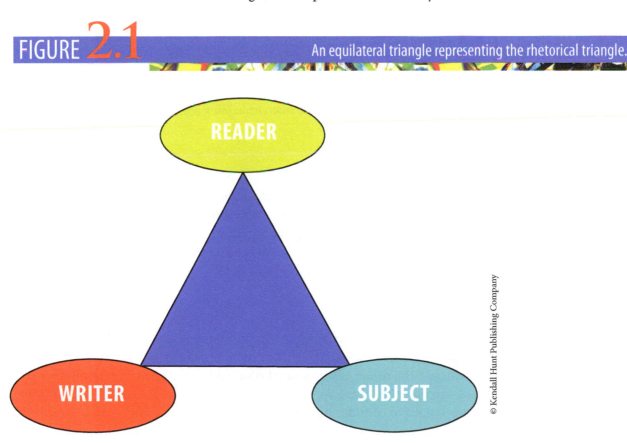

© Kendall Hunt Publishing Company

---
[1]Lloyd Bitzer, "The Rhetorical Situation." Philosophy and Rhetoric 1.1 (1968): 1-14. Print.

This image of an equilateral triangle—each side and angle are equal to each other—sets up the perfect analogy for how writing works. Each component—the subject, the writer, the reader—are of equal importance. If you are missing any one of these elements or do not fully understand the role each plays in a writing situation, then the text you produce will fall short of its intended purpose: to communicate. The *rhetorical* element is the relationship between these parts and the influence each has or plays on the others.

We can think of this rhetorical triangle in another way.

THE SUBJECT: the topic, issue, focus of a text, also the WHAT of a text

THE WRITER: the person(s) who is(are) composing a text, also the WHY of a text

THE READER: the person(s) who is(are) reading the text, also the HOW of a text

WHAT

The Subject: Some topics are highly specialized, such as quantum mechanics or impressionist art, and require a great deal of experience in the field or advanced coursework to fully understand, as they are not commonly used or experienced by most people. Other topics are less specialized because they are commonly experienced or studied by others. The subject matter helps to determine how much background information is needed, to what extent special vocabulary needs to be used, and how detailed or general a writer can be when explaining something to the reader.

WHY

The Writer: The reason why a writer writes something is what helps to shape what the writer needs to do in the actual text. The purpose of the text, whether to persuade, inform, entertain, persuade, or any number of other reasons, is what defines why the writer is writing about *this* subject at *this* time. The writer must make decisions about how to use words (and which ones) to create sentences that create paragraphs that create the final product.

HOW

The Reader: Who the writer imagines to be the reader directly impacts what choices the writer makes. The reader, then, is not just the instructor or fellow classmates. The reader is someone who would be interested in reading what you have written. What you have written will determine who reads it and vice versa. You will need to consider if your reader is an expert or a novice, well versed and read in the subject matter or new to it. Depending upon who you imagine your reader to be, your text will reflect it.

When we write, we make assumptions about who might read our text and why, and our own purpose informs what we are writing about. Thus, we need to keep these three components in constant dialogue with one another.

Starred *thought*

GENRE

There is fiction and non-fiction, technical and business, entertaining and informative, personal and argumentative genres in a variety of contexts (business, professional, personal, academic, multimedia) for a variety of reasons (to motivate others to take action, to verify some data point or decision, to reflect upon personal choices or experiences). There are a number of genres you might encounter in academia, and this textbook will take an in-depth look at several of the most often used. Here is a start, though, to give some idea of what is ahead.

Depending upon the text, purpose, and discipline, you will be asked to write *analyses*. In short, an analysis is when you take apart a large text or object to figure out what smaller parts are there. In some ways, you are dissecting a text, taking it apart to see how it functions, what its strengths and weaknesses are, what problems and solutions exists, or what the driving force is behind a text.

MEMOIR: This particular form of writing asks the writer to reveal insights about an experience to the reader. This kind of writing has dialogue, vivid details, and insightful reflection about the importance of that experience to some larger point. What that "point" is depends upon what the experience is and what the writer has learned. In some ways, the writer is analyzing his or her experience in order to convey meaning to the reader, yet this genre tends to be viewed as a more personal genre.

REVIEW: This particular form of writing asks the writer to evaluate a "thing" based upon criteria and show to what extent that "thing" meets the criteria. The "thing" could be a movie, a book, an advertisement, a new restaurant, or even an experience. This kind of writing includes a short summary or a brief description of what is being evaluated along with a detailed analysis of how it meets the standards or set of values that the writer establishes as important in the evaluation of the "thing."

RHETORICAL ANALYSIS: This particular kind of analysis focuses on how a text conveys meaning by looking at specific components of the text. Instead of evaluating the strength and weakness of a text's argument, the focus is on how the text has been put together. Rhetorical analysis is interested in the structure of the text, the kinds of support and sources used, the use of rhetorical strategies like *logos*, *pathos*, *ethos*, and the ways in which the writer engages the reader.

LITERARY ANALYSIS: This particular form of analysis asks a reader to interpret a literary text, which may be a novel, short story, poem, song lyrics, or drama/film. Typically, literary analysis focus on a theme, symbol, character, or setting and how these elements suggest a particular understanding of the text as a whole. Some literary analyses are fairly basic: Writers explain the impact of the setting upon the plot or explain the development of a character's choices in the action of the text. (There are several approaches to literary analyses, and the text you are analyzing often determines what you can say about it.) Some literary analyses are more complex as they examine multiple literary elements and their impact on the interpretation of a text or as they incorporate outside scholarship on the various interpretations of a text.

VISUAL ANALYSIS: This particular kind of analysis focuses on how we interpret nonwritten texts, such as artwork, performances (like dance or live plays), and film. Visual analysis is interested in how a nonwritten text communicates a meaning. Depending upon the text being analyzed, you will look at different components. For example, in artwork, you will look at color, shading, and placement of objects. You will look at how the painter used brushstrokes. You might consider if the painting is an oil painting or watercolor or if a canvas or wood was used. There are different elements we look at when we examine sculptures, film, or live plays. The end goal, however, is the same: to interpret what the text seems to be saying and ground that interpretation in analysis of the parts.

CRITICAL ANALYSIS: This particular form of writing asks readers and writers to examine an individual text (usually non-fiction) very carefully and, using a critical lens, analyze the issues raised by the author(s) of that text. You need to step-back from personal reactions you have about the topic and focus, instead, on *what the author's perspective is and why s/he holds that point of view.* The text and what it says and why ideas, perspectives, or issues are viewed the way they are is your only task. As you analyze the what and the why, you pay close attention to the claims the author is making, what evidence s/he is using, and any counterarguments that are or are not being addressed.

ARGUMENT-SYNTHESIS: This particular kind of writing is a blend of genres as explained previously. Typically, a writer will examine several texts (written, visual, and/or spoken), looking for ways they intersect each other and speak to a larger issue. Writers then discover an overarching theme or idea that all of these texts address. Out of this intersection, writers may discover that there are multiple ways of seeing an issue, from different perspectives and mediums, that will help them make an argument about some issue or idea. For example, a writer might analyze a visual text, such as a film about war, use historical records to show the context of that war, or incorporate a short story that depicts war, all in an effort to argue something about "war" in general or a specific war that the writer sees as insightful and worthy of consideration. Thus, the writer analyzes these distinct texts, synthesizes them, and then makes an argument about the issue they all address. This is the most complicated and complex kind of writing.

These give you a sample of how writing is varied, and as we begin our work within the genres, you will learn more about what they have in common and what makes them unique. You will be given opportunities to practice doing these different kinds of analysis, too, and we will build upon them as we move forward.

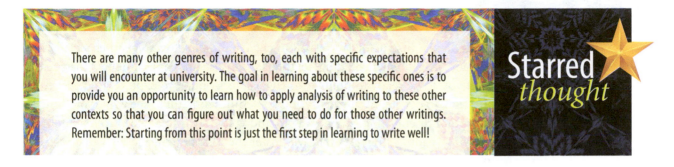

There are many other genres of writing, too, each with specific expectations that you will encounter at university. The goal in learning about these specific ones is to provide you an opportunity to learn how to apply analysis of writing to these other contexts so that you can figure out what you need to do for those other writings. Remember: Starting from this point is just the first step in learning to write well!

CRITICAL READING, THINKING, AND WRITING

Not only do we need to pay attention to writing, but we also need to examine how reading and thinking are part of the process for how writing works. When we write about a topic, we need to be able to know what we know and what we do not know so that we can direct our reading and research in the right direction. When we read, we adjust our attention depending upon our goals. Not all writing is the same, and neither is all reading the same. In the case of writing, we need to turn our attention to *active reading*, the kind that brings us close to the text and close to our own understanding of how a text works. If we can become skilled at analyzing other people's writing, then we can become skilled at critiquing our own. Reading and thinking critically also means that we engage texts of all sorts in a manner consistent with our intention to write critically about them. Let us turn our attention, then, to the ways we can engage texts with a critical eye and mind.

Consider the following dichotomy, a contrast between "active" and "passive" reading.

Active Reading	vs	Passive Reading
Movement		Stagnation
Action		Inaction
Questioning		Entertaining
Engaged		Uninvolved
Challenging		Accepting
Writing		Unquestioning
Opened up		Closed off
Multiple meanings		Singular meaning
Public		Private
Connecting		Restricted
Complexity		Simplicity
Possibility		Oversight

Pleasure reading is a kind of *passive reading* because we do not DO anything with the reading. It is an escape from the everyday busy life. It does not require much from us except enjoyment for its own sake.

In academia, instructors want you to engage in *active reading*, an especially important aspect when reading textbooks, novels, and assignments. Instructors want you to be ready to pounce, to engage, to wonder, to explore, to discover, to question, to debate. At university, it is sometimes difficult to see why something IS important or engaging, so one way to find your way into a text is to react to it by applying reading strategies that will foster the kinds of engagement that instructors want. As you practice active reading, you will begin to see what IS important and why. In turn, this realization helps you to become more successful writers because you are seeing the impact writing has upon a reader!

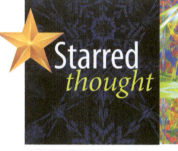

As you develop as a reader in academia, you will find that different texts in different courses require different kinds of reading. Some strategies might work better in one class than in another, or you might find that using them in tandem works for you. The goal is to try them out on multiple occasions in different courses to see what will become your method for active reading!

Here are some strategies for **active reading**:

Try these strategies at different times to evaluate which ones (or which combination) work the best and under what conditions. If you discover new strategies, share them with your class!

1. **HIGHLIGHTING:** As its name suggests, you are using a highlighter pen to highlight parts of a text. In History, you might highlight dates and events; in Mathematics, you might highlight an equation; in an English Literature course, you might highlight passages that explain a character's motivation. In other words, highlighting can be used universally but for different purposes. You might also consider using different colors for different kinds of highlighting. For example, you might use yellow to highlight passages in a

text, and you might use green to highlight key words or ideas. How you use colors to highlight is an individual practice, but the strategy is helpful across the board.

2. **POST-ITS:** If you have an aversion to writing or highlighting in your texts, you can opt for using post-its. They come in a variety of sizes, shapes, and colors to match your personal tastes and use. The idea is that you write on these pieces of paper what you would have highlighted or underlined. You might design your own method for what colors to use to mark important dates or important passages. You might even use one kind of post-it shape for your thoughts and another for what your instructor mentions or points out in class.

3. **UNDERLINING, CIRCLING, BOXING:** This is the most traditional approach to active reading. You simply use your pencil or pen and mark in your text those places that emerge as important to you. You might use circles, boxes, underlining or double-underlining, brackets, or any of your own shapes to mark the text. Whatever you choose to use, you are engaging that text, talking to it, talking back to it. This is where we begin to think critically about what is on the text and what our response is to it.

4. **DOODLES, THING-A-MA-BOBS, DOODADS:** Some readers create what we call "emoticons," a list of reactions that we place in the margins or in the middle of the page to call attention to some reaction we had. These "doodles" could be smiley faces where we found agreement or insight from what is on the page; we might use exclamation marks to indicate a strong disagreement or agreement with what the author has written; and we might create a whole set of other "thing-a-ma-bobs" to indicate our own idiosyncrasies when reading. This might include letters (e.g., "D" for a definition; "MP" for "major point"), numbers (e.g., to indicate a list of ideas that are not already numbered in the text), and even a star, an X, or some other mark that we ascribe meaning to that makes sense to only us.

Many students tend to use strategies they already know without really examining why or what alternatives may be better. The easiest method is simply highlighting without any writing to accompany it, but easier is not always the most effective, not if you want to engage at the level of inquiry expected at university. "Helpful" and "effective" depend upon what you are reading, why you are reading it, and what you want to get out of the reading. Some texts—especially in the natural sciences and social sciences—may require more marginal notes that point out formulas or results.

Starred *thought*

5. **Coversheet:** Another approach to writing in the book without actually marking the actual book is to use a sheet of transparent material (e.g., rice paper) that lays over the page and upon which you write. The idea is that you can see the page through the paper, and as you read you are underlining, highlighting, or doodading on the sheet of paper rather than on the original page. You can "see through" the paper. This is one way to still "mark" what is important or what is interesting while keeping the original text pristine.

6. **Dialectical Notebook:** This is the most advanced of the active reading strategies. Typically, this kind of active reading requires a notebook or journal where you fold one sheet of paper in half vertically. On the left side of the crease mark, you write down key ideas, notes, questions, and important passages that you find in the text. On the right side, you include your thoughts, your reactions, your questions, and any explanation about why you made the note in the first place. What you are creating is a dialogue, a conversation between what is in the text and how you are responding to it. This movement from what is there on the original page to what you are thinking about it is a dialectic: a move between the text and your thinking, between what is said literally on the page and what you are interpreting or seeing "in between" the lines. Because you are taking more time to write out your reactions to the text, the level of engagement with the text is higher. Thus, this is one of the most sophisticated strategies for active reading.

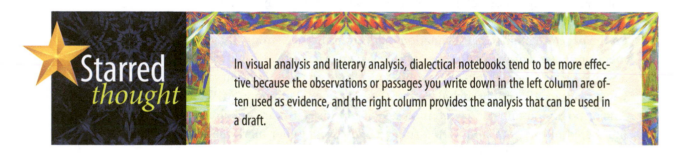

Starred *thought*

In visual analysis and literary analysis, dialectical notebooks tend to be more effective because the observations or passages you write down in the left column are often used as evidence, and the right column provides the analysis that can be used in a draft.

Read "Dancing with Professors" by Patricia Nelson Limerick and use one of the six strategies. Then, read "Entering the Conversation" by Mike Rose and use another strategy. Compare these.

DANCING WITH PROFESSORS:
THE TROUBLE WITH ACADEMIC PROSE

by Patricia Nelson Limerick

In ordinary life, when a listener cannot understand what someone has said, this is the usual exchange:

> *Listener:* I cannot understand what you are saying.

> *Speaker:* Let me try to say it more clearly.

But in scholarly writing in the late twentieth century, other rules apply. This is the implicit exchange:

> *Reader:* I cannot understand what you are saying.

> *Academic Writer:* Too bad. The problem is that you are an unsophisticated and untrained reader. If you were smarter, you would understand me.

The exchange remains implicit, because no one wants to say, "This doesn't make any sense," for fear that the response, "It would, if you were smarter" might actually be true.

While we waste our time fighting over ideological conformity in the scholarly world, horrible writing remains a far more important problem. For all their differences, most right-wing scholars and most left-wing scholars share a common allegiance to a cult of obscurity. Left, right, and center all hide behind the idea that unintelligible prose indicates a sophisticated mind. The politically correct and the politically incorrect come together in the violence they commit against the English language.

University presses have certainly filled their quota every year, in dreary monographs, tangled paragraphs, and impenetrable sentences. But trade publishers have also violated the trust of innocent and hopeful readers. As a prime example of unprovoked assaults on innocent words, consider the verbal behavior of Allan Bloom in *The Closing of the American Mind*, published by a large mainstream press. Here is a sample:

> If openness means to 'go with the flow,' it is necessarily an accommodation to the present. That present is so closed to doubt about so many things impeding the progress of its principles that unqualified openness to it would mean forgetting the despised alternatives to it, knowledge of which makes us aware of what is doubtful in it.

From *The New York Times*, © 1993 The New York Times. All rights reserved. Used by permission and protected by the Copyright Laws of the United States. The printing, copying, redistribution, or retransmission of this Content without express written permission is prohibited.

Is there a reader so full of blind courage as to claim to know what this passage means? Remember, the book in which this remark appeared was a lamentation over the failings of today's *students*, a call to arms to return to tradition and standards in education. And yet, in twenty years of paper grading, I do not recall many sentences that asked, so pathetically, to be put out of their misery.

Jump to the opposite side of the political spectrum from Allan Bloom, and literary grace makes no notable gains. Contemplate this breathless, indefatigable sentence from the geographer Allan Pred, and Mr. Pred and Mr. Bloom seem, if only in literary style, to be soul mates:

> If what is at stake is an understanding of the geographical and historical variations in the sexual division of productive and reproductive labor of contemporary local and regional variations in female wage labor and women's work outside the formal economy, of on-the-ground variations in the everyday context of women's lives, inside and outside of their families, then it must be recognized that, at some nontrivial level, none of the corporal practices associated with these variations can be severed from spatially and temporally specific linguistic practices, from languages that not only enable to conveyance of instructions, commands, role depictions, and operating rules, but that also regulate and control, that normalize and spell out the limits of the permissible through the conveyance of disapproval, ridicule and reproach.

In this example, 124 words, along with many ideas, find themselves crammed into one sentence. In their company, one starts to get panicky. "Throw open the windows; bring in the oxygen tanks!" one wants to shout. "These words and ideas are nearly suffocated. Get them air!" And yet the condition of this desperately packed and crowded sentence is a perfectly familiar one to readers of academic writing, readers who have simply learned to suppress the panic.

Everyone knows that today's college students cannot write, but few seem willing to admit that the professors who denounce them are not doing much better. The problem is so blatant that there are signs that students are catching on. In my American history survey course last semester, I presented a few writing rules that I intended to enforce inflexibly. The students looked more and more peevish; they looked as if they were about to run down the hall, find a telephone, place an urgent call, and demand that someone from the American Civil Liberties Union rush up to campus to sue me for interfering with their First Amendment rights to compose unintelligible, misshapen sentences.

Finally one aggrieved student raised her hand and said, "You are telling *us* not to write long, dull sentences, but most of our assigned reading is *full* of long, dull sentences."

As this student was beginning to recognize, when professors undertake to appraise and improve student writing, the blind are leading the blind. It is, in truth, difficult to persuade students to write well when they find so few good examples in their assigned reading.

The current social and political context for higher education makes this whole issue pressing. In Colorado, as in most states, the legislators are convinced that the university is neglecting students and wasting state resources on pointless research. Under those circumstances, the miserable writing habits of professors pose a direct and concrete danger to higher education. Rather than going to the state legislature, proudly presenting stacks of the faculty's compelling and engaging publications, you end up hoping that the lawmakers stay out of the library and stay away, especially, from the periodical room, with its piles of academic journals. The habits of academic writers lend powerful support to the impression that research is a waste of the writers' time and of the public's money.

Why do so many professors write bad prose?

Ten years ago, I heard a classics professor say the single most important thing—in my opinion—that anyone has said about professors: "We must remember," he declared, "that professors are the ones nobody wanted to dance with in high school."

This is an insight that lights up the universe, or at least the university. It is a proposition that every entering freshman should be told, and it is certainly a proposition that helps to explain the problem of academic writing. What one sees in professors, repeatedly, is exactly the manner that anyone would adopt after a couple of sad evenings sidelined under the crepe-paper streamers in the gym, sitting on a folding chair while everyone else danced. Dignity, for professors, perches precariously on how well they can convey this message: "I am immersed in some very important thoughts, which unsophisticated people could not even begin to understand. Thus, I would not *want* to dance, even if one of you unsophisticated people were to ask me."

Think of this, then, the next time you look at an unintelligible academic text. "I would not *want* the attention of a wide reading audience, even if a wide audience were to *ask* me." Isn't that exactly what the pompous and pedantic tone of the classically academic writer conveys?

Professors are often shy, timid, and even fearful people, and under those circumstances, dull, difficult prose can function as a kind of protective camouflage. When you write typical academic prose, it is nearly impossible to make a strong, clear statement. The benefit here is that no one can attack your position, say you are wrong, or even raise questions about the accuracy of what you said if they cannot *tell* what you have said. In those terms, awful, indecipherable prose is its own form of armor, protecting the fragile, sensitive thoughts of timid souls.

The best texts for helping us understand the academic world are, of course, Lewis Carroll's *Alice's Adventures in Wonderland* and *Through the Looking-Glass*. Just as devotees of Carroll would expect, he has provided us with the best analogy for understanding the origin and function of bad academic writing. Tweedledee and Tweedledum have quite a heated argument over a rattle. They become so angry that they decide to fight. But before they fight, they go off to gather various devices of padding and protection: "bolsters, blankets, hearthrugs, tablecloths, dish covers, and coal scuttles." Then, with Alice's help in tying and fastening, they transform these household items into armor. Alice is not impressed: " 'Really, they'll be more like bundles of old clothes than anything else, by the time they're ready!' she said to herself, as she arranged a bolster round the neck of Tweedledee, 'to keep his head from being cut off,' as he said." Why this precaution? Because, as Tweedledee explains, "it's one of the most serious things that can possibly happen to one in battle—to get one's head cut off."

Here, in the brothers' anxieties and fears, we have an exact analogy for the problems of academic writing. The next time you look at a classically professorial sentence—long, tangled, obscure, jargonized, polysyllabic—think of Tweedledum and Tweedledee dressed for battle and see if those timid little thoughts, concealed under layers of clauses and phrases, do not remind you of those agitated but cautious brothers, arrayed in their bolsters, blankets, dish covers, and coal scuttles. The motive, too, is similar. Tweedledum and Tweedledee were in terror of being hurt, and so they padded themselves so thoroughly that they could not be hurt; nor, for that matter, could they move. A properly dreary, inert sentence has exactly the same benefit; it protects its writer from sharp disagreement, while it also protects him from movement.

Why choose camouflage and insulation over clarity and directness? Tweedledee, of course, spoke for everyone, academic or not, when he confessed his fear. It is, indeed, as he said, "one of the most serious things that can possibly happen to one in a battle—to get one's head cut off." Under those circumstances, logic says tie the bolster around the neck and add a protective hearthrug or two. Pack in another qualifying clause or two. Hide behind the passive-voice verb. Preface any assertion with a phrase like "it could be argued" or "a case could be made." Protecting one's neck does seem to be the way to keep one's head from being cut off.

Graduate school implants in many people the belief that there are terrible penalties to be paid for writing clearly, especially writing clearly in ways that challenge established thinking in the field. And yet, in academic warfare (and I speak as a veteran), your head and your neck are rarely in serious danger. You can remove the bolster and the hearthrug. Your opponents will try to whack at you, but they seldom, if ever, land a blow—in large part because they are themselves so wrapped in protective camouflage and insulation that they lose both mobility and accuracy.

So we have a widespread pattern of professors' protecting themselves from injury by wrapping their ideas in dull prose, and yet the danger they try to fend off is not a genuine danger. Express yourself clearly, and it is unlikely that either your head—or, more important, your tenure—will be cut off.

How, then, do we save professors from themselves? Fearful people are not made courageous by scolding; they need to be coaxed and encouraged. But how do we do that, especially when this particular form of fearfulness masks itself as pomposity, aloofness, and an assumed air of superiority?

Fortunately, we have available the world's most important and illuminating story on the difficulty of persuading people to break out of habits of timidity, caution, and unnecessary fear. I borrow the story from Larry McMurtry, one of my rivals in the interpreting of the American West, though I am putting this story to a use that Mr. McMurtry did not intend.

In a collection of his essays, *In a Narrow Grave*, Mr. McMurtry wrote about the weird process of watching his book *Horseman, Pass By* being turned into the movie *Hud*. He arrived at the Texas Panhandle a week or so after filming had started, and he was particularly anxious to learn how the buzzard scene had gone. In that scene, Paul Newman was to ride up and discover a dead cow, look up at a tree branch lined with buzzards and, in his distress over the loss of the cow, fire his gun at one of the buzzards. At that moment, all the other buzzards were supposed to fly away into the blue Panhandle sky.

But when Mr. McMurtry asked people how the buzzard scene had gone, all he got, he said, were "stricken looks."

The first problem, it turned out, had to do with the quality of the available local buzzards, who proved to be an excessively scruffy group. So more appealing, more photogenic buzzards had to be flown in from some distance and at considerable expense.

But then came the second problem: how to keep the buzzards sitting on the tree branch until it was time for their cue to fly.

That seemed easy. Wire their feet to the branch, and then, after Paul Newman fires his shot, pull the wire, releasing their feet, thus allowing them to take off.

But, as Mr. McMurtry said in an important and memorable phrase, the film makers had not reckoned with the "mentality of buzzards." With their feet wired, the buzzards did not have enough mobility to fly. But they did have enough mobility to pitch forward.

So that's what they did: with their feet wired, they tried to fly, pitched forward, and hung upside down from the dead branch, with their wings flapping.

I had the good fortune a couple of years ago to meet a woman who had been an extra for this movie, and she added a detail that Mr. McMurtry left out of his essay: namely, the buzzard circulatory system does not work upside down, and so, after a moment or two of flapping, the buzzards passed out.

Twelve buzzards hanging upside down from a tree branch: this was not what Hollywood wanted from the West, but that's what Hollywood had produced.

And then we get to the second stage of buzzard psychology. After six or seven episodes of pitching forward, passing out, being revived, being replaced on the branch, and pitching forward again, the buzzards gave up. Now, when you pulled the wire and released their feet, they sat there, saying in clear, nonverbal terms: "We *tried* that before. It did not work. We are not going to try it again." Now the filmmakers had to fly in a high-powered animal trainer to restore buzzard self-esteem. It was a big mess; Larry McMurtry got a wonderful story out of it; and we, in turn, get the best possible parable of the workings of habit and timidity.

How does the parable apply? In any and all disciplines, you go to graduate school to have your feet wired to the branch. There is nothing inherently wrong with that: scholars should have some common ground, share some background assumptions, hold some similar habits of mind. This gives you, quite literally, your footing. And yet, in the process of getting your feet wired, you have some awkward moments, including the intellectual equivalent of pitching forward and hanging upside down. That experience—especially if you do it in a public place like a graduate seminar—provides no pleasure. One or two rounds of that humiliation, and the world begins to seem like a very treacherous place. Under those circumstances, it does indeed seem to be the choice of wisdom *to sit quietly on the branch*, to sit without even the *thought* of flying, since even the thought might be sufficient to tilt the balance and set off another round of flapping, fainting, and embarrassment.

Yet when scholars get out of graduate school and get Ph.D.s, and, even more important, when scholars get tenure, the wire is truly pulled. Their feet are free. They can fly wherever and whenever they like. Yet by then the second stage of buzzard psychology has taken hold, and they refuse to fly. The wire is pulled and yet the buzzards sit there, hunched and grumpy. If they teach in a graduate program, they actively instruct young buzzards in the necessity of keeping their youthful feet on the branch.

This is a very well established pattern, and it is the ruination of scholarly activity in the modern world. Many professors who teach graduate students think that one of their principal duties is to train the students in the convention of academic writing.

I do not believe that professors enforce a standard of dull writing on graduate students to be cruel. They demand dreariness because they think that dreariness is in the students' best interests. Professors believe that a dull writing style is an academic survival skill because they think that is what editors want, both editors of academic journals *and* editors of university presses. What we have here is a chain of misinformation and misunderstanding, where everyone thinks that the other guy is the one who demands dull, impersonal prose.

Let me say again what is at stake here: universities and colleges are currently embattled, distrusted by the public and state funding institutions. As distressing as this situation is, it provides the perfect setting and the perfect timing for declaring an end to scholarly publication as a series of guarded conversations between professors.

The redemption of the university, especially in terms of the public's appraisal of the value of research and publication, requires all the writers who have something they want to publish to ask themselves the question: Does this have to be a closed communication, shutting out all but specialists willing to fight their way through thickets of academic jargon? Or can this be an open communication, engaging specialists with new information and new thinking, but also offering an invitation to nonspecialists to learn from this study, to grasp its importance, and, by extension, to find concrete reasons to see value in the work of the university?

This is a country desperately in need of wisdom and of clearly reasoned conviction and vision. And that, at the bedrock, is the reason behind this campaign to save professors from themselves and detoxify academic prose. The context is a bit different, but the statement that Willy Loman made to his sons in *Death of a Salesman* keeps coming to mind: "The woods are burning, boys, the woods are burning." In a society confronted by racial and ethnic conflicts, a growing gap between the rich and the poor, and environmental dilemmas, "the woods are burning," and since we so urgently need everyone's contribution in putting some of those fires out, there is no reason to indulge professorial vanity or timidity.

Ego is, of course, the key obstacle here. As badly as most of them write, professors are nonetheless proud and sensitive writers, resistant to criticism. But even the most desperate cases can be redeemed and persuaded to think of writing as a challenging craft, not as existential trauma. A few years ago, I began to look at carpenters and other artisans as the emotional model for writers. A carpenter, let us say, makes a door for a cabinet. If the door does not hang straight, the carpenter does not say, "I will *not* change that door; it is an expression of my individuality; who cares if it will not close?" Instead, the carpenter removes the door and works on it until it fits. That attitude, applied to writing, could be our salvation. If we thought more like carpenters, academic writers could find a route out of the trap of ego and vanity. Escaped from that trap, we could simply work on successive drafts until what we have to say is clear.

Colleges and universities are filled with knowledgeable, thoughtful people who have been effectively silenced by an awful writing style, a style with its flaws concealed behind a smokescreen of sophistication and professionalism. A coalition of academic writers, graduate advisers, journal editors, university press editors, and trade publishers can seize this moment *and pull the wire*. The buzzards *can* be set free—free to leave that dead tree branch, free to regain their confidence, free to soar.

ENTERING THE CONVERSATION

by Mike Rose

If you walked out the back door of 9116 South Vermont and across our narrow yard, you would run smack into those four single-room rentals and, alongside them, an old wooden house-trailer. The trailer had belonged to Mrs. Jolly, the woman who sold us the property. It was locked and empty, and its tires were flat and fused into the asphalt driveway. Rusted dairy cases had been wedged in along its sides and four corners to keep it balanced. Two of its eight windows were broken, the frames were warped, and the door stuck. I was getting way too old to continue sharing a room with my mother, so I began to eye that trailer. I decided to refurbish it. It was time to have a room of my own.

Lou Minton had, by now, moved in with us, and he and I fixed the windows and realigned the door. I painted the inside by combining what I could find in our old shed with what I could afford to buy: The ceiling became orange, the walls yellow, the rim along the windows flat black. Lou redid the wiring and put in three new sockets. I got an old record player from the secondhand store for five dollars. I had Roy Herweck, the illustrator of our high school annual, draw women in mesh stockings and other objets d'redneck art on the yellow walls, and I put empty Smirnoff and Canadian Club bottles on the ledges above the windows. I turned the old trailer into the kind of bachelor digs a seventeen-year-old in South L.A. would fancy. My friends from high school began congregating there. When she could, my mother would make us a pot of spaghetti or pasta fasul'. And there was a clerk across the street at Marty's Liquor who would sell to us: We would run back across Vermont Avenue laughing and clutching our bags and seal ourselves up in the trailer. We spun fantasies about the waitress at the Mexican restaurant and mimicked our teachers and caught touchdown passes and, in general, dreamed our way through adolescence. It was a terrible time for rock 'n' roll—Connie Francis and Bobby Rydell were headliners in 1961—so we found rhythm and blues on L.A.'s one black station, played the backroom ballads of troubadour Oscar Brand, and discovered Delta and Chicago blues on Pacifica's KPFK:

I'm a man

I'm a full-grown man

As I fell increasingly under Mr. MacFarland's spell, books began replacing the liquor bottles above the windows: *The Trial* and *Waiting for Godot* and *No Exit* and *The Stranger*. Roy sketched a copy of the back cover of *Exile and the Kingdom*, and so the pensive face of Albert Camus now looked down from that patch of wall on which a cartoon had once pressed her crossed legs. My mother found a quilt that my grandmother had sewn from my father's fabric samples. It was dark and heavy, and I would lie under it and read Rimbaud and not understand him and feel

Reprinted with the permission of Free Press, a Division of Simon & Schuster, Inc., from *Lives on the Boundary: The Struggles and Achievements of American's Underprepared* by Mike Rose. Copyright © 1989 by Mike Rose. All rights reserved.

very connected to the life I imagined Jack MacFarland's life to be: a subterranean ramble through Bebop and breathless poetry and back-alley revelations.

In 1962, John Connor moved into dank, old Apartment 1. John had also grown up in South L.A., and he and I had become best friends. His parents moved to Oregon, and John—who was a good black-top basketball player and an excellent student—wanted to stay in Los Angeles and go to college. So he rented an apartment for forty dollars a month, and we established a community of two. Some nights, John and I and Roy the artist and a wild kid named Gaspo would drive into downtown L.A.—down to where my mother had waited fearfully for a bus years before—and roam the streets and feel the excitement of the tenderloin: the flashing arrows, the blue-and-orange beer neon, the burlesque houses, the faded stairwell of Roseland—which we would inch up and then run down—brushing past the photos of taxi dancers, glossy and smiling in a glass display. Cops would tell us to go home, and that intensified this bohemian romance all the more.

About four months after John moved in, we both entered Loyola University. Loyola is now coeducational; its student center houses an Asian Pacific Students Association, Black Student Alliance, and Chicano Resource Center; and its radio station, KXLU, plays the most untamed rock 'n' roll in Los Angeles. But in the early sixties, Loyola was pretty much a school for white males from the middle and upper middle class. It was a sleepy little campus—its undergraduate enrollment was under two thousand—and it prided itself on providing spiritual as well as intellectual guidance for its students: Religion and Christian philosophy courses were a required part of the curriculum. It denned itself as a Catholic intellectual community—promotional brochures relied on phrases like "the social, intellectual, and spiritual aspects of our students"—and made available to its charges small classes, a campus ministry, and thirty-six clubs (the Chess Club, Economics Society, Fine Arts Circle, Debate Squad, and more). There were also six fraternities and a sports program that included basketball, baseball, volleyball, rugby, soccer, and crew. Loyola men, it was assumed, shared a fairly common set of social and religious values, and the university provided multiple opportunities for them to develop their minds, their spirits, and their social networks. I imagine that parents sent their boys to Loyola with a sigh of relief: God and man strolled together out of St. Robert Bellarmine Hall and veered left to Sacred Heart Chapel. There was an occasional wild party at one of the off-campus fraternity houses, but, well, a pair of panties in the koi pond was not on a par with crises of faith and violence against the state.

John and I rattled to college in his '53 Plymouth. Loyola Boulevard was lined with elms and maples, and as we entered the campus we could see the chapel tower rising in the distance. The chapel and all the early buildings had been constructed in the 1920s and were white and separated by broad sweeps of very green grass. Palm trees and stone pines grew in rows and clumps close to the buildings, and long concrete walkways curved and angled and crossed to connect everything, proving that God, as Plato suspected, is always doing geometry.

Most freshman courses were required, and I took most of mine in St. Robert Bellarmine Hall. Saint Robert was a father of the church who wrote on papal power and censored Galileo: The ceiling in his hallway was high, and dim lights hung down from it. The walls were beige up to about waist level, then turned off-white. The wood trim was dark and worn. The floor combined brown linoleum with brown and black tile. Even with a rush of students, the building maintained its dignity. We moved through it, and its old, clanking radiators warmed us as we did, but it was not a warmth that got to the bone. I remember a dream in which I climbed up beyond the third floor—up thin, narrow stairs to a bell tower that held a small, dusky room in which a priest was playing church music to a class of shadows.

My first semester classes included the obligatory theology and ROTC and a series of requirements: biology, psychology, speech, logic, and a language. I went to class and usually met John for lunch: We'd bring sandwiches to his car and play the radio while we ate. Then it was back to class, or the library, or the student union for a Coke. This was the next step in Jack MacFarland's plan for me—and I did okay for a while. I had learned enough routines in high school to act like a fairly typical student, but—except for the historical sketch I received in Senior English—there wasn't a solid center of knowledge and assurance to all this. When I look back through notes and papers and various photographs and memorabilia, I begin to remember what a disengaged, half-awake time it really was. I'll describe two of the notebooks I found. The one from English is a small book, eight by seven, and only eleven pages of it are filled. The notes I did write consist of book titles, dates of publication, names of characters, pointless summaries of books that were not on our syllabus and that I had never read ("*The Alexandria Quartet*: 5 or 6 characters seen by different people in different stages of life"), and quotations from the teacher ("Perception can bring sorrow.") The notes are a series of separate entries. I can't see any coherence. My biology lab notes are written on green-tint quadrille. They, too, are sparse. There is an occasional poorly executed sketch of a tiny organism or of a bone and muscle structure. Some of the formulas and molecular models sit isolated on the page, bare of any explanatory discussion. The lecture notes are fragmented; a fair number of sentences remain incomplete.

By the end of the second semester my grades were close to dipping below a C average, and since I had been admitted provisionally, that would have been that. Jack MacFarland had oriented me to Western intellectual history and had helped me develop my writing, but he had worked with me for only a year, and I needed more than twelve months of his kind of instruction. Speech and Introductory Psychology presented no big problems. General Biology had midterm and final examinations that required a good deal of memorizing, and I could do that, but the textbook—particularly the chapters covered in the second semester—was much, much harder than what I read in high school, and I was so ill-adept in the laboratory that I failed that portion of the class. We had to set up and pursue biological problems, not just memorize—and at the first sign of doing rather than memorizing, I would automatically assume the problem was beyond me and distance myself from it. Logic, another requirement, spooked me with its syllogisms and Venn diagrams—they were just a step away from more formal mathematics—so I memorized what I could and squirmed around the rest. Theology was god-awful; ROTC was worse. And Latin, the language I elected on the strength of Jack MacFarland's one piece of bad advice, had me suffocating under the dust of a dead civilization. Freshman English was taught by a frustrated novelist with glittering eyes who had us, among other things, describing the consumption of our last evening's meal using the images of the battlefield.

I was out of my league.

Faculty would announce office hours. If I had had the sense, I would have gone, but they struck me as aloof and somber men, and I felt stupid telling them I was . . . well—stupid. I drifted through the required courses, thinking that as soon as these requirements were over, I'd never have to face anything even vaguely quantitative again. Or anything to do with foreign languages. Or ROTC. I fortified myself with defiance: I worked up an imitation of the old priest who was my Latin teacher, and I kept my ROTC uniform crumpled in the greasy trunk of John's Plymouth.

Many of my classmates came from and lived in a world very different from my own. The campus literary magazine would publish excerpts from the journals of upperclassmen traveling across Europe, standing before the Berlin Wall or hiking through olive groves toward Delphi. With the exception of one train trip back to Altoona, I had never been out of Southern California, and this translated, for me, into some personal inadequacy. Fraternities seemed exclusive and a little strange. I'm not sure why I didn't join any of Loyola's three dozen societies and clubs, though I do know that things like the Debate Squad were way too competitive. Posters and flyers and squibs in the campus newspaper gave testament to a lot of connecting activity, but John and I pretty much kept to ourselves, ragging on the "Loyola man," reading the literary magazine aloud with a French accent, simultaneously feeling contempt for and exclusion from a social life that seemed to work with the mystery and enclosure of the clockwork in a music box.

It is an unfortunate fact of our psychic lives that the images that surround us as we grow up—no matter how much we may scorn them later—give shape to our deepest needs and longings. Every year Loyola men elected a homecoming queen. The queen and her princesses were students at the Catholic sister schools: Marymount, Mount St. Mary's, St. Vincent's. They had names like Corinne and Cathy, and they came from the Sullivan family or the Mitchells or the Ryans. They were taught to stand with toe to heel, their smiles were inviting, and the photographer's flash illuminated their eyes. Loyola men met them at fraternity parties and mixers and "CoEd Day," met them according to rules of manner and affiliation and parental connection as elaborate as a Balinese dance. John and I drew mustaches on their photographs, but something about them reached far back into my life.

Growing up in South L.A. was certainly not a conscious misery. My neighborhood had its diversions and its mysteries, and I felt loved and needed at home. But all in all there was a dreary impotence to the years, and isolation, and a deep sadness about my father. I protected myself from the harsher side of it all through a life of the mind. And while that interior life included spaceships and pink chemicals and music and the planetary moons, it also held the myriad television images of the good life that were piped into my home: Robert Young sitting down to dinner, Ozzie Nelson tossing the football with his sons, the blond in a Prell commercial turning toward the camera. The images couldn't have been more trivial—all sentimental phosphorescence—but as a child tucked away on South Vermont, they were just about the only images I had of what life would be without illness and dead ends. I didn't realize how completely their message had seeped into my being, what loneliness and sorrow was being held at bay—didn't realize it until I found myself in the middle of Loyola's social life without a guidebook, feeling just beyond the superficial touch of the queen and her princesses, those smiling incarnations of a television promise. I scorned the whole silly show and ached to be embraced by one of these mythic females under the muted light of a paper moon.

So I went to school and sat in class and memorized more than understood and whistled past the academic graveyard. I vacillated between the false potency of scorn and feelings of ineptitude. John and I would get in his car and enjoy the warmth of each other and laugh and head down the long strip of Manchester , Boulevard, away from Loyola, away from the palms and green, green lawns, back to South L.A. We'd throw the ball in the alley or lag pennies on Vermont or hit Marty's Liquor. We'd leave much later for a movie or a football game at Mercy High or the terrible safety of downtown Los Angeles. Walking, then, past the *discotecas* and pawnshops, past the windows full of fried chicken and yellow lamps, past the New Follies, walking through hustlers and lost drunks and prostitutes and transvestites with rouge the color of bacon—stopping, finally, before the musty opening of a bar where two silhouettes moved around a pool table as though they were underwater.

I don't know what I would have found if the flow of events hadn't changed dramatically. Two things happened. Jack MacFarland privately influenced my course of study at Loyola, and death once again ripped through our small family.

The coterie of MacFarland's students—Art Mitz, Mark Dever, and me—were still visiting our rumpled mentor. We would stop by his office or his apartment to mock our classes and the teachers and all that " 'Loyola man' bullshit." Nobody had more appreciation for burlesque than Jack MacFarland, but I suppose he saw beneath our caustic performances and knew we were headed for trouble. Without telling us, he started making phone calls to some of his old teachers at Loyola—primarily to Dr. Frank Carothers, the chairman of the English Department—and, I guess, explained that these kids needed to be slapped alongside the head with a good novel. Dr. Carothers volunteered to look out for us and agreed to some special studies courses that we could substitute for a few of the more traditional requirements, courses that would enable us to read and write a lot under the close supervision of a faculty member. In fact, what he promised were tutorials—and that was exceptional, even for a small college. All this would start up when we returned from summer vacation. Our sophomore year, Jack MacFarland finally revealed, would be different.

When Lou Minton rewired the trailer, he rigged a phone line from the front house: A few digits and we could call each other. One night during the summer after my freshman year, the phone rang while I was reading. It was my mother and she was screaming. I ran into the house to find her standing in the kitchen hysterical—both hands pressed to her face—and all I could make out was Lou's name. I didn't see him in the front of the house, so I ran back through the kitchen to the bedroom. He had fallen back across the bed, a hole right at his sideburn, his jaw still quivering. They had a fight, and some ugly depth of pain convulsed within him. He left the table and walked to the bedroom. My mother heard the light slam of a .22. Nothing more.

That summer seems vague and distant. I can't remember any specifics, though I had to take care of my mother and handle the affairs of the house. I probably made do by blunting a good deal of what I saw and navigating with intuitive quadrants. But though I cannot remember details, I do recall feelings and recognitions: Lou's suicide came to represent the sadness and dead time I had protected myself against, the personal as well as public oppressiveness of life in South Los Angeles. I began to see that my escape to the trailer and my isolationist fantasies of the demimonde would yield another kind of death, a surrender to the culture's lost core. An alternative was somehow starting to take shape around school and knowledge. Knowledge seemed . . . was it empowering? No, that's a word I would use now. Then I felt freed, as if I were untying fetters. There simply were times when the pain and confusion of that summer would give way to something I felt more than I knew: a lightness to my body, an ease in breathing. Three or four months later I took an art history course, and one day during a slide show on Gothic architecture I felt myself rising up within the interior light of Mont-Saint-Michel. I wanted to be released from the despair that surrounded me on South Vermont and from my own troubled sense of exclusion.

Jack MacFarland had saved me at one juncture—caught my fancy and revitalized my mind—what I felt now was something further, some tentative recognition that an engagement with ideas could foster competence and lead me out into the world. But all this was very new and fragile, and given what I know now, I realize how easily it could have been crushed. My mother, for as long as I can remember, always added onto any statement of intention—hers or others'—the phrase *se vuol Dio,* if God wants it. The fulfillment of desire, no matter how trivial, required the blessing of the gods, for the world was filled with threat. "I'll plant the seeds this weekend," I might say. "Se vuol Dio," she would add. *Se vuol Dio.* The phrase expressed several lifetimes of ravaged hope: my grandfather's lost leg, the failure of the Rose Spaghetti House, my father laid low, Lou Minton, the landscapes of South L. A. *Se vuol Dio.* For those who live their lives on South Vermont, tomorrow doesn't beckon to be defined from a benign future. It's up to the gods, not you, if any old thing turns out right. I carried within me no history of assurances that what I was feeling would lead to anything.

Because of its size and because of the kind of teacher who is drawn to small liberal arts colleges, Loyola would turn out to be a very good place for me. For even with MacFarland's yearlong tour through ideas and language, I was unprepared.

English prose written before the twentieth century was difficult, sometimes impossible, for me to comprehend. The kind of reasoning I found in logic was very foreign. My writing was okay, but I couldn't hold a candle to Art Mitz or Mark Dever or to those boys who came from good schools. And my fears about science and mathematics prevailed: Pereira Hall, the Math and Engineering Building, was only forty to fifty yards from the rear entrance to the English Department but seemed an unfriendly mirage, a malevolent castle floating in the haze of a mescaline dream.

We live, in America, with so many platitudes about motivation and self-reliance and individualism—and myths spun from them, like those of Horatio Alger—that we find it hard to accept the fact that they are serious nonsense. To live your early life on the streets of South L.A.—or Homewood or Spanish Harlem or Chicago's South Side or any one of hundreds of other depressed communities—and to journey up through the top levels of the American educational system will call for support and guidance at many, many points along the way. You'll need people to guide you into conversations that seem foreign and threatening. You'll need models, lots of them, to show you how to get at what you don't know. You'll need people to help you center yourself in your own developing ideas. You'll need people to watch out for you. There is much talk these days about the value of a classical humanistic education, a call for an immersion in the humanities, a return to the great books. These appeals raise lots of suspicions, for such curricula have traditionally served to exclude working-class people from the classroom. It doesn't, of necessity, have to be that way. The teachers that fate and Jack MacFarland's crisis intervention sent my way worked at making the humanities truly human. What transpired between us was the essence of humane liberal education, and it enabled me to move far beyond the cognitive charade of my freshman year.

Name: _____ Date: _____

REFLECTIONS: USING ACTIVE READING STRATEGIES

Why did you choose the first strategy? How did it go?

Why did you choose the second strategy? How did it go?

You may find that one strategy was more helpful than the other, or they were equally effective. Speculate about why the results were what they were.

How do you define "helpful"? Would these same strategies work for all of your active reading? Why or why not?

PART 2

What Writing Is

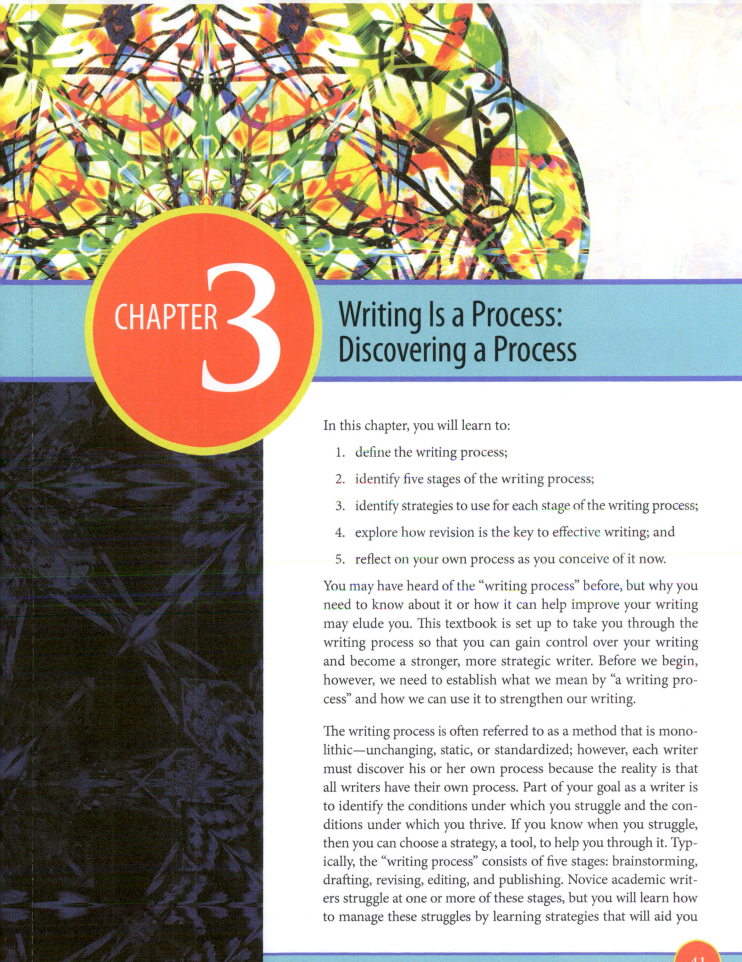

CHAPTER 3

Writing Is a Process: Discovering a Process

In this chapter, you will learn to:

1. define the writing process;

2. identify five stages of the writing process;

3. identify strategies to use for each stage of the writing process;

4. explore how revision is the key to effective writing; and

5. reflect on your own process as you conceive of it now.

You may have heard of the "writing process" before, but why you need to know about it or how it can help improve your writing may elude you. This textbook is set up to take you through the writing process so that you can gain control over your writing and become a stronger, more strategic writer. Before we begin, however, we need to establish what we mean by "a writing process" and how we can use it to strengthen our writing.

The writing process is often referred to as a method that is monolithic—unchanging, static, or standardized; however, each writer must discover his or her own process because the reality is that all writers have their own process. Part of your goal as a writer is to identify the conditions under which you struggle and the conditions under which you thrive. If you know when you struggle, then you can choose a strategy, a tool, to help you through it. Typically, the "writing process" consists of five stages: brainstorming, drafting, revising, editing, and publishing. Novice academic writers struggle at one or more of these stages, but you will learn how to manage these struggles by learning strategies that will aid you in overcoming those struggles. Keep in mind that YOUR writing process will not always follow this process in a lock-and-step fashion. Instead, you will learn that you might revise and edit simultaneously, or when you are drafting, you might need to go back and brainstorm. In other words, you might do one or more steps at the same time or you might reverse, back up, move forward, or start all over again. The writing process, therefore, is a *recursive process*. As you learn to write academically, you will likely need to adjust your process depending upon how much you already know about the topic, how familiar you are with the subject matter in a course, and how far along you are in a given writing project. Knowing what to do and when is learned over timed and with practice. Just like an athlete or a musician, you will need to practice these strategies. You are likely to fumble, but you need to get up, recover, and try again. This, too, is part of the writing process!

Starred *thought*

As you develop as a writer in academia, you will naturally gravitate toward certain subjects or disciplines, and you will learn how in each discipline to write, think, and use research in unique ways. Although the content changes, the ways we go about discovering a good topic or focus can be achieved using these various strategies, for they are transferrable across disciplines.

The stages of the writing process may be referred to by different names, or they may be described by what you do—as a strategy—during a particular stage. Let us take an in-depth look at these stages and the strategies you can use to move through them.

STAGE 1: BRAINSTORMING

In this first stage, known as brainstorming, prewriting, generating ideas, and invention, you are working out what is appropriate and doable for a given assignment. We all struggle coming up with a "good" idea, one we are excited about and want to explore. These strategies help us figure out what is worth our time and energy and what is not. This first stage is very important, so important, in fact, that the time you spend early in the writing process saves you time later.

One way brainstorming is helpful is in its simplicity. Writers have a lot of ideas in their head, and brainstorming allows writers to sift through them to discover what is the most interesting, timely, and appropriate for a given writing situation. Sometimes writers use brainstorming strategies to figure out what they already know and what they need to find out. Other times, writers use brainstorming strategies after they have completed reading and researching. In other words, this stage has strategies that can be utilized in different ways and at different times. After reading about a topic or researching a topic, it is time to begin writing about it. Taking the annotations you made during active reading, you have several ideas that need to be sifted through and analyzed for their potential for a focused writing topic. To work through those preliminary ideas, you need to eliminate dead-ends, uninteresting or trite topics, and ideas that are either too narrow or too broad. (All of this depends, of course, upon what the assignment is that you have to complete.)

In general, though, the strategies writers use in this first stage include the following:

> Reading/Researching
> Discussing/Talking
> Listing
> Webbing or Clustering
> Fastwriting
> Visualizing
> Outlining

RESEARCHING: Sometimes writers start with research because they are working on a topic about which they know very little, so they have to find out what the subject is all about. In cases this like, what matters in the field and what researchers in the field have already learned informs what a writer can say. Other times, writers need to examine what they already know about a subject in order to figure out what they do not know and need to find out. Novice writers, especially when writing about literature, fall into the trap of doing research about an author or story and become overwhelmed with information, and then they may lose their own voice because they are deferring to what others have said. In other words, research can be a useful strategy, but it needs to be approached carefully so that you, the writer, find your perspective first, which gives you your voice.

DISCUSSING AND TALKING: One of the best ways to explore a topic and its potential is by talking about it out loud with others. Class discussions are more formalized versions of this, yet talking with friends or family outside of class can also lead to some interesting areas to explore. "Bouncing" ideas off of others is a great way to gain insight into what you have not already thought about or considered. Taking notes during your discussion can then be used in one of the above mentioned strategies.

LISTING: As its name suggests, this strategy lists ideas that come to mind when you are thinking about a topic. This is an informal list; simply write down vertically or horizontally the words or phrases that come to mind when you are thinking about your topic. Do not censor yourself. Do not limit yourself. If there are ideas/words/phrases/questions that come to mind when you look over your annotations, write those down, too. Once you have several ideas listed, you can go back and eliminate the ones that seemed, at first, to be interesting, but that now bore you or make you roll your eyes or cringe. You are not wedded to anything on the list. They are simply ideas.

WEBBING OR CLUSTERING: An alternative to (or perhaps an addition to) listing ideas is using a *web* or *cluster* to lay out ideas spatially on the page. If used alone, you can place a key idea you have in a circle in the middle of a page and branch out (*web*) other ideas that link to that central idea. You have created a first-level web. (See Figure 3.1.)

FIGURE **3.1** First-level Webbing

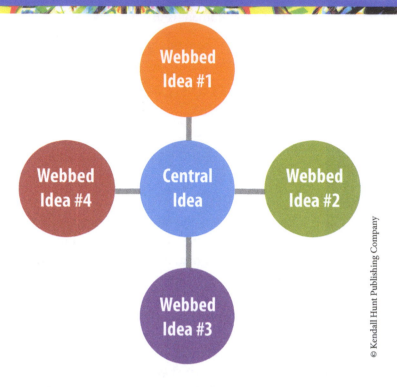

© Kendall Hunt Publishing Company

FIGURE **3.2** Second-level Webbing

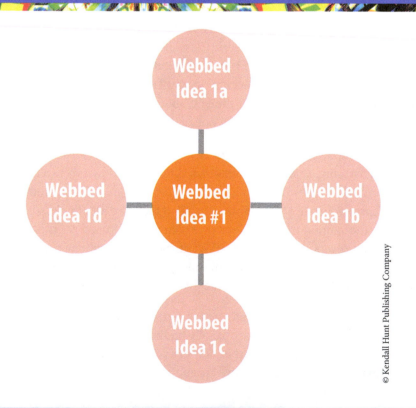

© Kendall Hunt Publishing Company

From the webbed ideas, you can continue adding on ideas until you exhaust the train of thinking for that central idea. You do not need to limit your "webbed ideas" to only four. In fact, the more you have, the more choices you have in what will make it into the next stage of writing and what will not make it.

After you have exhausted the first-level ideas that come from that central idea, you can build on to the web using second-level, third-level, etc., until you have completely exhausted the central topic (Figure 3.2).

You can also use this webbing/clustering strategy in combination with listing where you take an idea from the list you made and create a web for it. You can create multiple webs using several of the ideas from your list. These webs may lead you to seeing a group or *cluster* of ideas that could be shaped into sections or paragraphs for your essays. You can also use webbing/clustering to include the kinds of support you have for a given idea by including examples, explanations, paraphrases, or direct quotes (Figure 3.3).

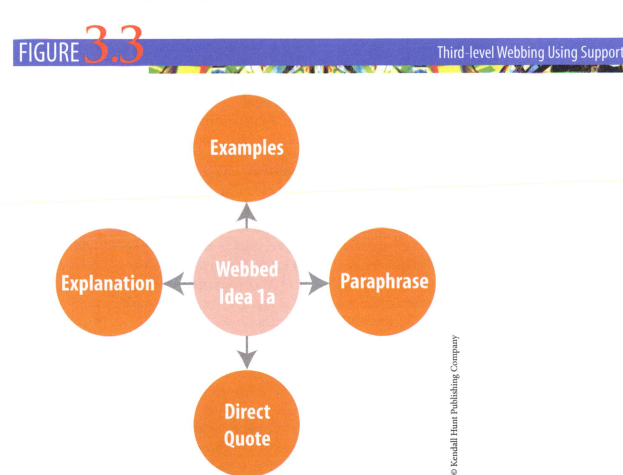

FIGURE 3.3   Third-level Webbing Using Support

© Kendall Hunt Publishing Company

These concepts are not written in stone, nor are they meant to be reproduced exactly as the images shown. The idea is that in brainstorming with this strategy you are exploring *possible* ideas, *possible* topics, and *possible* connections between ideas. These preliminary clusters and webs *might* lead to a working outline or a first draft.

FASTWRITING: You can use this strategy independently from listing, webbing, clustering, or in combination with them. If you are using it independently, then you take an idea and write for a set amount of time without stopping. You can start with writing for 3 minutes, nonstop. Write out whatever comes to mind. Do not censor yourself. Do not stop to correct spelling or reword your ideas. The idea is that we have an internal critic, a voice that prevents us from exploring ideas and trying out ideas to find out whether they are "good" or not. This voice demands perfection that cannot be achieved at this stage, nor should it be achieved at this stage. By writing without stopping, you are "outrunning" that critic in order to get out of your head the ideas that are there. We can sort them out after we have finished coming up with them!

If you find that your fastwrite led to a dead-end or you have written nonstop for 3 minutes and have exhausted that idea, then you simply omit it from your "possible topics" list and try another. When you find a topic that has potential, you will find yourself wanting more time to finish what you are thinking. If this happens, then take another 3 minutes to continue. You might find that after you have completed the second round, you are finding your focus. This could lead to a draft!

You can also follow this strategy with the listing or webbing/clustering. You choose an idea from your list or web and write for 3 minutes, nonstop. When the internal critic says, "No, that's a terrible/dumb/trite/silly idea," you simply write over that voice. You can even write out what that voice is saying, and once you have given it space on the page, it will often quiet itself or simply go away. This allows you to focus on the ideas rather than on evaluating them. (The writing process provides time later for evaluating the ideas.) After you write out your ideas—doing so for several of them—you then have the opportunity to evaluate them to see which is most appealing, interesting, or heartfelt.

VISUALIZING: Sometimes, we can explore topics that are better suited to sketching or drawing. For example, if you were to explore what new technology should be invented, you might draw out an imagined invention that could lead you to consider the different components, look, style, and uses it has. Another way visual brainstorming strategies can be helpful is for writers to "see" what they are thinking before beginning to use words, sentences, and paragraphs to explain that thinking. Another way to use visualizing is to draw out the essay you are imagining as a way of seeing how the various ideas fit together. It might look something like Figure 3.4.

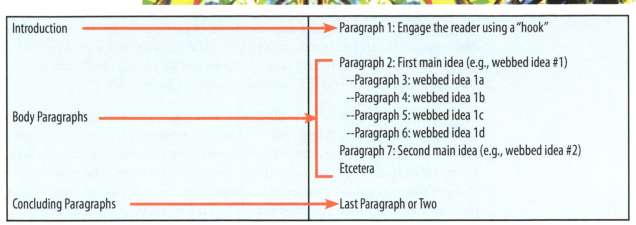

Introduction	Paragraph 1: Engage the reader using a "hook"
Body Paragraphs	Paragraph 2: First main idea (e.g., webbed idea #1) --Paragraph 3: webbed idea 1a --Paragraph 4: webbed idea 1b --Paragraph 5: webbed idea 1c --Paragraph 6: webbed idea 1d Paragraph 7: Second main idea (e.g., webbed idea #2) Etcetera
Concluding Paragraphs	Last Paragraph or Two

In other words, visualizing can sometimes be helpful in coming up with topics or in developing a possible organization/structure for your essay.

OUTLINING: This strategy can be helpful at the end of your brainstorming stage after you have a solid topic and some supporting ideas and just prior to drafting. Think of an outline as merely a tentative, possible structure for your essay. Outlines are meant to give you a place to start writing and how your essay might work. Of course, as you write the actual essay, the outline may change, and this is perfectly acceptable. In fact, change is typical in the writing process. A final outline can only be discerned after all of the paragraphs are in place and the essay is completed. This kind of outline, therefore, is a guide.

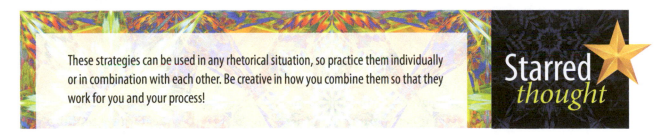

These strategies can be used in any rhetorical situation, so practice them individually or in combination with each other. Be creative in how you combine them so that they work for you and your process!

Starred *thought*

STAGE 2: DRAFTING

Many students in high school write for times-tests or simply write "one-and-done." However, very few "real" writing situations are under that kind of time pressure. Journalists and newscasters are often given only hours (or less!) to prepare their texts, but they are the exception. Most writers actually go through a process writing over extended periods of time, days, months, and even years, depending upon the project. At university, you will often be given an assignment with at least 1-week advanced notice—usually longer, though—to complete a written text. University expectations are that you will take that entire time to construct your essay, moving through brainstorming, drafting, revising, and editing before submitting the final product. Your individual instructors will not necessarily give you prompts or brainstorming activities to do in preparation for the submission of the essay. There is an expectation that you will do this on your own. This is why it is so important for you to gain control of your writing process, and when you get stuck, it is essential for you to have tools to help you get unstuck.

Drafting, therefore, may be very difficult because you are trying to put into words what is in your head, juggling multiple ideas, structuring and organizing information, and trying to figure out what you want to say, all in an effort to meet your instructor's expectations. To make matters even more complex, what you initially thought you were going to write can actually change because what writing does is put into coherency what you have not yet had coherent. Writers, in other words, have a general idea of what they want to say, but it is not until they actually say or write it that it becomes specific and concrete. Writers, then, often discover what they want to say by actually writing it out.

Some instructors call writing at this stage by a number of different names: initial draft, informal draft, zero draft, first draft, and preliminary draft. These names suggest that the nature of this writing stage is one where writers are meant to explore, examine, and discover how their ideas connect to an overall point. In an academic setting, what is expected in a "draft" ranges from having a completed draft where you have exhausted the connections between ideas to partial drafts where you have several paragraphs or pages but not necessarily all of the content. This stage, then, provides writers with the space to develop the content of the writing to the fullest extent so that they can go back and revise after getting some feedback on how to expand or develop their ideas further. This stage is often tough and labor intensive. You may find yourself starting and then stopping, only to start again.

STRATEGIES

1. **SIMPLY WRITE.** At some point, you just have to sit down and write out what you have been thinking about or discussing with others. You literally need to put the pen to paper or fingers on the keyboard. Write during a time that you are most productive. Many writers are best in the morning; others are best in the evening. Whatever time of day is your "best" time is when you set aside an hour to just do the work. As you build this into your daily routine, you may find that an hour is too short. Add on time as you become more productive.

   Also consider your environment. Some writers like to have music on in the background; others like silence. Some writers prefer to write at home in their pajamas; others like to write outside at the park or at the local coffeeshop. Some writers like to have tea or coffee at their side.

Others need clear, open space without any distractions. You are the writer, and part of realizing your writerly self is coming to know what *your* process looks like and what best engenders your writing. Try different locations, music, and times of day until you find the ones that are best suited to *your* writing style.

In academia, you may have to write under timed circumstances in the classroom or in a computer lab, yet these kinds of writing experiences are specific to coursework. In general, what we call "real" writing happens outside of the classroom, so as a writer, you will need to establish the kinds of habits that make "real" writing matter and work for you and your process!

Starred *thought*

2. **HANDWRITE OR WORD PROCESS.** If you usually sit down at the computer to draft, try writing by hand. Sometimes the blank screen is daunting, or it feels as if what appears on that screen is permanent even though we know there are "Backspace" and "Delete" keys. Others see the blank page of paper as daunting; in that case, try going to the computer first. The goal is to get the ideas down first before you begin to doubt the ideas. Once you have something to work with—a working draft—then you can begin to work on developing clearer connections between the ideas and work on deleting or adding to what you have.

This is a strategy to turn your attention to getting something on the page and not backtracking or correcting. Until you have something to work with, you are simply sabotaging your efforts. This way you are focusing on the writing, not correcting or "fixing" things. Do this for 3 to 4 minutes at a time. Then, turn the monitor on to read what you have written, and then do this all over again. After some time, say 15 minutes, you have part of a working draft that you can go back to and rework. Get it down first, and worry about getting it right later.

3. **START IN THE MIDDLE.** Rather than start with an introduction, start in the middle. Choose one of your main points or ideas from your brainstorming that you think will be part of the body section of your writing and start shaping that idea into paragraphs. Develop your point or idea as fully as possible, and then create another paragraph, focusing on the next point or idea you want to cover in your body section. Then, do it again with another idea. And again. And again. Once you have several paragraphs that might make up the "body" of your text, then you can begin to look at what threads bind them together, which could become a controlling idea (or thesis). After you have body paragraphs and can see how the ideas in them are connected, that is when it is time to construct a working introduction and conclusion.

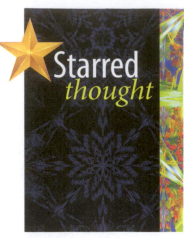

Starred *thought*

The reason this may be an effective strategy is because many inexperienced writers want to start their essays with an introduction, and they end up getting stuck. This is because many inexperienced writers are used to timed-writing situations where writers do not have a lot of time to revise or rework ideas. They have to know what they want to write as quickly and as simply as possible, so they develop a main idea with three main points and put that in an introduction. They follow-up with three paragraphs, one for each of those three main points, and conclude by stating what they wrote. This kind of writing, the five-paragraph exposition essay, is a simple "telling" of information or recalling a basic understanding.

At university, the kinds of writing you will do are typically complex, and because you will be given time outside of class to write, you will have time to explore, debate, argue, analyze, synthesize, and examine ideas (often from multiple perspectives or from one that is not necessarily your own), all in an effort to *take time* to figure out what you want to say. In these situations, it is not until you have done the *exploration* that you really *discover* what you want to focus on in your writing. In short, introductions tell your reader what they are about to read and what your focus is, but it is not until you have written your text that you know what that is. (After all, how do you know what you think until you have written it out?) Doing an introduction first stalls your *process for thinking* through the ideas. Thus, the introduction should be written last, after you have figured out what it is you think and how you want to frame it for your reader. That is the gift of drafting: You do not have to be psychic and know what you are writing until you have written it!

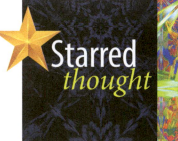

Starred *thought*

Writers begin writing with something in mind. They have a general understanding or set of ideas that they want to work on. The specifics, however, are discovered in the process of writing about these ideas. There are often connections between ideas that are not seen until they are on the page, and this is power of the process. It gives writers opportunities to discover the subtle connections that instructors want their students to find.

4. **RECORD YOURSELF "THINKING OUT LOUD":** Sometimes, writers get caught-up in the physical act of writing or typing out ideas. They find themselves stopping and correcting their writing rather than just writing to get their ideas out. This strategy, then, is meant to focus on your expressing your ideas without getting caught-up in this corrective practice that stops the "flow" of thinking. As you talk aloud about your ideas, you are likely to change your mind, discover some avenue of thinking that would not have

happened otherwise, or you may say something that "sounds good." You will then have all of that recorded and ready for review. You can omit what are dead-ends or off-topic and use what you do like and has potential. Then, you simply type out what you said and begin shaping it into a draft.

An alternative is to work with a family member, peer, or friend and have one of them ask you questions about your topic that you answer, recording the conversation. Out of this exchange, you may find some interesting avenues for writing. This is "bouncing ideas off of someone" who can help you discover your thinking or help you to clarify what you want to work on in your writing.

Starred *thought*

FINAL THOUGHTS ABOUT DRAFTING

Drafting allows writers the freedom to work out ideas, try new strategies, and "mess-up." This stage is not meant to be "perfect." In fact, it is a built-in rehearsal for your final product. The drafting stage should be viewed as a space to work out ideas. It is the practice before the big game, the rehearsal before opening night. At some point during this stage, you will have a complete, working draft that can be revisited in its entirety. When you have finished with your draft, a working draft that can be read by your peers during peer-review or read by your instructor for revision suggestions, you have ended this stage and can enter into the next one called revision.

Keep in mind, however, that you should try to come up with a rounded draft. Stopping in the middle or not finishing is simply that: unfinished. This, then, would not be a draft. You might ask "What if I get stuck? What if I can't finish the essay because I don't know what to go?" The beauty of the *drafting stage* is that you have the space and time built into the stage for these pauses. You have to realize that the "draft" is not the same thing as the "drafting stage." An incomplete draft is an incomplete draft. Consider what would happen when your instructor wants you to do a peer-review, and you have an incomplete draft, then you peer-review partners will not be able to provide you the most helpful feedback because they are only able to comment on part of what you have. They do not have the full picture or the full scope or range of your ideas. The "drafting stage" has to include time for your getting stuck, where you may have to put it aside for a day and come back to it. This is why "one and done" is a bad habit that undermines your best potential. You will have to build into your process time to procrastinate (if that is something that you do), time to struggle, time to write out your complete thinking. In other words, not finishing a draft, or having only part of a draft, needs to be built into the drafting stage.

Starred *thought*

Writers begin writing with something in mind. They have a general understanding or set of ideas that they want to work on. The specifics, however, are discovered in the process of writing about these ideas. There are often connections between ideas that are not seen until they are on the page, and this is the power of the process. It gives writers opportunities to discover the subtle connections that instructors want their students to find.

Read Anne Lamott's "Shitty First Drafts" and use an active reading strategy from Chapter 2. Pay attention to what Lamott's essay says about drafting and the purpose for it. What can you take away from her essay for your own process?

SHITTY FIRST DRAFTS

by Anne Lamott

Now, practically even better news than that of short assignments is the idea of shitty first drafts. All good writers write them. This is how they end up with good second drafts and terrific third drafts. People tend to look at successful writers, writers who are getting their books published and maybe even doing well financially, and think that they sit down at their desks every morning feeling like a million dollars, feeling great about who they are and how much talent they have and what a great story they have to tell; that they take in a few deep breaths, push back their sleeves, roll their necks a few times to get all the cricks out, and dive in, typing fully formed passages as fast as a court reporter. But this is just the fantasy of the uninitiated. I know some very great writers, writers you love who write beautifully and have made a great deal of money, and not *one* of them sits down routinely feeling wildly enthusiastic and confident. Not one of them writes elegant first drafts. All right, one of them does, but we do not like her very much. We do not think that she has a rich inner life or that God likes her or can even stand her. (Although when I mentioned this to my priest friend Tom, he said you can safely assume you've created God in your own image when it turns out that God hates all the same people you do.)

"Shitty First Drafts" from *Bird by Bird: Some Instructions on Writing and Life* by Anne Lamott, copyright © 1994 by Anne Lamott. Used by permission of Pantheon Books, an imprint of Knopf Doubleday Publishing Group, a division of Random House LLC. All rights reserved.

Very few writers really know what they are doing until they've done it. Nor do they go about their business feeling dewy and thrilled. They do not type a few stiff warm-up sentences and then find themselves bounding along like huskies across the snow. One writer I know tells me that he sits down every morning and says to himself nicely, "It's not like you don't have a choice, because you do—you can either type or kill yourself." We all often feel like we are pulling teeth, even those writers whose prose ends up being the most natural and fluid. The right words and sentences just do not come pouring out like ticker tape most of the time. Now, Muriel Spark is said to have felt that she was taking dictation from God every morning—sitting there, one supposes, plugged into a Dictaphone, typing away, humming. But this is a very hostile and aggressive position. One might hope for bad things to rain down on a person like this.

For me and most of the other writers I know, writing is not rapturous. In fact, the only way I can get anything written at all is to write really, really shitty first drafts.

The first draft is the child's draft, where you let it all pour out and then let it romp all over the place, knowing that no one is going to see it and that you can shape it later. You just let this childlike part of you channel whatever voices and visions come through and onto the page. If one of the characters wants to say, "Well, so what, Mr. Poopy Pants?," you let her. No one is going to see it. If the kid wants to get into really sentimental, weepy, emotional territory, you let him. Just get it all down on paper, because there may be something great in those six crazy pages that you would never have gotten to by more rational, grown-up means. There may be something in the very last line of the very last paragraph on page six that you just love, that is so beautiful or wild that you now know what you're supposed to be writing about, more or less, or in what direction you might go— but there was no way to get to this without first getting through the first five and a half pages.

I used to write food reviews for *California* magazine before it folded. (My writing food reviews had nothing to do with the magazine folding, although every single review did cause a couple of canceled subscriptions. Some readers took umbrage at my comparing mounds of vegetable puree with various ex-presidents' brains.) These reviews always took two days to write. First I'd go to a restaurant several times with a few opinionated, articulate friends in tow. I'd sit there writing down everything anyone said that was at all interesting or funny. Then on the following Monday I'd sit down at my desk with my notes, and try to write the review. Even after I'd been doing this for years, panic would set in. I'd try to write a lead, but instead I'd write a couple of dreadful sentences, XX them out, try again, XX everything out, and then feel despair and worry settle on my chest like an x-ray apron. It's over, I'd think, calmly. I'm not going to be able to get the magic to work this time. I'm ruined. I'm through. I'm toast. Maybe, I'd think, I can get my old job back as a clerk-typist. But probably not. I'd get up and study my teeth in the mirror for a while. Then I'd stop, remember to breathe, make a few phone calls, hit the kitchen and chow down. Eventually I'd go back and sit down at my desk, and sigh for the next ten minutes. Finally I would pick up my one-inch picture frame, stare into it as if for the answer, and every time the answer would come: all I had to do was to write a really shitty first draft of, say, the opening paragraph. And no one was going to see it.

So I'd start writing without reining myself in. It was almost just typing, just making my fingers move. And the writing would be *terrible*. I'd write a lead paragraph that was a whole page, even though the entire review could only be three pages long, and then I'd start writing up descriptions of the food, one dish at a time, bird by bird, and the critics would be sitting on my shoulders, commenting like cartoon characters. They'd be pretending to snore, or rolling their eyes at my overwrought descriptions, no matter how hard I tried to tone those descriptions down, no matter how conscious I was of what a friend said to me gendy in my early days of restaurant reviewing. "Annie," she said, "it is just a piece of *chicken*. It is just a bit of *cake*."

But because by then I had been writing for so long, I would eventually let myself trust the process—sort of, more or less. I'd write a first draft that was maybe twice as long as it should be, with a self-indulgent and boring beginning, stupefying descriptions of the meal, lots of quotes from my black-humored friends that made them sound more like the Manson girls than food lovers, and no ending to speak of. The whole thing would be so long and incoherent and hideous that for the rest of the day I'd obsess about getting creamed by a car before I could write a decent second draft. I'd worry that people would read what I'd written and believe that the accident had really been a suicide, that I had panicked because my talent was waning and my mind was shot.

The next day, though, I'd sit down, go through it all with a colored pen, take out everything I possibly could, find a new lead somewhere on the second page, figure out a kicky place to end it, and then write a second draft. It always turned out fine, sometimes even funny and weird and helpful. I'd go over it one more time and mail it in.

Then, a month later, when it was time for another review, the whole process would start again, complete with the fears that people would find my first draft before I could rewrite it.

Almost all good writing begins with terrible first efforts. You need to start somewhere. Start by getting something— anything—down on paper. A friend of mine says that the first draft is the down draft—you just get it down. The second draft is the up draft—you fix it up. You try to say what you have to say more accurately. And the third draft is the dental draft, where you check every tooth, to see if it's loose or cramped or decayed, or even, God help us, healthy.

What I've learned to do when I sit down to work on a shitty first draft is to quiet the voices in my head. First there's the vinegar-lipped Reader Lady, who says primly, "Well, *that's* not very interesting, is it?" And there's the emaciated German male who writes these Orwellian memos detailing your thought crimes. And there are your parents, agonizing over your lack of loyalty and discretion; and there's William Burroughs, dozing off or shooting up because he finds you as bold and articulate as a houseplant; and so on. And there are also the dogs: let's not forget the dogs, the dogs in their pen who will surely hurtle and snarl their way out if you ever *stop* writing, because writing is, for some of us, the latch that keeps the door of the pen closed, keeps those crazy ravenous dogs contained.

Quieting these voices is at least half the battle I fight daily. But this is better than it used to be. It used to be 87 percent. Left to its own devices, my mind spends much of its time having conversations with people who aren't there. I walk along defending myself to people, or exchanging repartee with them, or rationalizing my behavior, or seducing them with gossip, or pretending I'm on their TV talk show or whatever. I speed or run an aging yellow light or don't come to a full stop, and one nanosecond later am explaining to imaginary cops exactly why I had to do what I did, or insisting that I did not in fact do it.

I happened to mention this to a hypnotist I saw many years ago, and he looked at me very nicely. At first I thought he was feeling around on the floor for the silent alarm button, but then he gave me the following exercise, which I still use to this day.

Close your eyes and get quiet for a minute, until the chatter starts up. Then isolate one of the voices and imagine the person speaking as a mouse. Pick it up by the tail and drop it into a mason jar. Then isolate another voice, pick it up by the tail, drop it in the jar. And so on. Drop in any high-maintenance parental units, drop in any contractors, lawyers, colleagues, children, anyone who is whining in your head. Then put the lid on, and watch all these mouse people clawing at the glass, jabbering away, trying to make you feel like shit because you won't do what they want—won't give them more money, won't be more successful, won't see them more often. Then imagine that there is a volume-control button on the bottle. Turn it all the way up for a minute, and listen to the stream of angry, neglected, guilt-mongering voices. Then turn it all the way down and watch the frantic mice lunge at the glass, trying to get to you. Leave it down, and get back to your shitty first draft.

A writer friend of mine suggests opening the jar and shooting them all in the head. But I think he's a little angry, and I'm sure nothing like this would ever occur to you.

STAGE 3: REVISING

After you have a draft—a work in progress—that is rounded, then you might engage in a number of revision activities that will make your text more effective, clearer, more complete, and more appropriate for the rhetorical situation. How do writers know what is working and what is not? There are several strategies that help writers to gain new insight into their writing. Here are a few of the most often used.

STRATEGIES

READING ALOUD: One powerful way of improving your writing is to hear it. This can be done privately, where you read your text aloud in your own voice. This can also be done in a group where either you read your text to your peers or they read it to you. These all provide new ways of seeing your writing because you are hearing it. The change in medium (from print to speech) can provide you an opportunity to hear what is working. If you have peers reading to you, then take notes on where they have trouble getting through the words on the page or when they raise an eyebrow or wrinkle their foreheads. These are all ways that you are getting feedback on what readers are experiencing. Depending upon the readers' reactions, you will need to make modifications to the writing or replicate what works in other places in your writing. Stopping the readers when they stumble or wrinkle their face and asking what is going on gives insight into what readers are actually experiencing and not just what you imagined would be happening. If you want readers to have a different reaction, then you gain some insight into what is happening so that you can change it.

PEER-REVIEWING: This is not a "grading" session. This activity is meant to mimic a readership of your writing. That is, your readers are real people, like your peers, who can give you feedback on what is working and what is not working in your writing. Your instructor may have questions for you to use as your guide during peer-review, or you may be asked to develop some of your own or as a class. Either way, you and your readers—your peers—are meant to provide constructive feedback. Some questions that might help you shape constructive feedback are:

- As a reader, where do you get confused? Articulate what is confusing. Write it out or talk it out with the writer.
- As a reader, where are there gaps in the thinking? What might the writer do to bridge that gap? What additional information is needed?
- As a reader, are you pulled along, moved forward, through the ideas in the paper, in a smooth or rough way? If "rough," what might be causing this? What could the writer do to smooth it out?
- What do you, the reader, expect to happen in the text? Why? How might the writer make an adjustment in the draft to help meet that expectation?

- Where does the text really shine or come across as interesting, insightful, or having a "wow!" factor? Why does this work for you? How might the writer use this same strategy in other places in the text?

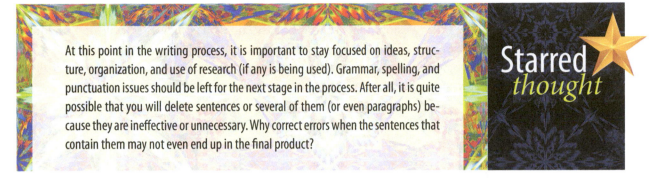

At this point in the writing process, it is important to stay focused on ideas, structure, organization, and use of research (if any is being used). Grammar, spelling, and punctuation issues should be left for the next stage in the process. After all, it is quite possible that you will delete sentences or several of them (or even paragraphs) because they are ineffective or unnecessary. Why correct errors when the sentences that contain them may not even end up in the final product?

Starred *thought*

Once your readers have provided you feedback on what is working and what is not working, then you go into the next stage in the process, which is typically called "revision." This stage is where you may be removing sentences, paragraphs, or whole ideas that may not fit into the text after you have re-seen them in the eyes of your readers. You might move sentences, paragraphs, or ideas around, add new ones, or put them in a different order. Revision is when the real work of writing begins, for you are now re-seeing your draft in a new way. You see what works and what does not, and you begin to think differently about your text now that others have read it and are a sounding board for you to rework your text into something more effective and more powerful!

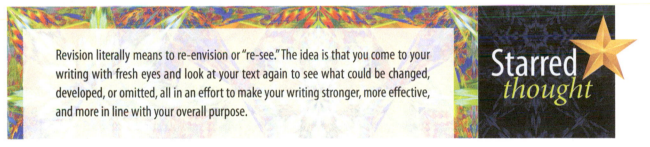

Revision literally means to re-envision or "re-see." The idea is that you come to your writing with fresh eyes and look at your text again to see what could be changed, developed, or omitted, all in an effort to make your writing stronger, more effective, and more in line with your overall purpose.

Starred *thought*

Some instructors may have you resubmit the revised draft, calling it a formal draft, a second draft, the next draft, or by some other name particular to your instructor. Whatever it is called, the intent is that with every revision (reworking/rewriting), you have a new text, and moving through multiple drafts and revisions makes each draft stronger and more effective. It makes what you want to say actually come out on the page.

Professional writers and experienced writers will often do all of these stages at the same time. They write a sentence, fix a comma splice or spelling error, add a sentence, read it aloud, read a source for more information, include a quote, leave the writing to think for a minute or two, come back to write several sentences or maybe delete several sentences, and then stop and start these all over again. Most novice writers, especially those who are first-year university students, do not always know what they are struggling with, or they get bogged down too soon in "correcting" errors before they have figured out what they want to really say. Sometimes, novice writers spend a lot of time on correcting and fixing their text that is not even kept in the final revision/final product, so they end up having wasted time on something that was not needed. If you find yourself fixing or rereading something you are writing on, this is okay, but you need to realize where you are in the process of writing so that you pay attention to the most important aspect of your text first.

STAGE 4: EDITING

Some instructors differentiate between editing and proofreading. Editing is typically thought of as examining sentences for style, variation, tone, and overall "sense." The next level of editing is usually concerned with how each sentence works with others in a paragraph. Does each sentence link clearly and logically to the next one? Do the parts of the sentences link well with each other?

In the publishing industry, writers provide a nearly perfect draft to their editor who then creates a document that needs to be formatted to fit the kind of publication they are doing. The editor and his or her team will create a "proof," a version of this finalized product, for the writer to review and approve. Hence, the *proof*reading is typically reserved for the nitty-gritty details related to grammar, mechanics, and usage. Does the subject agree with the verb in each sentence? Are the quotation marks, periods, and citations properly inserted? Are all of the words spelled correctly? Are the visuals on the page in effective positions?

STRATEGIES

SPELL AND GRAMMAR CHECKERS: Word programs have a built-in grammar and spell checker, which are useful tools to catch obvious errors or problems in a text; however, they are neither perfect nor always accurate or foolproof. If you use these tools, keep in mind that they are only ONE of the tools you should use. Consider, for example, that you spell the word "tow" when you really meant "two." The spell checker will not catch this because "tow" is a word; it is just not the one you meant to use. The grammar checker also sometimes marks long sentences with that green squiggly as an incomplete sentence or run-on, yet, in reality, you have used a beautiful compound-complex sentence. In short, these tools are just that: tools. You still must use other strategies to ensure you have made all of the corrections and have made them accurately.

READING ALOUD: Reading your work aloud or having someone else read it aloud is a good tactic, but for a slightly different reason than when you are drafting. When you read silently to yourself, you often will "fix" errors or overlook them because your brain "fixes" them. When you read aloud, you halt this autocorrection, and this gives you an opportunity to catch errors you would normally overlook. Having a reader read your work aloud is also a great tactic. When your reader stumbles, raises an eyebrow, or pauses, this could be an indication that there is an error. Also, having a set of eyes other than yours is a way to gain some objectivity. After all, you might not see an error because you have been so devoted to your writing and the ideas that you automatically "fix" it when you are reading it, or you might simply not see the error because you already know what you meant to write.

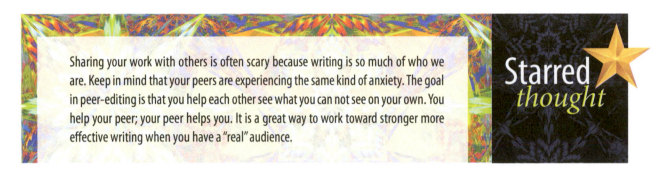

Sharing your work with others is often scary because writing is so much of who we are. Keep in mind that your peers are experiencing the same kind of anxiety. The goal in peer-editing is that you help each other see what you can not see on your own. You help your peer; your peer helps you. It is a great way to work toward stronger more effective writing when you have a "real" audience.

FOCUSED PEER-REVIEW: Peer-reviewing devoted strictly to editing can be helpful. We would call this "peer-editing." Another set of eyes reading a text is a great way to catch missing words or misspellings because the peer does not know what you have written until he or she reads it. The peer is not going to overlook or fix the errors that you are automatically fixing yourself because you are aware of your writing.

MINI-LESSONS: Asking your instructor to teach a few mini-lessons on specific areas of concern is also a good strategy. Your instructor will have tricks to teach you how to find and correct possessives, subject–verb agreement, pronoun–antecedent agreement, and many others. Do not be afraid to ask for help with specific elements of grammar and mechanics.

STAGE 5: PUBLISHING

The final stage in the writing process goes by many names: submission, final product, last or final draft, and publishing. If referred to as the "final draft," the idea is that all writing never really ends; there is always a possible revision, another "draft." However, we just stop the writing because the due date has arrived. This final draft, this final product, is what will need to be evaluated. In academia, this is when you get a grade.

The final product that you submit is what is polished, "pretty," complete, and ready for an official reading (by the instructor or by some other entity, such as a committee who reads college-entrance essays). The text is complete, intact, revised, edited, and polished. All of the hard work, labor, and time you devoted to getting your ideas down, and down accurately and effectively, is embodied in this final product. Sometimes, depending upon the assignment and purpose, you will have your work made available to the class (as in a class project), an undergraduate conference (where you present your work to other students, faculty, and staff outside of the classroom), or simply for your instructor. The submitting/publishing stage is a celebration of your hard work!

Name: _____ Date: _____

REFLECTIONS: MY WRITING PROCESS PROFILE

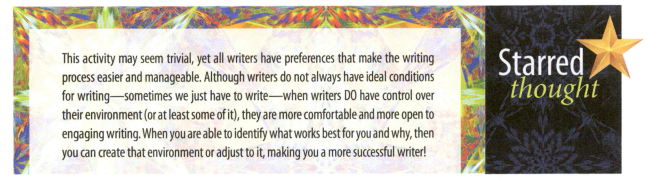

This activity may seem trivial, yet all writers have preferences that make the writing process easier and manageable. Although writers do not always have ideal conditions for writing—sometimes we just have to write—when writers DO have control over their environment (or at least some of it), they are more comfortable and more open to engaging writing. When you are able to identify what works best for you and why, then you can create that environment or adjust to it, making you a more successful writer!

Starred *thought*

1. Recall at least three different scenarios when you had to write, using the following questions to prompt your thinking.

   Location: Where were you?

   Occasion: Why were you writing? (For example, was it for fun, work, school?)

   Environment: What were the conditions? Consider: Who was there? Were you inside or outside? What was the temperature? Was it quiet or loud? Include anything else that captures the conditions of that writing moment.

   Response: How did it feel to be in that environment doing that kind of writing? How did you feel as a writer? What worked? What did not work?

   Speculation: Consider why you had the response(s) you did. What would have made the writing easier? More enjoyable?

   SCENARIO 1:

   Location:

   Writing Occasion:

   Environment/Conditions:

   Response:

   Speculation:

   SCENARIO 2:

   Location:

Writing Occasion:

Environment/Conditions:

Results:

Feelings:

Speculation:

SCENARIO 3:

Location:

Writing Occasion:

Environment/Conditions:

Results:

Feelings:

Speculation:

2. Examine your three scenarios to discover what you might call your ideal writing environment.

When do you prefer to write? Morning, afternoon, evening, night? Why?

Where do you prefer to write? At home, at school, in the library, outside? Why?

Do you prefer a quiet environment or do you need music or noise? Why?

Do you prefer natural or artificial light? Why?

Do you prefer to handwrite or type? Why?

Do you prefer having snacks on hand? What kind? Why?

Do you need a special drink, such as tea or coffee? Why?

3. When your ideal writing environment is not possible, what might you do to make it as comfortable as possible, based on your preferences?

CHAPTER 4

Writing Ethics

In this chapter, you will learn to:

1. distinguish between morals and ethics;

2. explain the complex nature of academic honesty and dishonesty;

3. explain why citing in academia is an issue of ethical behavior;

4. identity what forms of plagiarism exist;

5. explain why varying forms of plagiarism matter; and

5. explain the evolution of "copyright" laws and the ethics behind them.

There are many kinds of writers just as there are many kinds of writing. In academia, the writing you do is mostly based on reading about a subject matter and writing about it. Most of the time we are asked to use sources in our writing because we are entering into a kind of conversation that has been going on before we entered the course and will continue long after the course ends. Therefore, we must be aware of the authors we are reading and what information, insights, inspirations, and ideas they provide. As writers, we are obligated to use these sources to further our own understanding of the world, so we must use them wisely and accurately. This gives rise to the concept of *writing ethics*.

Ethics in writing is an extremely important aspect of writing, yet students often do not fully realize the reasons why. Because ethics is so valued in academia (and, in turn, in the workplace) and the nuances of ethics are often underappreciated or misunderstood, we are going to spend time on it in this chapter.

WHAT ARE ETHICS IN WRITING?

Let us define ethics, for ethics and morals are often used synonymously, but they are not exactly the same.

MORALS: religiously based, set of rules, external rule giver

ETHICS: socially and communally based, set of principles, internal rule giver

In academia, readers, writers, students, faculty, and administrators are bound by expectations and values that are outside of any given religion, for students may not all practice the same faith. Hence, the expectations for *ethics* in academia are based on communal, social, and academic values. Although these areas intersect, let us examine these components individually.

COMMUNAL EXPECTATIONS: At university, students are engaging in a special kind of writing, and all students engage in developing their own critical thinking in various areas or disciplines. Whether you are looking at the natural world and studying plant/animal life through observation or are studying literature in the Humanities and how a Shakespearean play has been interpreted over different centuries, students are entering into a preexisting conversation, one that other students started and later became the scholars and researchers you read now. They became the new generation of knowledgeable experts in their fields, and you someday might be, too! This means that writers need to give special attention to those who have come before them, the community of those who know and share their knowledge. This is done throughout acknowledging sources in writing and using the appropriate citation styles.

SOCIAL GENERATION OF KNOWLEDGE: Connected to this communal practice of knowledge sharing is *knowledge generation*. In the classroom (and across the courses students are enrolled), students and instructors read material, work on questions, and discuss information. There is a shared purpose within the classroom where the members of the class develop an understanding together. This kind of classroom knowledge is not cited as such. The knowledge is assumed to be shared because it has been socially constructed within the context of the classroom. Classmates may make a good point or observation that the class benefits from, and this also is assumed to be socially developed knowledge within the coursework and no citations are needed.

The exception to this is when your instructor or a guest lecturer provides information. Typically, the instructors are professionals and experts in their field. They have been studying the materials for years and have become part of the larger communal dialogue. Therefore, when they give lectures, writers tend to cite them as such, if those lectures are used as sources in the written part of coursework. You may notice, however, that instructors mention other scholars who have had an impact on their thinking when they mention names of scholars in discussion or in a presentation; they are paying homage to—and respect for—the ideas of those who have shaped their thinking.

ACADEMIC VALUE: The academic aspect of ethics is where students typically run afoul. When writers use another's ideas, words, or concepts, they must say "thank you"—this is how you should think of citations. It is more impressive for writers to insert citations—when needed and appropriate—than to claim they have come up with these ideas themselves. In other words, impress your readers with your expert use of sources and breadth of reading rather than simply trying to "sound" a particular way. Citing the work you have done while researching is an act of honor. You are honoring yourself by acknowledging others are helping to shape your thinking. You are honoring those who have spent many days or years, blood, sweat, or tears on issues or ideas that they cared deeply enough about to compose the texts you are using.

This ethical use of sources/research, then, is a complex interaction between the writer, the reader, and the subject matter. Some writing requires more research than others; some projects may require more research than others. However, when research is used, we owe it to ourselves, the original writer, and our readers to acknowledge the hard work everyone has contributed.

WHAT IS ACADEMIC DISHONESTY?

In academia, ethics are often referred to as either academic dishonesty or academic honesty. Being honest about what you are learning is part of the experience that is expected at university or college. Because these are places where people are learning a trade, skill, or knowledge to be successful and productive in a career, any shortcuts, lies, or misrepresentation of the truth used to achieve a grade, an award, a certificate, or a degree means the person is not truly qualified to hold such a designation. Consider the biology student who cheats on exams yet is accepted to a medical school to become a practicing doctor, or an English student who cheats on literature exams yet goes on to teach students the wrong information! In other words, the ethics in academia are aligned to what is expected and required in the public sphere and the workplace.

Academic dishonesty includes cheating, collusion, and plagiarism within the academic setting. *Cheating* is when an individual uses materials, methods, or actions to unfairly gain advantage over others. The typical example is taking in notes to an exam when there are no notes allowed. *Collusion* is when a group (two or more people) acts together to cheat. *Plagiarism* is using sources without citing them or citing them incorrectly in a public or published speech or in writing.

Starred *thought*

Each university will have its own policies for each of these dishonest academic acts, so you should be sure to read your student handbook or university handbook to know what the penalties are for each act. Better yet, take on the goal of learning honesty. If you do not understand something, be sure to get extra help so that you can be successful!

WHY CITING IS AN ACT OF ACADEMIC HONESTY AND WRITING ETHICALLY

Writers read, and when they read, *they* are learning from other writers. When *we* learn from these writers, and use *their* ideas in *our* own writing, we need to give *them* credit. They—like you—spend hours and energy on writing. We want to thank them for their hard work, late hours, and gift of sharing what they have learned and have come to understand. Citing sources, then, is an essential part of learning to write well, honestly, and ethically. Here are five important reasons why we cite accurately:

1. To say "thank you" to those who have come before us to teach us something we did not know

2. To differentiate our own thinking from those of others who have helped shape our thinking

3. To direct our readers where to go to find out more about the ideas we are using

4. To show an intelligent use of our research and breadth/depth of reading

5. To demonstrate our understanding of how to work with sources

When working with sources, writers are engaging in a relationship that the rhetorical triangle exemplifies in two ways. On one level, writers are *using* sources, and on another level, writers are *producing* materials that can become sources for others. These differences show us the two kinds of sources that are typically used in academic writing: *primary sources* and *secondary sources*.

- **PRIMARY SOURCES:** These texts are the basis for writing. Examples: stories and plays, direct observations of natural phenomenon, performances and artwork, student essays, policy documents, historical records, advertisements, speeches, products (such as toothpastes or cars).

  - Notice that whether primary or secondary, a writer (author) writes for someone (audience) on a topic (subject).

- **SECONDARY SOURCES:** These texts are about primary sources, usually written by scholars who are studying the same or similar primary source. Also, the texts and essays you compose are considered secondary sources.

  - Notice that when you are using these sources, you are the writer who is writing to an audience about the subject matter.

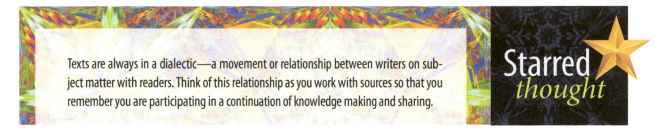

Texts are always in a dialectic—a movement or relationship between writers on subject matter with readers. Think of this relationship as you work with sources so that you remember you are participating in a continuation of knowledge making and sharing.

When we cite sources, we have to pay attention to several elements:

- The kind of sources we are using

- The ideas, concepts, and term/definitions those sources present

- The documentation style we need to use

There are many documentation styles used in academia. Some of the most well-known or often used are Modern Language Association (MLA), American Psychology Association (APA), Chicago Manual of Style (CMS or Turabian), Council of Science Editors (CSE), and Bluebook Law Review (Bluebook). The discipline you are writing in will often determine the documentation style.

Example of Discipline	Typical Documentation Style Used
English	MLA
Chemistry	CSE
History	CMS or Turabian
Sociology	APA
Law	Bluebook

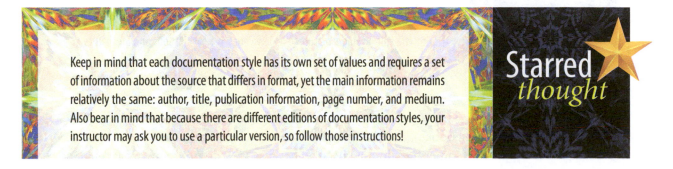

Keep in mind that each documentation style has its own set of values and requires a set of information about the source that differs in format, yet the main information remains relatively the same: author, title, publication information, page number, and medium. Also bear in mind that because there are different editions of documentation styles, your instructor may ask you to use a particular version, so follow those instructions!

Although the style or format of documentation will differ (that is, what the citations will actually look like), the reasons for citing remain the same throughout all styles.

- **DIRECT QUOTATION:** Whenever you use a word, phrase, sentence, or several sentences, you must use quotation marks around the verbatim language and include a citation.

- **PARAPHRASE:** Instead of using the author's exact words, you are explaining in your own words what a passage is saying or what the author's main ideas are. Although no quotation marks are needed, a citation is!

- **SUMMARY:** This sophisticated use of sources can be tricky. Typically you provide an introductory statement about the author, provide context for the material, and provide the main ideas in your own words. You then include a citation at the end.

If you are learning something new from the author, cite. If you are using the author's words or ideas that you did not have before, cite. If you are using the author's words or explanations for something you knew but did not yet write out yourself, cite.

WHAT COUNTS AS PLAGIARISM?

There are several levels of plagiarism.

1. **AN ERROR IN CITATION MECHANICS:** This is when there was an oversight, quite unintentional, by the writer. It usually includes missing a quotation mark or including quotation marks but missing the page number (or some combination thereof).

During the editing stage, be sure to review your work for citations and mechanics.

2. **IGNORANCE:** Sometimes writers use unusual sources or new media (such as ebooks), and there is no formalized way to cite them. In such cases, writers sometimes do not cite at all because they do not know what to do, nor have they asked for advice.

There are new editions of citation manuals that come out to address the changes in source mediums, such as the 2016 edition of MLA that now addresses how to cite ebooks that do not include page numbers. When in doubt, ask your instructor what to do!

3. **LAZINESS:** Although not strictly intentional or unintentional, "forgetting" to cite or thinking you will "come back later" to insert a citation creates plagiarism. This is why is it essential for you to work with sources carefully while you have them in front of you. (See Appendices A and B for strategies.)

Keeping careful notes when you are researching means you save time later when you begin to incorporate source material in your writing. Taking shortcuts during the researching stage or in the drafting stage will only create problems and potential plagiarism!

4. **INTENTIONAL DECEIT:** The most egregious form of plagiarism comes in the form of wholesale, verbatim, phrases, paragraphs, or conceptual ideas in a writer's essay that are not quoted or cited or that are misrepresented. It also includes:

having sources listed on the bibliography that you do not cite in your writing,

having sources cited in your paper that do not appear on the bibliography, or

saying that an author says something that the source actually does not say.

It also can be a paper that the student either bought or received free from an on-line company or person (either a friend or someone else). It also could be a recycled paper, submitted to another course that the student is taking or had taken in the past, OR a paper that is authored by another student who has given the essay to the current student.

As you can see, plagiarism is very serious because it means that the writer is not paying attention to his or her writing so that it holds up to scrutiny. If you want to communicate and be heard, you must be sure you work with sources carefully and honestly!

In summary, here are the different kinds of plagiarism, whether intentional or not:

Direct quotes missing on either side of the quoted material. Plagiarism.

Missing open or close quotes. Plagiarism.

Missing in-text citations altogether. Plagiarism.

Having partial in-text citations. Plagiarism.

Misrepresenting a source's ideas or saying it says something it does not actually say. Plagiarism.

Including sources on a bibliography without using them in your work. Plagiarism.

Using sources and quoting them, but not including them on a bibliography. Plagiarism.

So, there are many ways writers can unintentionally commit plagiarism, but it is still plagiarism, academic dishonesty, either way. This means that writers must have a strong understanding of how research is conducted, how to undergo a research process, and pay extra attention to punctuation and citation styles. In-depth explanation and exercises for researching and citing are found in Chapter 10 and Appendix A.

COPYRIGHT LAWS

Not only do writers have to pay attention to citing sources in their writing, but they also need to pay attention to the laws of copyright and digital files.

*COPYRIGHT

According to the US Copyright Office (2006), **copyright** is defined as "a form of protection grounded in the U.S. Constitution and granted by law for original works of authorship fixed in a tangible medium of expression. Copyright covers both published and unpublished works" (para. 1). Copyright protection covers any literary, dramatic, musical, and artistic work, including poetry, novels, movies, songs, computer software, and architecture. Ideas and facts cannot be copyrighted.

Copyright law has developed over several centuries. The chart on the following page shows the major milestones in U.S. copyright law history (Tedford & Herbeck, 2009, US Copyright Office, 1973). Each of the pieces of legislation is explained below.

*From *Becoming A Critic: An Introduction to Analyzing Media Content* by Rebecca M. L. Curnalia, Cary Wecht, and Amber L. Ferris. Copyright © 2014 by Kendall Hunt Publishing Company. Reprinted with permission.

COPYRIGHT ACT OF 1790. This was the first piece of intellectual property legislation from the federal government. It protected maps, charts, and books printed in the United States under copyright for 14 years from the date of copyright approval. At the end of the first 14 years, copyright could be extended once for another 14 years. After this time, the material would enter the **public domain**. Information in the public domain can be reproduced without paying fees to the creator(s). For example, Shakespeare's plays are within the public domain. Educators can print his plays in their texts without paying royalties.

1834 AMENDMENT. Music is added under copyright protection, both written and performed. Copyright protection was also extended to 28 years with the option of extending protection an additional 14 years.

1870 AMENDMENT. This amendment extended protection to the other fine arts: paintings, drawings, photographs, and sculptures.

1909 AMENDMENT. This amendment extended copyright ownership from 28 years with the option of an additional 28-year extension.

1912 AMENDMENT. Movies and motion pictures are now covered under copyright.

COPYRIGHT ACT OF 1976. This law abolished the renewal clauses and extended copyright to the way we view it today. Copyright under this law established creator rights to the life of the author plus 50 years. This law also outlined the principle of fair use. **Fair use** states that you can use copyrighted material for criticism, commentary, news and reporting, and teaching.

THE SONNY BONO COPYRIGHT TERM EXTENSION ACT OF 1998. This law established that newly issued copyrights extend protection through the life of the last living creator plus 70 years. The legislation also established that works by corporate authors copyrighted before January 1, 1978 would have extended copyright for 95 years after publication or 120 years after creation. This means that no new works will enter the public domain until 2019.

THE DIGITAL MILLENNIUM COPYRIGHT ACT OF 1998. This act extended copyright protection to the internet. The law also set guidelines for who would be liable for copyright infringements on the web. According to this legislation, internet service providers could not be held responsible if a user committed copyright infringement. If they do discover a user is violating copyright, they are obligated to post take down notices. If you've ever gone to YouTube to watch a clip from your favorite show and found that it was gone, that is most likely because that content was copyrighted and posting it was a violation of the law.

As you can see, copyright law has been extended over the years in both length of coverage and breadth of material eligible. Future laws will be enacted to deal with our ever-growing technological advances. One context that has been hotly debated in the courts is the issue of file-sharing.

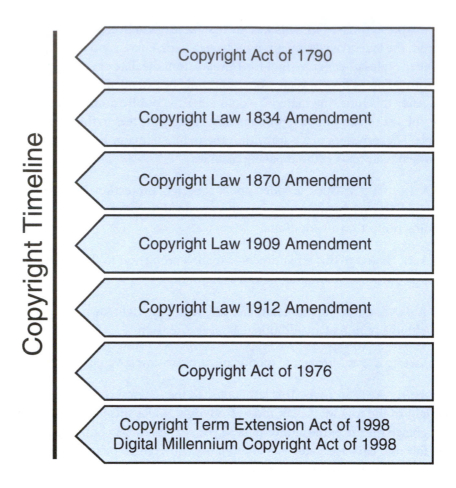

MP3 TECHNOLOGY AND COPYRIGHT. There are three major court cases that have tackled the issue of mp3 file sharing. The first case to be brought to the courts on this issue was *UMG Recordings Inc. v. MP3.com, Inc.* (2000). MP3.com had more than 80,000 CDs worth of songs on their website. Users could store, customize, and listen to songs from the database. In order to access the servers and download the songs, you had to prove you already owned the CD by inserting it in your computer when prompted or you had the option to buy the CD from an online retailer. UMG and several other music companies (including Sony, Capitol Records, BMG, Warner, etc.) sued the website for copyright infringement. The website attempted to argue for fair use; however, the courts ruled in favor of the music companies (*UMG v. MP3.com*, 2000). MP3.com was ordered to pay fines for copyright infringement, bankrupting the company.

The second landmark case with respect to music downloading was *A&M Records, Inc. v. Napster, Inc.* (2001). Napster was sued by A&M Records for copyright infringement. Napster was a network sharing company that allowed users to upload their music and download other music through a server. It was one of the first peer-to-peer (P2P) file sharing services. Even though Napster did not copy any of the music directly, the record company argued that it should still be liable because they knowingly encouraged, facilitated, and profited from others' copyright infringement. As with MP3.com, Napster tried to use fair use as a defense. As in the previous case, the courts sided with the record company. Napster was ordered to determine which content was copyrighted and what was not, which eventually led to the downfall of the company. This case established that companies could not assist users in copyright infringement and could be held accountable for users' actions.

The last case that impacted the downfall of free MP3 sharing and downloading was *MGM Studios, Inc. v. Grokster, Ltd.* (2005). After the rise of Napster, P2P sharing sites popped up all over the internet. New sites learned the lessons of Napster and avoided housing files on a centralized server. Grokster allowed for sharing of movies as well as MP3 files. The case made it all the way up to the Supreme Court, where the Court found that P2P networks willingly engage in illegal behavior, and therefore could be held liable for copyright infringement.

Overall, these cases show how technology can impact copyright laws. The lesson learned from these cases is that anyone who downloads copyrighted material without permission from the copyright holder is guilty of direct copyright infringement. Although some copying might be fair use, if you are using P2P networks, the networks have to be putting legal files on the web or they too can be sued for infringement.

PART 3 Genres

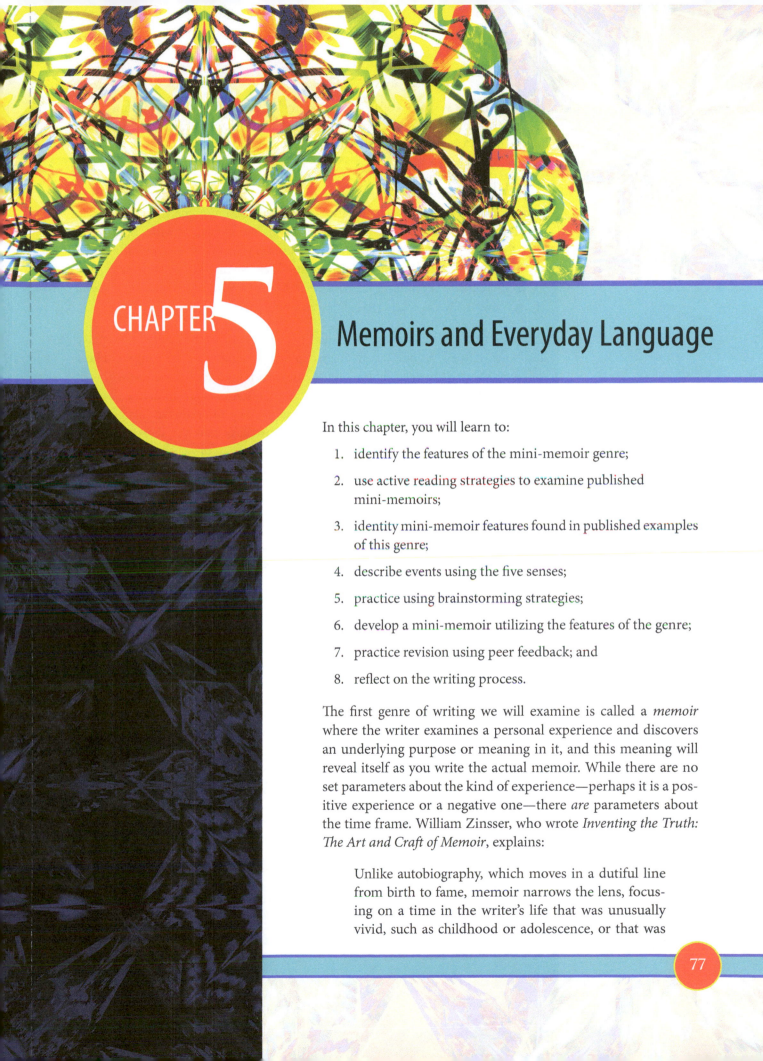

CHAPTER 5

Memoirs and Everyday Language

In this chapter, you will learn to:

1. identify the features of the mini-memoir genre;

2. use active reading strategies to examine published mini-memoirs;

3. identity mini-memoir features found in published examples of this genre;

4. describe events using the five senses;

5. practice using brainstorming strategies;

6. develop a mini-memoir utilizing the features of the genre;

7. practice revision using peer feedback; and

8. reflect on the writing process.

The first genre of writing we will examine is called a *memoir* where the writer examines a personal experience and discovers an underlying purpose or meaning in it, and this meaning will reveal itself as you write the actual memoir. While there are no set parameters about the kind of experience—perhaps it is a positive experience or a negative one—there *are* parameters about the time frame. William Zinsser, who wrote *Inventing the Truth: The Art and Craft of Memoir*, explains:

> Unlike autobiography, which moves in a dutiful line from birth to fame, memoir narrows the lens, focusing on a time in the writer's life that was unusually vivid, such as childhood or adolescence, or that was

framed by war or travel or public service or some other special circumstance....[A] good memoir is [...]a work of history, catching a distinctive moment in the life of both a person and a society. (15)

Because memoirs can be lengthy, a *mini-memoir*, one that captures a specific moment in time, allows for writers to focus on a very specific moment or event and its impact upon the writer's sense of self. Mini-memoirs use description, narration, and vivid details to show the reader what that experience was like; in fact, the writer tries to recreate the experience for the reader so that the impact might be shared with the reader and may even change the reader's own sense of self. Memoirs, even in their briefest form, should have a powerful message because the experience, itself, was powerful enough that the writer wanted to tell the reader about it!

One way to study writing and our identity as writers is to write about language and how we use it. A good way to begin exploring the nature of language and how it is shaped by its users is by looking at our own language that we use with our friends and family. This "everyday language" is often referred to as the "unofficial" language or the familial, informal language. Amy Tan refers to this personal language as the "mother tongue," that is, the language that she shares with her mother.[1] Richard Rodriguez describes it as a "private" language in his book-length memoir about his own education.[2] What these writers describe is a language that is shared between members of a small community, typically the family unit or even one that extends to close neighbors and friends. Typically, this particular use of language includes references to activities and events that are known only by the members of this community, and the language used is often marked by inside jokes, references to ideas or words that have special meaning only to those who know its particular reference, and what might be called slang or insider language.

WHAT'S NEXT?

Read the following mini-memoir by Keith Gilyard. As you read, choose at least one active reading strategy suggested in Chapter 2 of this textbook and apply it to your reading. Pay special attention to the following:

1. Places where Gilyard uses an informal language and where he uses formal language: What do you notice about when and where he uses these?

2. Moments that show personal experience where Gilyard describes his "first lessons."

3. Places where Gilyard provides guideposts that link the overall memoir together.

---

1. Amy Tan, "Mother Tongue." *The Threepenny Review* 43 (1990): 7-8. Print.
2. Richard Rodriguez, *Hunger of Memory: The Education of Richard Rodriguez.* New York: Bantam Books, 1982. Print.

FIRST LESSONS

by Keith Gilyard

Some events come before the memory. Completely beyond the veil of vagueness. Just no way to recall. The only knowledge I have of the times came through eavesdropping. I could not deal with direct questioning because it was clear that made me a bug. Try to open up the past and I would get shrugged off with stares like roach spray. So I just kept listening and observing and drawing my own conclusions, trying to get a sense of what the pre-memory was all about. That's important to me because it's a part of life too and it's a lot like the wind, you know, you can't see it but it can kick your rump pretty good if it blows hard enough.

I hit the scene uptown in 1952 on a Sunday afternoon. I think I started out as a good reason for all to be happy, but there was a curious error on the take-home copy of my birth certificate. In the space where the name of the father belongs my own name was written in. His was left off the document altogether. That error, however committed, was my first omen.

I hadn't yet cut a tooth when I received omen number two. A fire broke out in our apartment. Started in back of the refrigerator. My mother detected it first, yanked my one-year-old sister out of her bed, snatched me up from the crib, and hustled on outdoors. She didn't bother to arouse her husband/my dad. It's a blessing he managed to get out on his own. I've always thought that was a horrible thing for her to do although by the time I heard the story, with the influence I was under, I felt he probably deserved it. And I have chuckled about the event on numerous occasions since. But at other times I have pictured my father lying dead in a robe of bright yellow flames and felt my own palms moisten with fear. There was no doubt something cruel going on in our little world.

The signs persisted like ragweed. Sad events that would be revealed to me in tale. The tale of the perfectly thrown frying pan, you know, it's more feistiness than I would like to see in a woman of mine. Sherry and I were, in one sense, beneath it all. Down on the floor knocking over and spilling everything. But we also assumed a role in the power play as it was we who became its center. Mama took that battle also; as far back as we can remember we had the distinct impression that we belonged to her exclusively. We were her objects of adornment and possession, always dressed for compliments. Pops could get no primary billing in that setup. When I think back now to my earliest remembrances I sense him only as a haze in the background. And even as I reel forward again and he begins to crystallize for me, it's quite some time before he appears essential. Moms, on the other hand, was ranked up there next to sunlight from the beginning.

That's a long way to come from Ashford, Alabama. Way down by the Chipola River. Little Margie, with stubbornness her most celebrated trait. Might as well whip a

Reprinted from "First Lessons" from *Voices of the Self: A Study of Language Competence* by Keith Gilyard. Copyright © 1991 Wayne State University Press, with the permission of Wayne State University Press.

tree, they would say, if you were figuring on whipping her for a confession. At least you spare your own self some pain. And she was real close to her few chosen friends. If she liked you she could bring you loyalty in a million wheelbarrows. Labeled "good potential," she worked far below it. Skated her way through school. Folks have camped just outside her earshot for years whispering, "She's smart so she could do better if. . . ."

Ammaziah, though bright, didn't have a chance to skate through school. He had to work on a farm northeast of Ashford, going up toward the Chattahoochee. "He's just a plain nice man" is the worst thing I have ever heard anybody outside of our own household say about him. And I guess it would be hard not to like a big and gentle Baptist with a basic decency who could hold his liquor and had a name you could make fun of.

He liked to watch all the horses run and all the New York women too. Couldn't lick either gamble. He hadn't developed enough finesse for the big town. I know he tried hard at times but whenever he put together two really good steps irresponsibility would rear up and knock him back three. He couldn't be any Gibraltar for you.

All this going on around our heads. The big folks. Both destined to be enshrined in the best-friend-you-could-possibly-have hall of fame, provided they could keep each other off the selection committee. But they still hung out together. Hadn't fully understood the peace that can crop up here and there amid the greatest confusion. And right in the middle of 1954 came daughter number two. Judy ate well and slept a lot, then less, and grew to be a good partner to knock around with as we caromed off the walls of the Harlem flat and tumbled forward.

In the early reaches of memory events swirl about like batches of stirred leaves. No order or sequence. I remember we had two pet turtles. One had a yellow shell. The other's was red. We kept them in a bowl with a little plastic palm tree and tiny cream-colored pebbles. Sherry fed them and I poured in the fresh water. Well the turtles were a bit frisky. They often climbed out of the bowl and we had to overturn tables and cushions and chairs to find them. I don't recall how many times we went on this chase but it was all over one morning when they were found under the sofa with their bellies ripped open by rats. For a long time afterward I would associate rats with turtlemeat first, rather than cheese, which I guess isn't exactly a good start toward a high IQ.

So the turtles died early on. But I can't tell you whether that was before the back of my head was split open on the front stoop. There was a bunch of us out there preparing to run a dash down 146th Street. Victory wasn't the main thing in these races. Just please don't come in last or you would be the first one to get your mother talked about and everything. I had poor position inside along the rail next to this chubby girl, but as we came thundering past the front of the building I began to pull away from her. I was getting away from the last spot for sure when she reached out and pushed me down. My head banged hard into the edge of a concrete step and the blood started dripping down the back of my neck and I started screaming like crazy. Then I had to get shaven bald in one spot and look like a jerk so I could get patched up right. But that was better still than being last. I mean I had heard Pee Wee Thomas, who was in school already, tell Tyrone that the reason he was so slow was because whoever Tyrone's father was had to be slow too not to have been able to get away from Tyrone's ugly damn mama.

There was a babysitter we went to sometimes down on Seventh Avenue. Her name was Janine and she had boy-girl twins, Diane and Darnell, who were a few months older than Sherry. She was real nice and let us drag our toys all over the house, but whenever her husband, Butch, would come home early in the afternoon she would round us up quickly and herd us into the kids' room. We were under strict orders not to come out and of course we didn't. But she never said anything about peeping. The first time was at Darnell's suggestion. We crept up to the door and cracked it with the stealth of cat burglars. I couldn't see over Sherry and the twins so I crouched to the floor and never did get a look at the action. Darnell almost burst out laughing and we retreated to the farthest corner of the room. We sent Judy off to play with some blocks.

"What is they doin Sherry?" I whispered as I took a seat atop Darnell's wagon.

"Oh you so stupid Keith."

"Well I ain't see so good."

"Oh you just so stupid. Tell him Darnell." She and Diane were giggling.

"No you Sherry."

"No Darnell you."

"It's your brother. You 'pose to."

"I can't. I don't know for real."

"You know for real."

"No I don't."

"Then why you laughin?"

"I was laughin at you." And they all started laughing at each other. Then Darnell came and whispered in my ear: "They doin nasty."

"NASTY OOOOH NAS–." Darnell clamped his hand over my mouth. "You gotta be quiet Keith or we can't go no more."

I was quiet. And got to go many times before I decided, or was it Diane who decided, that we could do some nasty of our own. But we announced our intentions first and Sherry squealed and Janine gave both of us a spanking. Barely five, I was mad I had to wait.

I remember one Saturday we were coming home from the beauty parlor with my mother. I had on my cowboy get up, six-shooters at my sides. We were walking well up in front of her as usual, trained to stop at the corner. That morning, however, I took it into my head to go dashing across Eighth Avenue on my own. I think I saw my father but I'm not sure. I know I didn't look for any traffic lights. I tripped about halfway across and couldn't get to my feet again. I was struggling hard but my coordination had deserted me. Like scrambling on ice. There was a screeching of brakes and then the most gigantic bus imaginable was hovering over me. I still couldn't get the feet to work together. I was somehow yanked from under the bus, dragged the rest of the way across the street and, with my own pistols, beaten all the way up the block. It was a fierce thrashing and there were folks out there imploring my mother to stop. But verbal support was all I received. Wasn't anybody out there going to risk tangling with Moms. I have never fallen in any roadway, nor been pistol-whipped, since.

One evening we were digging into some fruit cocktail after dinner and heard a great ruckus out in the hallway. The cops were chasing these two drug addicts and they were headed for the roof. "They's junkies I know" said a man across the hall. Sherry had mentioned something about junkies to me before, but when the police paraded them down the stairs stark naked with their hands cuffed behind their backs it was the first time I had a good opportunity to see what they actually looked like. It was somewhat disappointing, however, for they looked just about like everybody else.

I was bringing a loaf of bread home from the store when I saw this gray dog getting his neck chewed off in a dogfight on the corner. I dropped my bag to go save him and was trying to push my way through the circle of gamblers and spectators when this huge man hoisted me up onto his shoulder. He thought I merely wanted a better view. Before I could figure a way to get down another man rescued the dog, though he was cursing the poor animal, and green bills changed hands around the circle.

Sherry had gone off to kindergarten and I decided to give Judy a sex change operation while our mother was asleep. I slipped her into a change of my clothing as I kept reassuring her. "You know it gon be more fun. You know it right?" She was properly willing. We had to roll the pants up at the bottom and her feet couldn't make it down into the toes of my sneakers but we could live with that. But we were dissatisfied with her hair. Such soft long braids. Boys get away with that now but not in '57.

'You gotta cut it."

"Then I be a boy Keith? I finish that I be a boy?"

"Yeah you'll be one. It gon be more fun too."

Scissors please. She wouldn't cut it in one fell swoop like I wanted her to do. She started nibbling at the edges. Tiny dark patches falling gently to the floor. As she became more relaxed, however, she began to clip at a faster pace and made a clearing on one side all the way to the scalp. I was urging her to clip even faster, "go head Judy go head," when Sherry came charging into the apartment, saw what was taking place, let out a long and soulful "Ooooooooh I'm gonna tell Ma," and ran into the other room to awaken her. I began to sweat.

"You made me" Judy accused.

"No I didn't and you gon git in trouble and git a beatin too."

"You made me."

"I did not."

"Yes you did."

"I DID NOT." I had to get loud to prove my innocence. Moms was already approaching fast like an enraged lioness and I wanted no part of her fury. She slashed me across the legs with her strap and cast me aside. I was getting off light. Unbelievably so. But Judy got it all.

Maybe I could have stood up for Judy, but by then I was taking the vast majority of the whippings in the household. So I guess I figured what the heck, Judy could stand to share some of the weight. She may have become a trifle less eager to pursue my ideas of fun but I was sort of growing bored with running around the house with her all morning anyway. I mean Sherry was bringing home books and fingerpaintings all the time and making kindergarten seem like the hip thing.

It was all right I suppose. Artwork and musical chairs and fairy tales. The biggest kindergarten thrill for me, however, was the chance to come home along Eighth Avenue unescorted. Sherry didn't get out until three o'clock and my mother didn't embarrass me by picking me up like I was a baby, so every day I had a three-and-a-half-block distance to negotiate as I pleased. Or at least I took it that way.

Some of us would go scampering along the Avenue. Anything could happen out there. The side streets were tall and narrow with hallways no more interesting than our own. But Eighth Avenue, well, that was the real world. We stuck our noses into the barber shop, the shoe repair shop, the fish market, the bars. The conversation was mostly baseball and whores. Willie Mays was clearly the Prince of Uptown, and the next best thing you could be was a pimp. We threw stones at sleeping winos and followed the vegetable wagon all the way down to 140th Street waiting for the horse to move his bowels in the middle of the street. Then we'd stay and watch the cars run over the large piles of dung. Every time a tire scored a bull's eye we'd shout "Squish" and spin about with glee. Don't let it be a truck that scored. Ecstasy. Sometimes we would run straight across 148th Street to Colonial Park to play tag and rock fight and climb the hill until the guilt snuck up on us one by one and then, each according to his conscience, we would begin to head for home.

From the very beginning my mother couldn't understand why it should take me over an hour to walk less than four blocks, especially when it meant showing up with my new jacket all muddy or my pants ripped at the knee, you know, the kinds of things you never notice until your mother points them out. And she made all her points clear with that belt. I tried telling her that the clock on the kitchen wall must be broken or something because I always ran straight home, but she wouldn't buy it. I eventually had to come around. And that's when I really got jammed.

There was a substitute teacher for our class one day and she didn't know the proper time to dismiss us. It must have been going on 12:30 and she was still reading us a story about Curious George. Our class was at the end of the hall, so when the other classes let out we couldn't hear them. There was no impatient parent to rescue us. The substitute just kept on and on about this wonderful monkey.

Finally she sensed something was wrong and asked us what time we were supposed to let out.

"Twelve o'clock" we chorused.

"Oh no" she exclaimed. "Are you sure?"

"We get out twelve o'clock" some of us repeated, as general chatter erupted about the room. Louis went up to her and said, "We get out when the two hands is straight up. That's twelve o'clock right?" She ran out of the room. When she returned a few moments later she was shouting "Hats and coats everybody. Hats and coats now. We're late."

Late was the last word I needed to hear. She couldn't let us out of there fast enough to suit me. I sprinted home as swiftly as possible, scaled the six flights of stairs in record time, and as I burst into the apartment out of breath my mother, as I knew she would be, was waiting for me belt in hand. She backed me up against the door with her stern voice.

"Haven't I told you about not coming straight home from school?" I caught my breath. I was sure glad I was armed with the truth.

"Ma we had a substitute. We had a substitute Ma and she didn't know what time to let us out. I ran all the way home."

"Boy don't tell that barefaced lie. I'll take the skin off your backside for lyin to me."

"But I ain't lyin Ma. I ain't."

"Shut up boy! Ain't no teacher can keep no class late like that."

"But she was readin us a story."

"Shut up I said. Don't be standin there and givin me no cold-ass argument." She drew back the strap and I cringed in terror. I sidestepped her, as the first blow crashed against my thigh, and took off for the living room. She was right behind me. I dove to my knees and stuck my head under the couch. It was one of the several defensive maneuvers I had developed by then. I was always mortgaging my rear to save my head. Wasn't going to let anybody beat me in the head. Which was all right with Moms.

"You ain't accomplishin nothing by stickin that behind up there like that boy. That's the part I want any old how. I'll teach you yet about not payin me no mind." She had that talking-beating rhythm in high gear. You know how you had to receive a lecture to go along with your whipping. And can't anyone on earth hand out a more artistic ass whipping than a Black woman can. Syncopated whippings: Boy didn't I lash lash tell you about lash lash lying to me? Lash lash lash lash hunh? Lash hunh boy? Lash lash lash hunh boy? Hunh? I was always supposed to answer these questions although my answering them never stopped anything and sometimes made matters worse, especially if I was giving the wrong answers as I was that day. Although I was hollering my head off I still managed to insist upon my innocence. To no avail. Lash lash lash I will break your behind lash if necessary lash boy. Do you hear me? Do you lash lash hear me?

I heard and I felt and it hurt both ways. After the beating I continued to proclaim my innocence. Only stopped when she became angry all over again and threatened me with more punishment. Afterwards I complained to my sisters on occasion, but it was weeks before I mentioned the incident to my mother again. She just gave me a warm smile and said, "I'll tell you something Keith. It all evens out."

Sibling rivalry stalked me from behind. I was getting intensive reading lessons from Sherry and had made progress to the point where I was ready to show off for Moms. We had her cornered on the sofa and I was holding the book out in front of me. Sherry was on my right, ready to help if I faltered, so I started reading something like:

> "See here," said Don. "Here are blue flowers. We want blue flowers.
> Let us get blue flowers."

It was something along those lines, you know, and I was performing well. My mother was beaming and I had her undivided attention until Judy came out of somewhere, slid the edge of a razor blade into the side of my face clear to the bone, narrowly missing my eye, and ripped a deep diagonal clean past my ear.

Blood popped out everywhere. I spent what seemed like hours with my head ducked under a running faucet. Towels. Compresses. Mercurochrome. Bandages. Then my mother seized a high-heeled shoe and beat Judy worse than she had beaten me for almost getting myself killed out on the Avenue.

My little sister never apologized. In fact she used to taunt me about this incident as she was later becoming a favorite target for my aggression. No matter what I did to her. Kick her, trip her, whatever. She would just keep repeating, "So I cut you in the face."

"Do it again" I would retort most angrily.

"I did it already."

"I dare you to do it again. I'll push you out the window."

"No you won't."

"Yes I will."

"No you won't."

"I will so." .

"Then I'll cut you in your face again."

"Then come on. Come on if you still think you so big and bad."

"I ain't scared."

"Come on then sucker."

"I'll cut you right in the face again."

"What you waitin for then fraidy cat?"

"I did it already."

She was about as mean a three year old as you will ever find.

Actually I had my hardest battles with Sherry. She was good for teaching me things but when her mood shifted I had to watch out. She gave me my next permanent scar by pressing a hot steam iron to the back of my hand. Burned off a circle of flesh. I later shattered a light bulb against the bridge of her nose but she escaped unharmed. I think you can say we were taking this rivalry thing a bit too seriously.

At times my sisters would double-team me. We were heavily into words now and when my sisters discovered that to stifle mine was the best weapon they could use against me, it led to some of the unhappiest moments I can recall. They had found my fledgling sensitivity, clutched it about the windpipe, and squeezed. They teased me and baited me but whenever I began to reply they would shout as loudly as they could to obscure what I was saying. Their favorite lines were "Am sam sam sam sam. Am sam sam sam sam." As soon as I parted my lips they would start chanting and send me straight to tears. I would wipe aside the water, swallow hard to compose myself, and fall apart all over again. I could rumble and accept insults but I couldn't ever deal with not being allowed to speak. Their am sam curse was too devastating. I had neither the sense to ignore nor the strength to attack.

I don't recall much about a whole pregnancy but when my mother left for the hospital one night in June of '58 there was only a single wish ringing in my consciousness: BOY. And I knew I would get a brother because it was the only thing that could even the score. He would be my guarantee to be heard because wasn't anybody going to brainwash little brother but me. I alone would teach him how to bound down the stairs two at a time and sneak to the park. And he'd be the real thing. No imitation like Judy. No turncoat like Sherry. I knew I would have to handle his fights for him but that was fine as long as he listened to me and helped me beat the am sam curse. We'd start our own "Ooma booma booma booma" or something like that. Fix them good.

When the phone rang my grandmother, who was up from Alabama, reached it first. I watched her smile as she spoke. As she turned toward me she was saying, "Yeah he standin right here. You know he can't wait to hear the news." She handed me the receiver.

"Hi Ma."

"Hi" she answered dreamily. "You finally have another sister."

I was condemned. I dropped the receiver and walked out of the room in a daze. Debra Lynn showed up a few days later with a head full of wild hair. She was a beauty, and from that day to this she has never been out of my heart. But she couldn't be a brother.

I had just one more summer to pass on 146th Street. Farmer Gray cartoons in the morning. The Jocko Show in the afternoon. Sit down and rock Debra Lynn for a spell or jump up and go wild to the rhythm of my first favorite record, "Tequila," by the Champs. And I was beginning to tread more lightly about the apartment, trying to avoid all scars and bruised feelings, overjoyed at any opportunity to go outside. Just give me the playground or send me to the corner grocery so I can squeeze in as much Eighth Avenue as possible before I have to hurry back. I couldn't shoot a basketball high enough to make a goal but I began learning how to dribble and saw my first pair of dead wide open eyes on a fat man lying amid a crowd in front of the fish market with a thin jagged line of blood across the width of his throat.

On Sundays, for religion, we went up on the hill. Skipping along the hexagon-shaped tile in Colonial Park. Darting up the steps to Edgecomb Avenue. Stopping in the candy store on St. Nicholas to load up. Leaning forward for leverage to finish the climb up to the church. I was always impressed by this particular house of the Lord. Tremendous gray and white cinder blocks. Polished maple pews in the main service room. Red carpet, stained windows, and gigantic organ pipes. And the Lord, he owned the best singers available. There was nothing like a gorgeous soprano wailing and sweating under influence of the spirit and a hot wig. There were always old women with blue dye in their hair shrieking and swooning during the sermon as folks around them grabbed hold of them while exclaiming, "Yes Lord. I see you done come to us." With women like that falling out in droves you had to believe. And Pops was up in the front row with the rest of the deacons. A broad-shouldered frame in a gray or blue suit. Sometimes wore white gloves to serve communion. He always winked at us when he passed by.

The first grade brought a teacher, Miss Novick, who we thought was the top genius on the planet. She was going to turn us all into little scientists she would say. And there was invariably one experiment or another for us to observe.

She placed a glass jar, two small candles in holders, and a box of matches on her desk. She raised the jar and candles over her head and waved them slowly for all to see.

"I have here a glass jar and two simple candles. Can everyone see them?"

"Yes Miss Novick" we replied, speaking as everyone.

"See them James?"

"Yeah."

"See them Karen?"

"Uh hunh."

"See them John?"

"I sees it."

"Okay." She returned the objects to her desk, lit the candles and held them overhead. Our eyes were transfixed with magic show expectations.

"Now the candles are lit. You see? Rosanne? Ryan? Keith?" I gave a nod of affirmation. Then she lowered the candles to the desk and lifted the jar, upside down, as we inched forward in our seats.

"Now who can tell me what will happen if I set this jar down over one of these flames? Can anyone tell me? James?" He could not. He was smart but stumped. Sat looking dumb with his face greased and his eyes bulged and his index finger glued to his chin.

"How about you Barbara?"

"You gonna catch the des' on fire Miss Novick."

"YEAAHHHHHHHHH. . . ."

"No, little scientists. No. No. No. We will not harm the desk. Anyone else? . . . No? . . . Well let us observe."

She placed the jar over one of the candles and we stared eagerly at both flames until the one inside the jar died out. Miss Novick surveyed our puzzled faces and smiled.

"Now why did that happen class?"

"You mean why it went out?"

"Yes Harold. Can you tell me why?"

"Because you put that jar on there. You made it go out Miss Novick. You did it."

"Sure Harold. But how could I do it with only the jar?"

"I don't know. Was there some water in there?"

"There wasn't Harold. We all looked at the jar together, remember?"

"Oh yeah."

"Anyone else?" Miss Novick was extremely patient and thoroughly flustered us all before giving us our first formal explanation concerning oxygen.

I liked the prospect of becoming a resident scientist up at P.S. 90 (strange what faith I had in the public school system up there), and when the announcement came later that fall that we were moving into a house out in Queens I was, at first, a bit disheartened. I knew there were scientific experiments elsewhere but I wasn't so sure I could get another Miss No-vick or even more important, in a related field, another Eighth Avenue.

I wasn't anti-Queens; all I knew about the place was that it was over a bridge somewhere. But I surely had no beef with Harlem. I didn't recoil at the sight of its streets as I would at other times later in life. I had no sense of society being so terrible. I was there and I fit.

On another level, however, I guess I did welcome a chance to leave the apartment I was associating more and more with misunderstanding and pain. *House* sounded like more space to stay out of the way of others.

So at the age of six it was time for a crossing. My young mind poised for any game that came along. Could play the middle or skirt the fringe as I saw fit. Just come out stepping light and easy, you know, and if it gets hectic remember to cover in the clinch. The point was to hold the defense together while all about me from complex fabrics of frustration and rejection and sensitivity and conflict and hope and loneliness and resignation and reticence and wonderment and bewilderment and romantic notions and romantic disappointments, from all this and more, the imposing offense was being woven.

And the bridge bowed gracefully and beckoned. Bore me upon its majestic back and arched me high above the cold and swirling dark waters of that November toward another shore, and another truth, which all should know: Most times a bridge is just another two-way street.

Discuss your observations about Gilyard's text with a partner, answering the following questions in your journal.

1. What pattern(s) do you see when you review where and when Gilyard uses informal and formal language? What is he trying to show his readers about his experience?

2. Choose one of the moments where Gilyard shows his "first lessons." What does Gilyard do in the writing that *shows* readers this moment?

3. Looking at the guideposts where Gilyard links his experiences together, what is the overall theme he is using?

4. What is Gilyard's ultimate conclusion about his experience?

WHAT'S NEXT?

Now that you have read Gilyard's mini-memoir and answered some preliminary questions, you are ready to examine how a mini-memoir functions and what the typical expectations are for this particular writing genre.

FEATURES OF THE MINI-MEMOIR

There are several important expectations or features of a mini-memoir. They are what make this genre unique.

FIRST-PERSON POINT OF VIEW: The most obvious expectation for this genre is the use of first-person perspective. Because the nature of this writing is based on personal experience—YOURS—it only makes sense that you would use first-person point of view (I, me, we, our). The immediacy of the experience is made more apparent by the use of first-person and engages your reader in a one-on-one dialogue. In the end, you want your reader to identify with you and your recollection; so using first-person pronouns is the best method for doing so.

VIVID DETAILS: These are used to show, rather than simply tell, the experience. Writers use all the senses to describe a situation. The use of strong action verbs, adjectives and adverbs, similes, and figurative language all contribute to the retelling of your experience for someone who was not originally there. Reread Gilyard's text and identify places where he uses vivid imagery, figurative language, and narrative. How would omission of these details affect the tone of his memoir?

DIALOGUE: Dialogue in a memoir can make the experience you are describing come alive and resonate with a reader. Keep in mind that you do not want to use dialogue for your entire memoir, but you do want to include moments that seem especially important in relating your experience to your reader. Notice how

Gilyard uses dialogue in his text. Where does he include dialogue? What is the purpose for those moments? To what extent does it add to the overall point he is making?

ANECDOTES: These are the particular moments of an experience that help to show the reader what is important about it. They are vivid recollections of what happened that an author shares with the reader in an effort to bring the reader into the moment and share in the experience. The moments you choose to share must connect with the overall point of your memoir or they end up masking the true purpose of your sharing the experience in the first place. Reread Gilyard's text, noticing how he has chosen very specific moments to recount. Choose two and explain how these contribute to his overall point.

DIALECTICAL WRITING: Like dialectical reading, dialectical writing is used to describe the experience in general and reflect on its importance specifically. This movement from describing and detailing experience to reflecting on and explaining it is essential in memoirs. This movement must be controlled and purposeful so that you are showing both what happened and why it is worth remembering. The details, dialogue, and anecdotes that you choose for your memoir should in some way reflect or connect to an overall point, so you must consciously choose specific moments in your experience that are significant and directly link to an overarching theme or main point. Dialectical writing is something that is "peppered" throughout a memoir, gently guiding your readers to see your experience and understand why they should see it the way you do.

SO WHAT?: What makes a memoir successful is having the experience you describe resonate with a reader. After all, the goal of a memoir is to take a personal experience and invite your reader to see its significance for not only you, the writer, but also for the reader. The overall point of your memoir, the "a-ha" moment where all that you have written comes together under a main idea, is the answer to the "so what?" of experience. Why is this experience, among the many that you could recollect, important enough for a reader to take notice? What do you think Gilyard's "a-ha" is? What is the "so-what" of Gilyard's "first lessons"?

WHAT'S NEXT?

Now that you have some experience with memoirs, let us read another mini-memoir. As you read Amy Tan's "Mother Tongue," use active reading strategies to note where you see these features of a memoir appearing in her text.

MOTHER TONGUE

by Amy Tan

I AM NOT a scholar of English or literature. I cannot give you much more than personal opinions on the English language and its variations in this country or others.

I am a writer. And by that definition, I am someone who has always loved language. I am fascinated by language in daily life. I spend a great deal of my time thinking about the power of language—the way it can evoke an emotion, a visual image, a complex idea, or a simple truth. Language is the tool of my trade. And I use them all—all the Englishes I grew up with.

Recently, I was made keenly aware of the different Englishes I do use. I was giving a talk to a large group of people, the same talk I had already given to half a dozen other groups. The nature of the talk was about my writing, my life, and my book, *The Joy Luck Club.* The talk was going along well enough, until I remembered one major difference that made the whole talk sound wrong. My mother was in the room. And it was perhaps the first time she had heard me give a lengthy speech—using the kind of English I have never used with her. I was saying things like, "The intersection of memory upon imagination" and "There is an aspect of my fiction that relates to thus-and-thus"—a speech filled with carefully wrought grammatical phrases, (burdened, it suddenly seemed to me, with nominalized forms, past perfect tenses, conditional phrases—all the forms of standard English that I had learned in school and through books, the forms of English I did not use at home with my mother.

Just last week, I was walking down the street with my mother, and I again found myself conscious of the English I was using, the English I do use with her. We were talking about the price of new and used furniture and I heard myself saying this: "Not waste money that way." My husband was with us as well, and he didn't notice any switch in my English. And then I realized why. It's because over the twenty years we've been together I've often used that same kind of English with him, and sometimes he even uses it with me. It has become our language of intimacy, a different sort of English that relates to family talk, the language I grew up with.

So you'll have some idea of what this family talk I heard sounds like, I'll quote what my mother said during a recent conversation which I videotaped and then transcribed. During this conversation, my mother was talking about a political gangster in Shanghai who had the same last name as her family's, Du, and how the gangster in his early years wanted to be adopted by her family which was rich by comparison. Later, the gangster became more powerful, far richer than my mother's family, and one day showed up at my mother's wedding to pay his respects. Here's what she said in part:

Copyright © 1989 by Amy Tan. First appeared in The Threepenny Review. Reprinted by permission of the author and the Sandra Dijkstra Literary Agency.

"Du Yusong having business like fruit stand. Like off the street kind. He is Du like Du Zong—but not Tsung-ming Island people. The local people call putong, the river east side, he belong to that side local people. That man want to ask Du Zong father take him in like become own family. Du Zong father wasn't look down on him, but didn't take seriously, until that man big like become a mafia. Now important person, very hard to inviting him. Chinese way, came only to show respect, don't stay for dinner. Respect for making big celebration, he shows up. Mean gives lots of respect. Chinese custom. Chinese social life that way. If too important won't have to stay too long. He come to my wedding. I didn't see, I heard it. I gone to boy's side, they have YMCA dinner. Chinese age I was 19."

You should know that my mother's expressive command of English belies how much she actually understands. She reads the Forbes report, listens to Wall Street Week, converses daily with her stockbroker, reads all of Shirley MacLaine's books with ease—all kinds of things I can't begin to understand. Yet some of my friends tell me they understand fifty percent of what my mother says. Some say they understand eighty to ninety percent. Some say they understand none of it, as if she were speaking pure Chinese. But to me, my mother's English is perfectly clear, perfectly natural. It's my mother tongue. Her language, as I hear it, is vivid, direct, full of observation and imagery. That was the language that helped shape the way I saw things, expressed things, made sense of the world.

LATELY, I've been giving more thought to the kind of English my mother speaks. Like others, I have described it to people as "broken" or "fractured" English. But I wince when I say that. It has always bothered me that I can think of no way to describe it other than "broken," as if it were damaged and needed to be fixed, as if it lacked a certain wholeness and soundness. I've heard other terms used, "limited English," for example. But they seem just as bad, as if everything is limited, including people's perception of the limited English speaker.

I know this for a fact, because when I was growing up, my mother's "limited" English limited *my* perception of her. I was ashamed of her English. I believed that her English reflected the quality of what she had to say. That is, because she expressed them imperfectly her thoughts were imperfect. And I had plenty of empirical evidence to support me: the fact that people in department stores, at banks, and at restaurants did not take her seriously, did not give her good service, pretended not to understand her, or even acted as if they did not hear her.

My mother has long realized the limitations of her English as well. When I was fifteen, she used to have me call people on the phone to pretend I was she. In this guise, I was forced to ask for information or even to complain and yell at people who had been rude to her. One time it was a call to her stockbroker in New York. She had cashed out her small portfolio and it just so happened we were going to go to New York the next week, our very first trip outside California. I had to get on the phone and say in an adolescent voice that was not very convincing, "This is Mrs. Tan."

And my mother was standing in the back whispering loudly, "Why he don't send me check, already two weeks late. So mad he lie to me, losing me money."

And then I said in perfect English, "Yes, I'm getting rather concerned. You had agreed to send the check two weeks ago, but it hasn't arrived."

Then she began to talk more loudly, "What he want, I come to New York tell him front of his boss, you cheating me?" And I was trying to calm her down, make her be quiet, while telling the stockbroker, "I can't tolerate any more excuses. If I don't receive the check immediately, I am going to have to speak to your manager when I'm in New York next week." And sure enough, the following week there we were in front of this astonished stockbroker, and I was sitting there red-faced and quiet, and my mother, the real Mrs. Tan, was shouting at his boss in her impeccable broken English.

We used a similar routine just five days ago, for a situation that was far less humorous. My mother had gone to the hospital for an appointment, to find out about a benign brain tumor a CAT scan had revealed a month ago. She said she had spoken very good English, her best English, no mistakes. Still, she said, the hospital did not apologize when they said they had lost the CAT scan and she had come for nothing. She said they did not seem to have any sympathy when she told them she was anxious to know the exact diagnosis since her husband and son had both died of brain tumors. She said they would not give her any more information until the next time and she would have to make another appointment for that. So she said she would not leave until the doctor called her daughter. She wouldn't budge. And when the doctor finally called her daughter, me, who spoke in perfect English—lo and behold—we had assurances the CAT scan would be found, promises that a conference call on Monday would be held, and apologies for any suffering my mother had gone through for a most regrettable mistake.

I think my mother's English almost had an effect on limiting my possibilities in life as well. Sociologists and linguists probably will tell you that a person's developing language skills are more influenced by peers. But I do think that the language spoken in the family, especially in immigrant families which are more insular, plays a large role in shaping the language of the child. And I believe that it affected my results on achievement tests, IQ tests, and the SAT. While my English skills were never judged as poor, compared to math, English could not be considered my strong suit. In grade school, I did moderately well, getting perhaps Bs, sometimes B + s in English, and scoring perhaps in the sixtieth or seventieth percentile on achievement tests. But those scores were not good enough to override the opinion that my true abilities lay in math and science, because in those areas I achieved As and scored in the ninetieth percentile or higher.

This was understandable. Math is precise; there is only one correct answer. Whereas, for me at least, the answers on English tests were always a judgment call, a matter of opinion and personal experience. Those tests were constructed around

items like fill-in-the-blank sentence completion, such as "Even though Tom was
_____, Mary thought he was _____." And the correct answer always seemed to
be the most bland combinations of thoughts, for example, "Even though Tom
was shy, Mary thought he was charming," with the grammatical structure "even
though" limiting the correct answer to some sort of semantic opposites, so you
wouldn't get answers like "Even though Tom was foolish, Mary thought he was
ridiculous." Well, according to my mother, there were very few limitations as to
what Tom could have been, and what Mary might have thought of him. So I never
did well on tests like that.

The same was true with word analogies, pairs of words, in which you were supposed
to find some sort of logical, semantic relationship—for example, "sunset" is to
"nightfall" as _____ is to_____." And here, you would be presented with a list of
four possible pairs, one of which showed the same kind of relationship: "red" is
to "stoplight," "bus" is to "arrival," "chills" is to "fever," "yawn" is to "boring." Well,
I could never think that way. I knew what the tests were asking, but I could not
block out of my mind the images already created by the first pair, "sunset is to
nightfall"—and I would see a burst of colors against a darkening sky, the moon
rising, the lowering of a curtain of stars. And all the other pairs of words—red, bus,
stoplight, boring-just threw up a mass of confusing images, making it impossible
for me to sort out something as logical as saying: "A sunset precedes nightfall"
is the same as "a chill precedes a fever." The only way I would have gotten that
answer right would have been to imagine an associative situation, for example,
my being disobedient and staying out past sunset, catching a chill at night, which
turns into feverish pneumonia as punishment, which indeed did happen to me.

I HAVE been thinking about all this lately, about my mother's English, about
achievement tests. Because lately I've been asked, as a writer, why there are not
more Asian-Americans represented in American literature. Why are there few
Asian-Americans enrolled in creative writing programs? Why do so many Chinese
students go into engineering? Well, these are broad sociological questions I can't
begin to answer. But I have noticed in surveys—in fact, just last week—that Asian
students, as a whole, always do significantly better on math achievement tests
than in English. And this makes me think that there are other Asian-American
students whose English spoken in the home might also be described as "broken"
or "limited." And perhaps they also have teachers who are steering them away
from writing and into math and science, which is what happened to me.

Fortunately, I happen to be rebellious in nature, and enjoy the challenge of
disproving assumptions made about me. I became an English major my first
year in college after being enrolled as pre-med. I started writing non-fiction as a
freelancer the week after I was told by my former boss that writing was my worst
skill and I should hone my talents toward account management.

But it wasn't until 1985 that I finally began to write fiction. And at first I wrote
using what I thought to be wittily crafted sentences, sentences that would finally

prove I had mastery over the English language. Here's an example from the first draft of a story that later made its way into *The Joy Luck Club,* but without this line: "That was my mental quandary in its nascent state." A terrible line, which I can barely pronounce.

Fortunately, for reasons I won't get into today, I later decided I should envision a reader for the stories I would write. And the reader I decided upon was my mother, because these were stories about mothers. So with this reader in mind—and in fact, she did read my early drafts—I began to write stories using all the Englishes I grew up with: the English I spoke to my mother, which for lack of a better term, might be described as "simple"; the English she used with me, which for lack of a better term might be described as "broken"; my translation of her Chinese, which could certainly be described as "watered down"; and what I imagined to be her translation of her Chinese if she could speak in perfect English, her internal language, and for that I sought to preserve the essence, but not either an English or a Chinese structure. I wanted to capture what language ability tests can never reveal: her intent, her passion, her imagery, the rhythms of her speech and the nature of her thoughts.

Apart from what any critic had to say about my writing, I knew I had succeeded where it counted when my mother finished reading my book, and gave me her verdict: "So easy to read."

Discuss your observations about Tan's text with a partner, answering the following questions in your journal:

1. Where do you see Tan using the memoir features? Identify at least one place in the text where you see vivid details, anecdotes, and dialectical writing.

2. Where do you see Tan using dialogue? Does Tan use dialogue differently than Gilyard? Explain.

3. Locate the guideposts where Tan links her anecdotes together. How do they build upon each other and ultimately connect to her overall point?

4. What is Tan's ultimate conclusion about her experience? In other words, what is the "so what" or "a-ha" in Tan's memoir? Where is it located?

WRITING YOUR OWN MINI-MEMOIR

Compose a mini-memoir about a personal, significant experience related to learning about language. Your mini-memoir, then, is a genre of writing that focuses attention on a specific moment in time and in a specific place. You will want to capture the setting, the circumstances, and the people who were involved and explain how these contributed to the overall experience.

You will need to meet the expectations of this genre, so your writing will include a personal, first-hand experience. You should attempt to capture the experience of a specific time and place by using vivid details, dialogue, and anecdotes so that the reader can share in the recollection. Alternatively, you might consider writing a collage mini-memoir where you choose three or four experiences that are linked in some way. For example, in your brainstorming activities, did you find yourself recollecting negative experiences? Positive ones? Were they all linked to something specific? You can create several sections in your mini-memoir that show this link.

The use of "I" is embraced as a necessary element in the writing, for it is, after all, your experience. Memoirs also rely on memory, which can sometimes be elusive, but writers of memoirs rely on their creative abilities to fill in the gaps as honestly as possible. This genre also requires that you *reflect back* on your previous experience from the position you are in today. This is dialectical writing. All writing is persuasive on some level, so part of your goal when writing a memoir is to "persuade" your reader that the experience you detail has significance and is worthy of attention, just as Gilyard and Tan did, yet you are not offering a typical "thesis" in this genre, for the purpose of this kind of writing is revelation and reflection. Typically, the "a-ha" moment, the realization of the experience's significance (the "so what?") comes late in your essay, that is, in the last paragraph or two.

BRAINSTORMING FOR THE MINI-MEMOIR

LISTING PROMPTS

1. Make a fast list of experiences you have had with writing, whether good, bad, or indifferent. Reach back to the time between grades 8 and 12. Spend 1 minute making this list. Don't think too much, but do try to capture a few chronological experiences. Just list.

2. Make a fast list of experiences you have had with a specific kind of writing or writing experience when you were in grade 8, then grade 9, and then grade 12. Spend 1 ½ minutes making this list. Don't think too much, but do try to capture a few similar experiences in chronological sequence.

3. Paying particular attention to formal education experiences during this time period, make a list of questions that have always nagged you about essays, grammar, peer-reviewing, creative writing, instructor pet-peeves, and sharing writing with others. Spend 1 minute making this list of questions.

FASTWRITING PROMPTS

1. Choose an item from any listing prompt #1. Now, just start fastwriting about the item; perhaps start with a story, a scene, a situation, a description, or a memory. Just follow the writing to see where it leads. Spend about 5 minutes on this one.

2. Choose one of the items from listing prompt #2. Writing in the present tense, describe what you see, hear, feel, and do. Write for 2 minutes. Then, skip a line and choose another moment. Write for 2 minutes. Skip a line. Write for 2 minutes.

    Writing about individual moments and then putting them together in one essay is called a collage essay. (You can separate each anecdote you develop using a few spaces or a short line, centered, between the individual sections.) The idea is that each memory acts alone, showing a reader the importance of a single moment in time, yet the accumulation of these moments tells a larger narrative about your experiences.

    If you choose to try this more creative strategy, be sure to capture several poignant moments that are linked to each other by the same topic. In this case, the chronology of your writing experiences should reveal something significant that links them all together even though they are separated from each other in time and on the page.

3. Consider one of the questions you wrote in listing prompt #3, and try answering it. Do not try to come up with THE answer; rather, explore what might be the many answers to that question. Fastwrite for 5 minutes without stopping.

VISUAL PROMPTS

1. In the middle of a blank page, put the word "writing" in a circle. This is your main topic. What comes to mind when you think of "writing"? (Don't censor yourself!) With every idea, create a first-level cluster by drawing a line from the center circle to another circle in which your related idea goes. Do this several times with the main topic.

    Then, create a second-level cluster, coming up with ideas related to what is in the circle. Do this several times until you exhaust two or three second-level ideas.

2. Draw a picture of what the ideal setting would be for you to feel comfortable with writing or for writing. (Don't worry about being a "bad" artist.) Where are you? Who is there? What is there? What is the temperature? What are you wearing? What are you sitting on? What smells are there? What do you hear?

WHAT'S NEXT?

Now that you have developed some potential experiences to write about, choose a drafting strategy from Chapter 3 and create a first draft. As you develop your anecdotes, use vivid details to make them come alive for your reader. Try the "Show, Don't Tell" strategy below.

SHOW, DON'T TELL, YOUR EXPERIENCE: USING THE 5 SENSES TO DESCRIBE

Below are the five senses and the ways they can capture different parts of our experience:

SIGHT: This sense can be used to describe what we see by focusing on:

location (far/near) and appearance (light/dark; color; size; shape).

SOUND: This sense can be used to describe what we hear by focusing on:

location (far/near) and the quality of the sound's tone (high/low pitch) or volume (loud/quiet).

SMELL: This sense can be used to describe what we smell by focusing on:

location (far/near) (e.g., the stronger the smell, the closer it is); time (past/present) (e.g., the stronger the smell, the more recent in time it is); age (old/new) (e.g., the weaker the smell, the older it might be, as in the case of perfume); and aroma (see taste).

TASTE: This sense can be used to describe what we taste by focusing on:

the taste response: sweet/spicy/salty/sour/bitter/metallic/umami.

TOUCH: This sense can be used to describe what we feel by focusing on:

the qualities of physical touch: hard/soft; natural/synthetic; rough/smooth; hot/cold.

As you recollect your experiences, use the above senses to capture:

1. What you saw

2. What you heard (beyond just dialogue)

3. What you smelled

4. What you tasted

5. What you physically felt

DESCRIBE YOUR EXPERIENCE USING THE FIVE SENSES

Writer: _____ Reader: _____

PEER-REVIEW FOR MEMOIR DRAFT 1

1. What do you think is the *real* story in my essay? In other words, what idea or theme is lurking beneath the accounts of my experiences and observations?

2. Where can I add more details and reflection to help my writing come alive or to show you what I am trying to say?

3. Where do I seem to be too obvious or too general about my experience? Write some questions here to help me be more specific and insightful.

4. Where do I unnecessarily explain things that are better revealed by *showing* rather than *telling*?

5. What, in your own words, is the answer to the "so what"? What is the significance of my sharing this experience with you? Is it expected?

Name: _____ Date: _____

REFLECTIONS: MEMOIR WRITING

Which of the brainstorming strategies helped you the most? Why do you think they were the most helpful?

What did you find to be the hardest part about writing a memoir?

What did you find to be the easiest part about writing a memoir?

What would you do differently when writing a memoir next time?

If you had more time, what would you work on in the memoir?

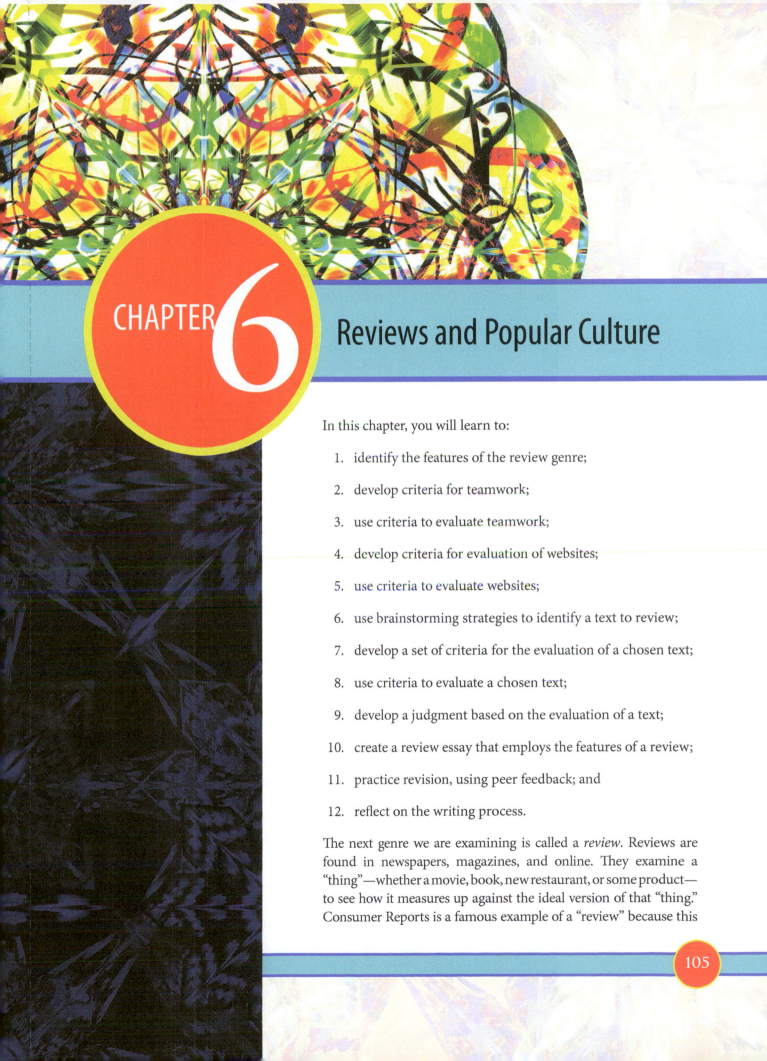

CHAPTER 6

Reviews and Popular Culture

In this chapter, you will learn to:

1. identify the features of the review genre;

2. develop criteria for teamwork;

3. use criteria to evaluate teamwork;

4. develop criteria for evaluation of websites;

5. use criteria to evaluate websites;

6. use brainstorming strategies to identify a text to review;

7. develop a set of criteria for the evaluation of a chosen text;

8. use criteria to evaluate a chosen text;

9. develop a judgment based on the evaluation of a text;

10. create a review essay that employs the features of a review;

11. practice revision, using peer feedback; and

12. reflect on the writing process.

The next genre we are examining is called a *review*. Reviews are found in newspapers, magazines, and online. They examine a "thing"—whether a movie, book, new restaurant, or some product— to see how it measures up against the ideal version of that "thing." Consumer Reports is a famous example of a "review" because this company examines many and various items, such as cars and appliances, to provide consumers information about the products that will inform their purchasing choices. The criteria Consumer Reports uses are determined by the product under review, and these criteria are used systematically and fully across the "things" they are reviewing. For example, if they are reviewing cars, they decide what elements—criteria—are important for SUVs, trucks, passenger cars, and sedans. Some of the criteria may apply across the types of cars, such as safety, but other considerations, such as price or engine type, will become more or less important depending upon the kind of vehicle under review. Once the "thing" is identified and appropriate criteria are listed, Consumer Reports evaluates the "thing" to see how well it matches that set criteria. Once the evaluation is complete, then there is a judgment made about whether or not the item in question is recommended and why.

Similar reviews are conducted in other areas. Rotten Tomatoes is a great example of movie reviews. You should note that there are often "professional" reviewers, actual movie critics, who provide their evaluation of a film, and even common, everyday users who provide their feedback. Sometimes, the everyday movie-goer may rate a film much higher than a professional reviewer, and this is because the criteria each party uses differs. You might also see "reviews" on other websites, like Amazon or iTunes or GooglePlay, where users of the site provide widely varying accounts of how useful or good a product is.

This is why criteria matter; they make evaluation of a "thing" systematic and consistent for those who use reviews. As a reviewer, you need to let your readers know exactly what criteria you are using to provide common ground. Your readers need to know what you are reviewing, what criteria you are using, and what leads you to make the judgment that you have. You can not assume that all of your readers would review the "thing" using the same criteria, which is why you need to be explicit about what you are using, how you are applying it, and what the end result is.

FEATURES OF THE REVIEW

There are several important expectations or features of a review. They are what make this genre unique.

"THING": "Thing" is a word used as a placeholder for what you are reviewing. If you are examining a movie, then that is your "thing." If you are reviewing shampoo, then that is your "thing." What you must keep in mind and address is that not all movies are equal. There are genres of movies: action, science fiction, thriller, horror, comedy, and so forth. Notice, too, that within each of those are sub-genres. For comedy, there are romantic comedies, slapstick, spoof, and others. Thus, you must be VERY clear about what kind of "thing" you are examining.

CRITERIA: This element lists the expectations most people would have of the "thing." Ask yourself, "What would most people expect to see in a perfect version of the 'thing' I am examining?" If you are examining a comedy that is a spoof, your criteria will include elements that may not be expected in, say, a romantic-comedy. You also may find that some criteria are more important than others. If this is the case, then you must let your readers know so that they understand why your evaluation is what it is. The criteria are essential for you and your readers because that is the whole basis for making the evaluation.

EVALUATION: The evaluation is where you actually analyze the "thing" to see how well it stacks up against the *expected* criteria. Reviews do not necessarily have to have 100% of all the criteria to indicate it is exceptional. Depending upon the criteria and the weight you give them, the evaluation will reflect what is emphasized. You, the reviewer, however, must provide the justification for that evaluation. You need to ask yourself how much of "x" criterion is needed for the "thing" to meet the threshold for meeting the expectation. You also need to take into consideration all results (i.e., from each evaluated criterion) to make a judgment.

JUDGMENT: After you have analyzed the "thing" for how well it meets the set of criteria, you must then decide, objectively, what the final result is. Does this "thing" meet enough of each criterion to justify a recommendation to try it, buy it, watch it, use it, invest in it, etc.? In order for you to make this judgment, you must show the reader the extent to which the "thing" has met or not the set of criteria, and this is accomplished through the use of evidence.

EVIDENCE: It is not enough to simply say that the "thing" has "x" criterion. Your reader wants to know how you came to the conclusion you did. What did you look at, how did you decide the extent to which it did or did not meet the criteria, and what evidence do you have? For example, if you examine a new mobile phone that has come onto the market, you might say that one of the criterion is color. If the mobile phone comes in three colors (black, white, and silver), does that mean it has met the threshold for that criterion? If not, then what would have met it? If not, why not? You might say that compared to other kinds of mobile phones, this particular one does not offer enough of a variety of colors, which should be at least five different colors. In other words, you have to show the reader what the evidence is or would be expected as "proof" that the criterion has been met.

BALANCED VIEW: When it comes to popular culture, "things" like movies, TV shows, and music are highly personal. Everyone has their "favorite" based on personal taste. However, reviews are not about personal tastes; they are about evaluation of a thing based on pre-established criteria. This means that you must take yourself and your own affinity for the "thing" out of the assessment, for you are providing as objective of a review as possible. Nothing is perfect or beyond reproach, so reviewers must be able to see the shortcomings of a "thing" just as much as what is successful about it. Therefore, you must remove your own biases from the evaluation—which is what the criteria are meant to help you do—and acknowledge a weakness, which may be that not every single criterion was met or it was only partially met.

THIRD-PERSON POINT OF VIEW: Another way to gain some objectivity is to use third-person point of view. In other words, "I" is not appropriate for this genre.

What "you" liked or did not like is not what a review is. A review stays focused on the criteria and how well the "thing" meets them. Saying a comedy made you laugh is not going to persuade your reader; your sense of humor may not be what someone else's sense of humor is. Therefore, you, the writer, must take a clinical view of the "thing" to say why the film is funny and how the humor is either universally appealing or, perhaps, only appreciated by a select few.

REVIEWING AND EVALUATING WEBSITES CRITICALLY USING CRITERIA

The following is an exercise that will give you some experience with a review using criteria. Because there are reviews on the web for all sorts of products, services, and entertainment, and because writers use the internet for information gathering and research, it is important that they can distinguish between valid and invalid sites. This is an exercise to help you learn how to evaluate websites for authenticity, reliability, and usability.

PURPOSE

The purpose of this project is twofold. First, the internet is a place where we all go to learn about various topics, and, no doubt, to which you will turn for your review essay, at least in part. Because the internet is not monitored for accuracy or reliability, we have the task of distinguishing between good and bad sources of web information. Second, working together in groups is an important social skill, one which helps us accomplish a task more quickly by delegating responsibility for a part of the work, being held accountable for our part in a project, and sharing what we learned in our research with our group members. Below, identify what criteria need to be used for effective group work, and explain why.

CRITERIA FOR EFFECTIVE TEAMWORK:

1.

Why?

2.

Why?

3.

Why?

4.

Why?

5.

Why?

Use these criteria to evaluate your teamwork!

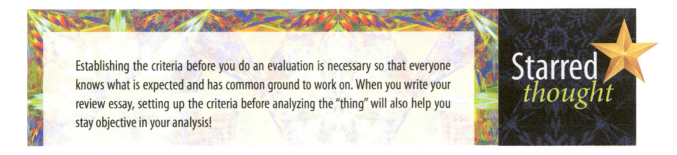

Establishing the criteria before you do an evaluation is necessary so that everyone knows what is expected and has common ground to work on. When you write your review essay, setting up the criteria before analyzing the "thing" will also help you stay objective in your analysis!

Starred *thought*

Now, take a look at the following websites that provide criteria by which we can analyze websites critically. Note what criteria are similar and dissimilar on both sites, what the criteria are, and how we are supposed to use them.

1. "Evaluating Web Sites: Criteria and Tools" is sponsored by the Olin & Uris Libraries at Cornell University. **http://olinuris.library.cornell.edu/ref/research/webeval.html**

2. "Evaluating Web Pages: Techniques to Apply & Questions to Ask" is sponsored by the UC Berkeley Library. **http://www.lib.berkeley.edu/TeachingLib/Guides/Internet/Evaluate.html**

INDIVIDUAL WORK: After you have read through the information on these two websites, fill out the following section which summarizes **five criteria** that will help you to analyze the quality of online information. This entry should include a list of five criteria, what each criterion is, how each is supposed to be applied to a website, and why it is important to have that criterion as part of the evaluation. Be prepared to share and discuss your journal entry in the next class.

CRITERION 1:

What is it?

How is it used?

Why do we use it?

Criterion 2:

What is it?

How is it used?

Why do we use it?

Criterion 3:

What is it?

How is it used?

Why do we use it?

CRITERION 4:

What is it?

How is it used?

Why do we use it?

CRITERION 5:

What is it?

How is it used?

Why do we use it?

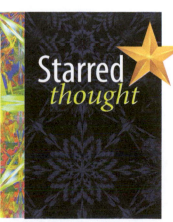

When we evaluate websites, we really need to use as many of the criteria as possible because sometimes one criterion may be essential to the validity of the whole site. For example, if you are examining a medical site about the current status of cancer research, the author of the site may be legitimate and the content may be unbiased, but the information is based on data from 10 years ago. While the site meets two or three criteria, the fact that it is out of date makes the information suspect. If you use at least five criteria, you are more likely to ensure that the website has valid and appropriate information for your purposes!

Starred *thought*

GROUP WORK: Working in teams of **five**, discuss your lists and compile a *master list of five criteria* that you all agree to use in evaluating websites. (You will need to negotiate with your group members which five criteria you want to use, for you may not all have the same ones listed.) Once you have agreed upon five criteria, apply them to a website. As a group, you need to decide whether or not your website is authentic, reliable, and usable for academic research, which is your judgment of the website (the "thing" in this case).

Name: _____

REVIEW YOUR TEAMWORK

NOTES:

Score each member for each criterion using 1 as the lowest and 3 as the highest.

Group Member	Criterion 1:	Criterion 2:	Criterion 3:	Criterion 4:	Criterion 5:	Totals

REFLECTION:

a. What was, for you, the most *surprising thing* that you learned today about evaluating websites?

b. What was, for you, the most challenging thing about working in groups?

WRITING YOUR OWN REVIEW ABOUT POPULAR CULTURE

Here are some considerations for structuring your review.

INTRODUCTION: The introduction may be one to two paragraphs. Typically, reviewers "hook" their readers in the first paragraph with an engaging introduction that includes the "thing" under review and a brief summary (if needed) of the "thing." To determine if you need a summary, you need to consider how "popular" and "mainstream" the "thing" is. *Star Wars: Episode VII* is well known in America; however, not everyone in America may have seen it. Thus, you may need to provide a short summary of the basic plot, a snippet that might be found on the back of the DVD. You may choose to tell your reviewers upfront what your judgment is, depending upon whether you think your readers will welcome your judgment or not. If not, then you might choose to leave the judgment for the end, similar to how you leave the "a-ha" in a memoir at the end. The judgment functions as your controlling idea for your review.

BODY PARAGRAPHS: Writers will examine the "thing" based on a number of criteria that will be broad enough to cover the major, expected features of the "thing." The criteria should be specific enough to address the genre of the "thing" being examined and any sub-genre considerations. With each criterion, writers will also include examples from the "thing," or support/evidence, as a way of showing the readers how they have analyzed the criteria. After the analysis and support, the writer could make a judgment of that criterion. Alternatively, the writer can wait until after all criteria have been examined to provide an overall judgment.

For your review, you should include at least one secondary source, a professional online review of the "thing" that helps to advance your analysis. Be sure to use the QuACing method when you use the source. (See Appendix A, p. 301.) You will also address at least one weakness in the "thing" to show a level of unbiased judgment. More creatively inclined writers may want to include "stills" in their essay. These are images of scenes that capture some criterion you are examining. For example, if you want to examine costuming in a film, then you might include a frame from the film that shows the costumes. You would then refer to it in your essay, explaining what the still is showing and how it fits into your review. Remember: If stills are included, then there must be a correct in-text citation and accompanying entry on the bibliography page.

> Stills are images captured from a film and are similar to a photograph that captures an element you are reviewing. For example, if you are reviewing a film, you might include a still of a scene showing a character's reaction or costume (depending on what criterion you are looking at); if you are reviewing a play, you might have a still of the set or an actor. The "stills" you choose should link directly to your criteria and must be cited!

Starred *thought*

CONCLUSION: If the writer has delayed the judgment of the "thing" until the conclusion, then the conclusion must announce the overall evaluation. If the judgment is provided in the introduction, then the conclusion needs to provide a bookend to the review, moving beyond a simple reiteration of the judgment, perhaps articulating some kind of insight into the "thing" or possible improvements that might be made on the "thing."

BRAINSTORMING

Try using "listing" from "Stage 1: Brainstorming" suggestions from Chapter 3 to work out possible topics.

LISTING

1. Make a list of personal items (e.g., shampoos, shaving creams, cologne).

2. Make a list of films you hate.

3. Make a list of films you love.

4. Make a list of places you have visited.

5. Make a list of places where you have eaten.

6. Make a list of new technology you have purchased (e.g., smartphones, laptops, gaming systems).

Now, try using "fastwriting" from Chapter 3 to push further into examining possible topics.

FASTWRITING

1. After you have made the lists, choose one item from one of the lists that seems the most interesting. Fastwrite for 1 minute about why.

2. Choose another item from another list that is equally interesting. Fastwrite for 1 minute about why.

3. Do this several times until you hone in on one topic that is the most interesting and exciting for you.

4. Next, examine the "thing" you have chosen. What similarities does this "thing" have in common with the other items on your list? Dissimilarities?

EXPLORING FURTHER

Now that you have worked out some of the details of the "thing" and your interest in it, work on the following:

What is the "thing" that you are reviewing? Provide a short description or summary.

Who would be interested in this "thing"?

What "genre" (type of) does this "thing" fall under?

What criteria are expected in the ideal version of this "thing"? Make your list exhaustive.

Of this exhaustive list, which five criteria are the most important to making the ideal version of the "thing"?

Explain why each of the criteria is important. What function does each serve?

Now, consider how you will judge the "thing" based on those criteria and what evidence you will need to use to show your reader that your judgment is viable.

CRITERION #1:

Judgment:

Evidence 1A:

Evidence 1B:

CRITERION #2:

Judgment:

Evidence 2A:

Evidence 2B:

CRITERION #3:

Judgment:

Evidence 3A:

Evidence 3B:

CRITERION #4:

Judgment:

Evidence 4A:

Evidence 4B:

CRITERION #5:

Judgment:

Evidence 5A:

Evidence 5B:

Given all of your analysis, what is your overall judgment of the "thing"? How does this judgment evolve out of that analysis? In other words, what elements are weighted?

WHAT'S NEXT?

Now that you have completed some prewriting, it is time to turn that into a draft. Choose one of the "drafting strategies" from Chapter 3 to create your first draft.

Writer: _____   Reader: _____

PEER-REVIEW FOR REVIEW DRAFT 1

1. Are you familiar with the "thing"?

   - Extremely familiar. I know it, use it, own it, tried it….

   - Heard of it but never saw it, tried it, touched it…

   - Huh?

2. Is there enough summary of the "thing" for you to know what the "thing" is? Is there too much summary?

3. Examine the essay. NOTE: If there are any missing elements, be sure to note them here so that I know where to go and what to revise.

   a. Highlight, in yellow, the criteria.

   b. Underline the use of evidence. Is each persuasive? Does the evidence actually link to the criterion?

   c. Circle the judgment I have made about each criterion. Does the judgment actually link to the evaluation of the criterion?

   d. Highlight in orange where I include a flaw. Is this enough to show I am balanced in my review? Explain.

4. What is the overall judgment of the "thing"?

5. How convincing is this review? In other words, did I convince you of my judgment of the "thing" over-
    all? Where might I make my case stronger? What should I do?

6. What is your favorite part of the essay? Why is it your favorite?

7. Is there a bibliography? Does it follow the appropriate document design and style?

Name: _____ Date: _____

REFLECTIONS: REVIEW WRITING

Describe your writing process for this review. What strategies did you use?

Compare your process for writing a review to writing a memoir. Was it different or the same?

What did you find to be the hardest part about writing a review?

What did you find to be the easiest part about writing a review?

What would you do differently when writing a review next time?

If you had more time, what would you work on in the review?

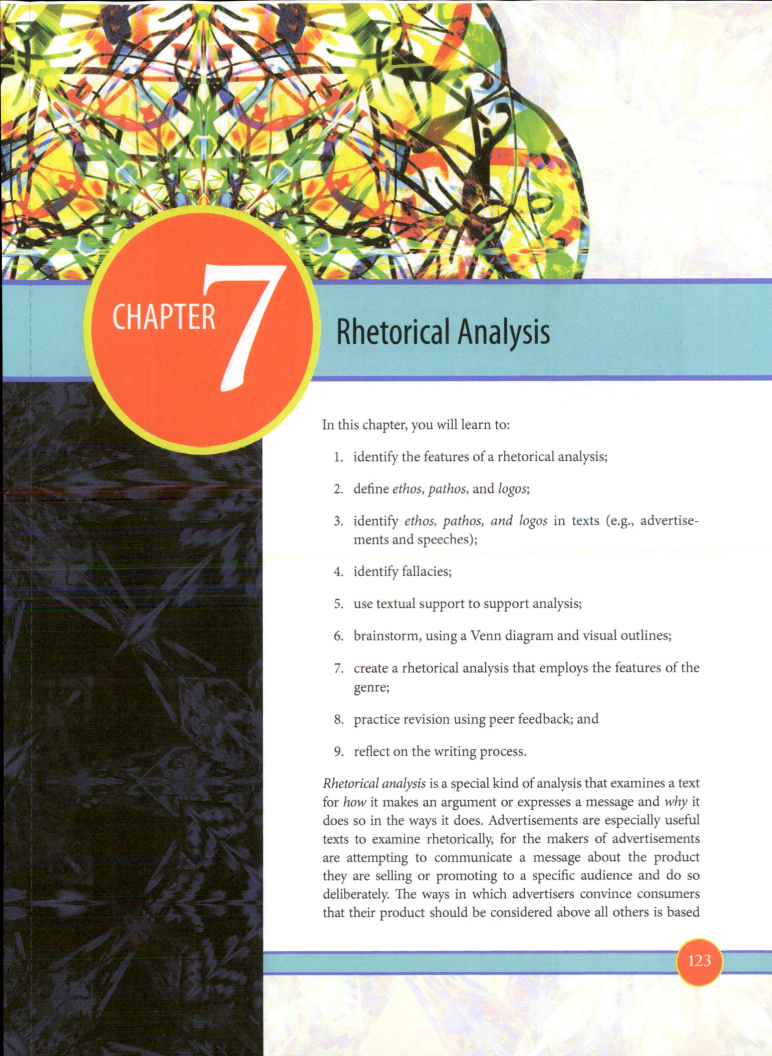

CHAPTER 7

Rhetorical Analysis

In this chapter, you will learn to:

1. identify the features of a rhetorical analysis;

2. define *ethos*, *pathos*, and *logos*;

3. identify *ethos, pathos, and logos* in texts (e.g., advertisements and speeches);

4. identify fallacies;

5. use textual support to support analysis;

6. brainstorm, using a Venn diagram and visual outlines;

7. create a rhetorical analysis that employs the features of the genre;

8. practice revision using peer feedback; and

9. reflect on the writing process.

Rhetorical analysis is a special kind of analysis that examines a text for *how* it makes an argument or expresses a message and *why* it does so in the ways it does. Advertisements are especially useful texts to examine rhetorically, for the makers of advertisements are attempting to communicate a message about the product they are selling or promoting to a specific audience and do so deliberately. The ways in which advertisers convince consumers that their product should be considered above all others is based on assumptions that advertisers make of their audience. In some ways, they are depending upon assumptions about and habits of people to entice buyers to purchase the items for sale. Although some rhetorical analyses are extremely complex and examine all possible permutations of meaning in a text, the kind you will be doing in this chapter will provide an introduction to the kinds of things kaleidoscopic thinkers begin with when doing rhetorical analysis. To do this, we will focus on three elements that make up a basic argument: the three aspects of the rhetorical triangle.

Starred *thought*

When examining texts rhetorically to see who the intended audience is, we must be careful that we do not overly generalize; this can lead to stereotyping, which is problematic. However, advertising works because companies make assumptions about the people's habits based upon what that particular audience is likely to value, want, or need. This is why commercials that air during *Shadowhunters or Vampire Diaries* are quite different than what is aired during *60 Minutes* or *Anderson Cooper 360⁰* episodes; the audiences for these are significantly different from each other.

THREE BASIC RHETORICAL STRATEGIES

Recall from Chapter 2 the explanation of the what, why, and how aspects of the rhetorical triangle. Let us add to that three more terms that are needed to understand the rhetorical situation. These are *logos*, *ethos*, and *pathos*. Aristotle, an ancient writer who wrote extensively on rhetoric, used these terms to explain the ways people persuade others. We apply them today in the following way.

LOGOS

As part of the "subject" aspect of the rhetorical triangle, *logos* is where logical and analytical reasoning, data, facts, and common sense are used to explain the subject matter or content. Writers/speakers use these to "prove" a point they are making or to persuade someone that an idea is valid or viable. *Logos* could be considered more formal because it often includes research and data, but common sense is also valuable though not necessarily "formal."

This kind of argument tool is based on two kinds of facts and reasons, given to us from Aristotle:

HARD EVIDENCE: facts, clues, statistics, testimonies, witnesses

REASON/COMMON SENSE: habits of mind and cultural assumptions

For example:

- **STATISTICS:** A manufacturer of car seats will use safety data from car crash testing to prove that its product is safe.

- **FACTS AND TESTIMONIALS:** A person wanting a raise at work will provide his or her attendance record, productivity data, and letters of recommendation to the employer.

- **COMMON SENSE:** A professor wanting to have his or her students attend class will point out that to learn the materials for a test, students must be in class.

ETHOS

As part of the "writer/speaker" aspect of the rhetorical triangle, the writer must ensure that he or she is presenting information that is credible, authentic, and usable because the writer's choices show the writer's ethical qualities. The kinds of information (and the place from which the writer gets source information) indicates his or her ethical stance or character. The writer must ensure that the source material is coming from reliable sources. Moreover, the writer's *ethos* is determined by *how* the writer uses the sources. There is an ethical component expected of the writer to ensure that he or she is presenting the source material accurately, within context, and with appropriate citations. A writer's reputation is a part of *ethos* because a writer's words reflect the writer's character.

This kind of argument tool not only relies on the writer appearing honest or likeable but also on the writer being able to affirm an identity and share values with the audience.

For example:

- If Oprah says that we need to pay attention to our children's use of cell phones, people tend to listen because she is known to be charitable and is well-liked.

- A movie critic with several years of experience in the film industry has more *ethos* than a general moviegoer. The critic has more authority to make recommendations.

When arguing for a position on a controversial subject, you will have more *ethos* if you acknowledge that the opposition has a good point (you *concede*). This shows your reader that you have at least understood that there is another way of seeing the issues, and this makes you appear more reasonable.

> Source material should come from experts in the field—individuals who have established credentials (such as education, training, or experience) that make their contribution to the subject matter trustworthy and not just a personal opinion. In academic settings, writers use "peer-reviewed" articles because they are vetted by others in the field who have expertise to judge the value and validity of the information.

Starred *thought*

PATHOS

As part of the "reader" aspect of the rhetorical triangle, *pathos*, commonly known as "argument from heart," is used to elicit feelings from the audience in order to persuade them. Once a writer knows who the audience is, then the writer can identify the assumptions, values, and cultural views that might be shared and tap into those to elicit an emotional response that will aid in persuading the readers to act, think, or believe a certain way. Writers may use images, words, or arguments to achieve this effect. This kind of argument tool appeals to our sense of humanity or being humane and often influences us to make decisions based upon our feelings (e.g., joy, fear, anger, sympathy, pity, love). They are used to get us to buy things, to go places, to believe ideas.

For example:

- Hire a beautiful/handsome model to sell shampoo, and people will buy the products that promise to do the same for them.

- Show palm trees, warm water, and people laying out on the beach relaxed, and people will want to go to Jamaica for vacation.

- Create an advertisement with cute, cuddly animals, and people will want to give a donation to their local animal shelter to make a difference in those animals' lives.

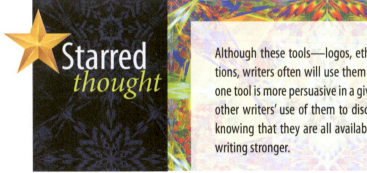

Starred *thought*

Although these tools—logos, ethos, pathos—are distinct and have specific functions, writers often will use them in tandem to persuade their readers. Sometimes, one tool is more persuasive in a given context than another, so you will have to study other writers' use of them to discover when and why to use which one. However, knowing that they are all available to you builds your repertoire for ways to make writing stronger.

FALLACIES

As we analyze the rhetoric of advertisements and speeches, we may discover that the authors of those texts are inadvertently (and sometimes purposely!) creating problems in reasoning. Advertisements and speeches are making an argument to buy or invest in a product or take a course of action, so they are often filled with fallacies. A "fallacy" is a flaw in the structure of an argument that results in authors creating conclusions that are invalid or, at least, suspect. If we can recognize these in others' texts, then we, too, can learn to avoid them in our own thinking and writing.

The *Encyclopedia of Philosophy*, a peer-reviewed online source, lists more than 200 different kinds of fallacies! What follows is a partial list of the names, definitions, and examples of several common fallacies.

1. ***Ad hominem:*** This Latin term literally means "against the man." This fallacy consists of an attack on the person making the argument rather than on the argument itself. People who commit this fallacy hope that if they can get you to dislike the person making the argument, you will conclude that the argument is bad. Of course, who makes an argument doesn't have much to do with the quality of the argument.

   Example: I see your evidence that if whaling continues at the current rate, whales will become extinct, but I don't believe it. Aren't you a member of that crazy PETA group? They are nothing but domestic terrorists, and so are you.

   A specific type of the *ad hominem* fallacy is called the "You Too" fallacy. This fallacy is committed when one person tries to deflect an accusation by accusing the accuser of being guilty of the same offense. You might think of it as the "Two Wrongs Don't Make a Right" fallacy.

   Example: I don't think you should be warning me about the dangers of binge drinking. Didn't I see you double-fisting beers at a party last weekend?*

   Example: He can't possibly know the answer; he isn't smart.

2. ****Appeal to force:*** When someone tries to convince you that an argument is correct by threatening you in some way, he or she has engaged in the "Appeal to Force" fallacy. Sometimes the threat is direct, but most times in the real world it is veiled or takes the form of political or economic pressure.** Imbedded in this fallacy are two others, both devoted to tapping into one's emotions.

   Example: Senator, I'm sure that you'll find my pro-choice argument convincing. As a side note, the donations that my pro-choice group usually makes to your campaign are under consideration at this very moment, and I hope I can argue in good conscience that they should be made at the same level this year.*

3. **Scare tactic:** This fallacy presents an issue in terms of exaggerated dangers or fears. The goal is to scare people into reacting to the issues and dismiss other options available for dealing with a problem.

   Example: If we don't do something about the economy today, we will have another depression, people will riot, and no one will be able to do anything about it!

*Content within asterisks from *Critical Approaches to Reading, Writing and Thinking* by Ric Baker & Vivian Beitman. Copyright © 2015 by Ric Baker & Vivian Beitman. Reprinted by permission of Kendall Hunt Publishing Company.

4. **Sentimental appeal:** This fallacy appeals to the emotion of love or romantic sentiments that can cloud our ability to see the irrationality of excessive emotions.

   Example: A Coca-Cola polar bear commercial uses animated polar bears who act like humans to make us feel "warm and fuzzy."

5. **Bandwagon appeal or **appeal to the masses:** If you argue that a claim is true because lots of people believe it, you've committed the fallacy of "Appeal to the Masses." But how many people believe a claim has nothing to do with whether it's actually true? At one time most people believed the sun revolved around the earth, but of course that didn't make it so.

   Example: You don't believe in Bigfoot? How could thousands of people who believe in Bigfoot be wrong?**

   Example: Everyone is buying the iPhone; it must be a great phone.

6. ***Arguing from ignorance:** The fallacy of "Arguing from Ignorance" happens when an arguer asserts that a claim is true because you can't prove it false (or less often, that it's false because you can't prove it true). As you've learned, though, you need good evidence before you accept a claim. How could a lack of evidence prove a claim? Of course it can't.

   Example: I know ghosts exist because no one has proven that they don't.

7. **Begging the question:** This fallacy means that the conclusion of the argument is simply a restatement of the premise. The "Begging the Question" fallacy is tricky because there are many different ways to say the same thing, and so therefore you might not realize right away that the evidence is just the conclusion in different words.

   Example: Jennifer Lawrence is the most beautiful woman alive. I know that's true because she's incredibly pretty.

   A particular subtype of this fallacy is called circular reasoning. This occurs when the conclusion is dependent on premises for its support, and the premises are in turn dependent on the conclusion for their support.

   Example: We know that Mayor Richardson is an honest person. His autobiography says he never told a lie as an adult, and we can be sure his autobiography is reliable, because he's so honest.*

   Example: The Bible says God exists, and since the Bible was written by God, He must exist.

8. ***Burden of proof:** The "Burden of Proof" fallacy is committed when someone makes a claim and then says that it's up to you to prove the claim

wrong. The burden of proof, however, is rightfully on the person making the claim; if you want other people to believe something, you have to give evidence.

Example: The Greek god Zeus actually exists. Prove that he doesn't.

9. **COMPLEX QUESTION:** The "Complex Question" fallacy means asking two questions but disguising them as only one question, and assuming that the first question has been answered when it hasn't.

Example: When did you start stealing things?

10. **EITHER/OR:** The "Either-Or" fallacy happens when an arguer artificially narrows choices or consequences of an argument down to two options. In fact, there are usually many more than two possible choices in the real world.

Example: Either the soul can be scientifically detected, or it doesn't exist.**

Example: America: love it or leave it.

11. **FAULTY ANALOGY:** *A "False Analogy" occurs when someone tries to use an analogy as evidence in an argument when the similarity between the two things being compared is only superficial. A good analogy, one that would carry weight in an argument, compares two things that have essential similarities.

Example: Since my car is red and can go really fast, your car, which is also red, must be able to go really fast as well.*

Example: The body is like an intricate watch. If a watch is broken, then you replace the broken piece, and it works perfectly again.

12. ***FALSE AUTHORITY:** As you learned, expert testimony can be a reliable form of evidence. The fallacy of "False Authority" is committed when someone tries to use the testimony of an expert to support his or her argument, when the expert's proficiency lies outside of the area about which he or she is testifying. The person committing the fallacy hopes that you will be wowed by the fact that the person is an expert in one field, without noticing that the person is not actually an expert in the field under question.

Example: Bill Gates says that the foreign policy of Pre-emptive War is bad, so therefore you shouldn't support it.**

False authority is also a claim is based on the expertise of someone who lacks appropriate credentials.

Example: The martial arts champion gave "two thumbs up" to Jackie Chan's recent film.

13. ***GUILT BY ASSOCIATION:** When someone attempts to discredit an argument or belief by pointing out that someone who is widely disliked also held that belief, he or she is engaging in the fallacy of "Guilt by Association," who believes a claim has nothing to do with the truth value of that claim.

   Example: You oppose animal experimentation? You know who else opposed animal experimentation? Hitler.

   Hitler also believed in working hard to accomplish his goals, but that doesn't automatically discredit the idea that you need to work hard; this should help you understand why the person holding an idea is not as important as the evidence and logic supporting the idea.*

14. **DOGMATISM:** The fallacy in which a claim is supported on the grounds that it's the only conclusion acceptable (therefore no debate is needed) within a given community.

   Example: It is clear to anyone who has thought about it that global warming could be controlled if people would use public transportation.

15. **EQUIVOCATION:** The fallacy in which a lie is given the appearance of truth, or in which the truth is misrepresented in deceptive language.

   Example: *Women* need to worry about *man*-eating sharks. OR

   You were out until 3:00 AM, but you tell your parents you were not out *all* night.

16. **POST HOC, ERGO PROPTER HOC:** This Latin term means "after this, therefore because of this." It is also known as "Faulty Causality." **The fallacy of "False Cause," or "*Post Hoc,*" happens when one assumes that because one event happened after another event, the first event had to have caused the second event. Often, events are purely coincidental, and causation must be demonstrated.

   Example: Several of the people who discovered King Tut's tomb later died tragic deaths. His tomb must be cursed.

   Many superstitions arise from this fallacy. For example, if you see a black cat and then later have bad luck, did seeing the black cat cause your bad luck?

   A subtype of this fallacy is "Mistaking Correlation for Causation." This fallacy is committed when someone assumes that because two events occur together, one must have caused the other. Of course, it could be a coincidence, or a third event could be the root cause of the other events.

   Example: The economy always seems to go south whenever a Republican president is in the White House. It seems that Republican presidencies cause economic downturns.**

Example: We never had any problem with the furnace until you moved into the apartment.

17. **Non sequitur:** This Latin term means "it does not follow." A fallacy in which claims, reasons, or warrants fail to connect logically; one point does not follow from another.

    Example: Walk on a crack, and break your mother's back.

    Example: A rabbit's foot on your keychain is good luck.

18. **Hasty generalization:** A fallacy in which an inference is drawn from insufficient data.

    Example: I loved the hit song, so I'll love the album it's on.

    Example: Josue had been to that doctor twice and had to wait an hour to see the doctor. That happens every time!

19. ***Moving the goalposts:** The fallacy "Moving the Goalposts" means asking for evidence from your opponent that fits certain criteria, and then when your opponent provides that evidence, changing the criteria. In this way, your opponent is never able to prove the argument, despite meeting the criteria you yourself set.

    Example: Amanda is a very stingy person. Do you have any evidence that she gives to charity? Oh, she gave to the American Cancer Federation last year? Well, that was only one charity. Oh, she also gave to the MS Foundation? Well, she didn't give more than $5,000.00, so she is definitely stingy.

20. **Naturalistic fallacy:** The "Naturalistic" fallacy is committed when an arguer assumes that because something is natural, it must be good. Of course, many human-made substances are good, and many naturally occurring substances (like uranium) are harmful.

    Example: Chemotherapy shouldn't be used to treat cancer; it's just shooting chemicals into your body. Instead, cancer should be treated with all-natural herbs.

21. **Red herring:** The "Red Herring" fallacy means including irrelevant details in an argument to distract an opponent's attention. In this way, the person committing the fallacy hopes that the irrelevant material will be taken as evidence supporting the unrelated conclusion (and you learned how important it is for evidence to be relevant).

    Example: Perhaps passing the healthcare reform bill is an ethical necessity, but are we spending enough money on national defense? Do we want Iran attacking our troops while we are debating healthcare?

22. **SLIPPERY SLOPE:** The "Slippery Slope" fallacy occurs when an arguer suggests that taking an action will inevitably give rise to a chain of events that will lead to undesirable consequences, when the chain of events is not very likely, and the arguer makes no attempt to prove that it is likely.

   Example: If we cut taxes, the government will go bankrupt, and the United States will become a Third World country.*

   Example: If I don't get an A in this class, I won't get into medical school.

23. **MORAL EQUIVALENCE:** The fallacy in which no distinction is made between serious issues, problems, or failings and much less important ones.

   Example: That parking attendant who gave me a ticket is as bad as Hitler.

24. ****STRAW MAN:** When a person misrepresents an opponent's argument to make it sound ridiculous so that he or she can refute the ridiculous argument instead of the real one, the person has committed the "Straw Man" fallacy. The arguer hopes that the mischaracterized argument will be mistaken for the real argument and probably also hopes that the ridiculous characterization will make his or her opponent look ludicrous.

   Example: You believe that the drinking age should be lowered? Why would you argue that it is a good idea to have thousands of drunken teenagers running around?**

   Example: *Person A:* I don't think children should run into the busy streets. *Person B:* Well, I think that it would be foolish to lock up children all day with no fresh air.

HOW DO I DO A RHETORICAL ANALYSIS?

PRINT ADVERTISEMENTS

Now that we have examined the introductory elements of a rhetorical analysis, let us rhetorically analyze two fashion advertisements and then examine a speech. The same principles of rhetorical analysis apply to each kind of text, but how we discuss them is slightly different. The analysis of visuals requires that we look at what is pictured, including location and color, while written speeches require looking at words and where they are located and what they mean. Examine the following illustrations.

Nancy White / Shutterstock.com

Nancy White / Shutterstock.com

Use a Venn diagram on the next page to compare the images. In the left hand column, list all of the items you see in the Paris version; in the right hand column, list all of the images you see in the New York version. See if you can pair up any images that are found in both. For example, notice that shoes are used in both advertisements, but high-heels are used in the Paris version while boots are used in the New York one.

See if you can pair up any images that are found in both along the dividing line in the middle, and the images that are only found in one of the images, place those closer to the outside lines.

Venn Diagram for Comparison	
Paris Fashion	New York Fashion

WHAT'S NEXT?

Use the questions below to sort through and analyze what you have in the Venn diagram.

1. What do the items suggest about Paris? Consider:

    What can a visitor to Paris see or do?

    What kind of weather is there?

    What kind of clothing is worn there?

2. What do the items suggest about New York? Consider:

    What can a visitor to New York see or do?

    What kind of weather is there?

    What kind of clothing is worn there?

3. What do the advertisers see as common elements in both cities? Why might these be common?

4. What do the advertisers see as unique elements in each city? Why might these be unique?

5. What do the advertisers think is important to people who would visit Paris? How do you know?

6. What do the advertisers think is important to people who would visit New York? How do you know?

7. Taken together, what does the Paris fashion advertisement seem to be saying:

    about Paris or Parisians?

    about people who would want to visit Paris?

8. Taken together, what does the New York fashion advertisement seem to be saying:

    about New York or New Yorkers?

    about people who would want to visit New York?

9. What is the argument the advertisers are making about each?

    City?

    Citizens?

    Visitors?

WHAT'S NEXT?

Now that you have examined the images, consider HOW the advertisers are making their argument(s).

1. *Logos*:

   What kinds of facts, clues, statistics, testimonies, witnesses are being used, if any?

   What kind of reason or common sense is being used, if any?

   How do the advertisers use *logos*?

   Why does the use of *logos*, if used, persuade the audience to accept the argument?

   What fallacies, if any, are there? Explain how they function.

2. *Ethos*:

   What is the *ethos* of the advertisers?

   How do the advertisers establish their *ethos*?

   Why does the use of *ethos*, if used, persuade the audience to accept the argument?

   What fallacies, if any, are there? Explain how they function.

3. *Pathos*:

   What emotions, if any, are being tapped into in the images?

   How do those emotions get conveyed?

   Why does the *pathos*, if used, persuade the audience to accept the argument?

   What fallacies, if any, are there? Explain how they function.

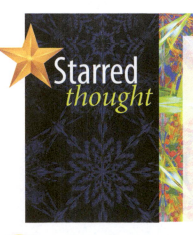

Starred *thought*

Keep in mind that advertisements have obvious messages: buy this, use this, go here. The key to a rhetorical analysis is to see behind the obvious to reveal what is lurking behind that message. Think of it this way: The Paris fashion advertisement obviously wants you to buy into the idea that "Paris is always a good choice," but so does the New York advertisement, so why do they want you to believe that and how do they get you to believe that? THAT is what a rhetorical analysis does—it reveals how the speaker/author is working out ways to convince you that THIS product, place, service, etc., is the one that will give you whatever it is they say it will give you.

RESEARCHING

Consider, too, what some research on the two cities might reveal. You might, for example, look up tourist information.

How many people visit Paris/New York every year?

From where do the visitors come?

When do they go?

How long do they stay?

Are there any "hot spots" or "must see" places?

Finding out information about the locales may provide some insight into why the advertisers chose the images they did. You could also consider why certain elements were NOT included. For example, wine and cheese are often associated with France, yet these are not included as images in the advertisements. Why not? Did the advertisers think these might not be needed or not useful? Many people think of New York as being crowded and the city that "never sleeps," yet the advertisement does not seem to address this. Why not? Did the advertisers think these might not be needed or not useful?

In other words, sometimes doing some research on the product, service, event, or idea advertised can provide some insights into why advertisers use or do not use certain elements to persuade their audience to "buy into" what is being advertised. As you examine other advertisements, pay attention to whether the advertisement is in a magazine or on the TV; notice WHO is pictured and HOW they are dressed; notice what words there are and what font is used; examine WHAT colors are used and the meanings of those colors; notice WHEN you see the advertisement (morning, afternoon, night) and why that might matter. These are the clues you have that will help you to define who the advertisers think their audience is and what the advertisers think their viewers value or believe.

SPEECHES

Speeches are also great texts to examine rhetorically because there is a speaker, subject, and audience more directly discernible. For our purposes, here, we are examining the written form of a speech, so we must stay within the bounds of what is written.

Starred *thought*

Because we are reading a written text here, we are restricted to looking at words, phrases, sentences, and the order of ideas. If we were to listen to the speech, we could examine the speaker's voice, intonation, pronunciation, enunciation of words, and other oral elements. If we were to watch the speech, we would have all of these elements available to us in addition to gestures, eye contact, and facial expressions. This shows us that rhetorical analyses can become very complex as we add on elements!

WHAT'S NEXT?

Read the following speech by President Roosevelt regarding World War II to get a sense of what it is about and to whom the President is speaking.

THE PRESIDENT'S WAR MESSAGE, DECEMBER 8, 1941

by Franklin D. Roosevelt

Yesterday, December 7, 1941—a date which will live in infamy—the United States of America was suddenly and deliberately attacked by naval and air forces of the Empire of Japan.

The United States was at peace with that Nation and, at the solicitation of Japan, was still in conversation with its Government and its Emperor looking toward the maintenance of peace in the Pacific. Indeed, one hour after Japanese air squadrons had commenced bombing in Oahu, the Japanese Ambassador to the United States and his colleague delivered to the Secretary of State a formal reply to a recent American message. While this reply stated that it seemed useless to continue the existing diplomatic negotiations, it contained no threat or hint of war or armed attack.

It will be recorded that the distance of Hawaii from Japan makes it obvious that the attack was deliberately planned many days or even weeks ago. During the intervening time the Japanese Government has deliberately sought to deceive the United States by false statements and expressions of hope for continued peace.

The attack yesterday on the Hawaiian Islands has caused severe damage to American naval and military forces. Very many American lives have been lost. In addition American ships have been reported torpedoed on the high seas between San Francisco and Honolulu.

Yesterday the Japanese Government also launched an attack against Malaya.

Source: Franklin D. Roosevelt, "The President's War Message, December 8, 1941."

Last night Japanese forces attacked Hong Kong.

Last night Japanese forces attacked Guam.

Last night Japanese forces attacked the Philippine Islands.

Last night the Japanese attacked Wake Island.

This morning the Japanese attacked Midway Island.

Japan has, therefore, undertaken a surprise offensive extending throughout the Pacific area. The facts of yesterday speak for themselves. The people of the United States have already formed their opinions and well understand the implications to the very life and safety of our Nation.

As Commander-in-Chief of the Army and Navy I have directed that all measures be taken for our defense.

Always will we remember the character of the onslaught against us.

No matter how long it may take us to overcome this premeditated invasion, the American people in their righteous might will win through to absolute victory.

I believe I interpret the will of the Congress and of the people when I assert that we will not only defend ourselves to the uttermost but will make very certain that this form of treachery shall never endanger us again.

Hostilities exist. There is no blinking at the fact that our people, our territory, and our interests are in grave danger.

With confidence in our armed forces—with the unbounded determination of our people—we will gain the inevitable triumph—so help us God.

I ask that the Congress declare that since the unprovoked and dastardly attack by Japan on Sunday, December seventh, a state of war has existed between the United States and the Japanese Empire.

WHAT'S NEXT?

Now, reread it, using active reading strategies, paying attention to the elements of the rhetorical triangle.

- Use highlighting to mark places where the president is using *logos*, and try to distinguish between facts and common sense forms of *logos*.

- Use "underlining, circling, or boxing" to mark the places where you see the president showing his *ethos*.

- Use "doodles, thing-a-ma-bobs, or doodads" to mark places where you feel an emotion (note what kind of emotion it is), which is an indication that *pathos* is being used.

The evidence you will use for your analysis will include actual words (diction), phrasing (set of words), and ideas that are imbedded in the text. For an example of an "idea imbedded in the text," consider the fact that the President of the United States is the one giving the speech. The highest office in the country gives the speaker, the President, implicit authority, and this is part of the *ethos* component. This authority is an understood element, so the "evidence" is simply stating that this is what is accepted as part of the role of a U.S. President. What the President says or what his political leanings are can also be part of *ethos*, and those are additional aspects that you can examine. Research can help you identify and explain what those aspects are to better develop your interpretation of speaker's *ethos*.

WHAT'S NEXT?

Using your annotations, fill in the following sections by identifying the various ways each rhetorical device is being used in the speech and the evidence you have for each. As you identify the device and the ways it is used, think of how you might show that to your readers in a logical, structured way. Notice how the first exercise may function as a *working outline* or structure for how you deliver your analysis.

A WORKING VISUAL OUTLINE

A working visual outline can be helpful for writers who like to visualize how they might structure their analyses. Sometimes color and images can help writers think through the way the text appears on the page. In each box, fill in the information for each component to help you categorize the rhetorical elements.

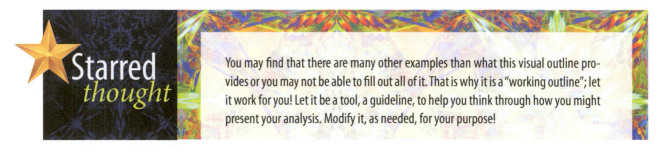

Starred *thought*

You may find that there are many other examples than what this visual outline provides or you may not be able to fill out all of it. That is why it is a "working outline"; let it work for you! Let it be a tool, a guideline, to help you think through how you might present your analysis. Modify it, as needed, for your purpose!

Logos (Subject)

- Facts:
  - evidence from text:
- Data:
  - evidence from text:
- Common Sense:
  - evidence from text:

Ethos (Writer)

- Authority:
  - evidence:
- Trustworthiness:
  - evidence:
- Character:
  - evidence:

Pathos (Audience)

- Emotion 1:
  - evidence:
- Emotion 2:
  - evidence:
- Emotion 3:
  - evidence:

Source: Deborah Scaggs.

Visual Outline 2

If you prefer a more linear way of outlining, you might consider the next example, which is a more traditional form of an informal outline. Fill in the information for each component to help you categorize the rhetorical elements and provide examples to support them.

- *Logos* (Subject):

  Logos' Definition:

  Facts:

    evidence from text:

  Data:

    evidence from text:

  Common Sense:

    evidence from text:

- *Ethos* (Speaker):

  Ethos' Definition:

  Authority:

    evidence:

  Trustworthiness:

    evidence:

  Character:

    evidence:

- *Pathos* (Audience):

  Pathos' Definition:

  Emotion 1:

    evidence:

  Emotion 2:

    evidence:

  Emotion 3:

    evidence:

Taken together, what do your visual outlines suggest is the message Roosevelt is conveying beyond just going to war? *How* do the rhetorical devices *work together* to convey that message? Why is that effective?

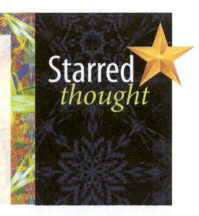

Whichever tool you prefer, remember that in a rhetorical analysis, the specific elements you are examining are contributing to an overall message the advertisement or speech is attempting to achieve, so you always have to connect the individual parts to the whole. Diagrams, outlines, and drawings can be helpful in visualizing the connections so that you can "see" how they fit together. Try out the different ways of thinking through the organization to see which one works best for you and your purpose!

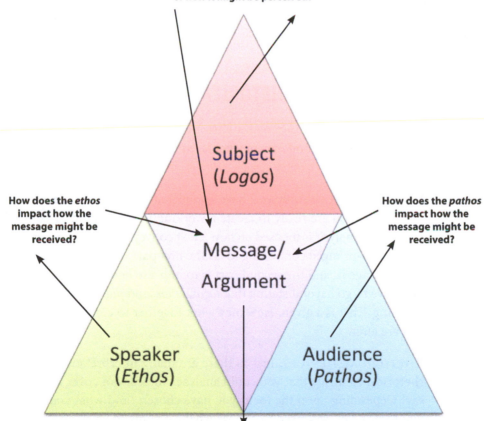

How does the *logos* impact what the message might be or how it might be perceived?

Subject
(*Logos*)

How does the *ethos* impact how the message might be received?

Message/
Argument

How does the *pathos* impact how the message might be received?

Speaker
(*Ethos*)

Audience
(*Pathos*)

Taken together, what is the message? How do these rhetorical devices shape the way the message is conveyed? How do these methods work to achieve persuasion?

© Kendall Hunt Publishing Company

RESEARCHING

For speeches, you can do some research to find out more about the context. In the case of Roosevelt's speech, it might be interesting to locate some newspapers from that time period before Japan attacked Pearl Harbor to see what Americans were being told about the war in Europe and their general impression of what Americans thought their role was in it. Then, examining newspapers after the attack to see what happened to Americans' perception might provide some valuable insight into what Roosevelt was trying to achieve in his speech.

Starred *thought*

Context is extremely important for all writing, and when examining texts rhetorically, context becomes essential. Finding out what was going on in the culture at the time an advertisement aired or was published or when a speaker gave a speech provides much needed information in determining what the meanings might be. For example, a speech given in 1941 might have a very different reception if given now because the world, people, and governments in power have changed. Therefore, contextualizing the time, place, and concerns of the day will impact how we interpret texts!

FEATURES OF A RHETORICAL ANALYSIS

Now that we have examined a rhetorical analysis of advertisements and of a speech, we have a good idea of what is expected in this genre of writing. Here are the features.

INTERPRETATION: After you have completed the analysis and have conducted prewriting, you are ready to create a working interpretation or controlling idea. Rhetorical analysis is focused on how a text conveys a message, so you will need to have a two-pronged controlling idea. The first part will be to identify *what* the actual message is, and the second part is to indicate *how* that message in conveyed. You have to go beyond stating that *logos*, *ethos*, and *pathos* are used to convey the meaning. That is a given. *How* they work together to convey the message is what you are after.

RHETORICAL DEVICES: Just as there are many interpretations, there are many rhetorical elements that you could analyze. You cannot cover them all in one essay! Depending upon the focus you have chosen (and what your instructor asks you to do), you will need to choose what elements to work on. For the purposes here, you will focus on the three specific elements examined in this chapter: *logos*, *ethos*, and *pathos*. These are the parts that will help you to make an interpretation of the whole.

Textual Support: You have to be very explicit in what constitutes evidence for *logos*, *ethos*, and *pathos*. Do not assume that your readers will have the advertisement or speech in front of them, nor assume that they see it the same way as you do. When you argue that a particular element is functioning in a particular way, you have to explain to your readers how that is possible.

> **Advertisements:** Because a rhetorical analysis of an advertisement is based on something visual that is simply not "quotable," the support you use is based on *describing* what is in the advertisement and *explaining* how that *implies* meaning and how it might be *interpreted*. If there is written text in an advertisement, then you will quote that using quotation marks and an in-text citation.

> **Speeches:** Because there is written text (i.e., words, phrases, sentences) in a speech, you will be using that as evidence. Additionally, a rhetorical analysis taps into what is NOT said directly but *implied*. Therefore, you will need to explain your thinking, the reasoning behind what you say is there in the speech but not actually said in words. You will have to include quotation marks around the written text that you are examining and provide the in-text citation for it. Your bibliography will include the primary text (the advertisement or speech) and any secondary sources (i.e., research) you used.

Secondary Sources: For a rhetorical analysis, your goal is not to find out what others have said about the advertisement or speech but what the circumstances were behind the development of the text. In other words, you are *contextualizing* the conditions around which the advertisement or speech was created and why that is important to understanding the message conveyed in it. Use secondary sources about the historical time period or social or cultural conditions that the primary text was written in *if that information helps you to support your interpretation.* You might consider researching the author's background. For example, in the Paris and New York fashion advertisement, finding out who the creators were might help you to figure out what their end goal was beyond just selling a product or idea. Examining Roosevelt's foreign policy in the 1940s might help shed light on why he says what he says in his speech.

Structure: In the first paragraph or two, you need to establish the text(s) you are analyzing along with the author(s). You also should briefly describe what the advertisement is advertising (on the surface) or what the speech is about in a few sentences. You need a controlling idea that will indicate what the message is behind the literal message, and identify how the author of the text has achieved this. This is typically found within the first paragraph or two. The controlling idea should be more than a list of the rhetorical devices you examined. You must tell your reader what the *connection* is between the elements and *how they function* to create a *message*.

The rest of the essay—the body paragraphs—is devoted to the interpretation of the primary text where you make a point that supports the interpretation and then provide the textual support for it. The conclusion is not simply a restating of the introduction. Instead, think of the conclusion as a final thought about what impact your analysis has on the interpretation of the primary text or what new insights your interpretation provides for the primary text. This is pushing beyond just a restatement of what you said you would do and acts more like a justification for why your interpretation is valid or valuable.

THIRD-PERSON POINT OF VIEW: Rhetorical analyses do not use "I" or other first person pronouns because the focus is on analysis in the academic sense of being objective and quieting the personal reactions or feelings about the topic itself. If you find yourself being persuaded by an advertisement or speech, you should ask yourself how that is happening. What is it that the author is tapping into about values and ideas that he or she thinks the audience shares?

WRITING YOUR OWN RHETORICAL ANALYSIS

Locate one printed advertisement or one written speech and analyze the rhetorical triangle components of subject, author, and audience, emphasizing the rhetorical strategies of *logos*, *ethos*, and *pathos*. You will analyze these components and develop an overall controlling idea of what the advertisement's or speech's argument is and how that is conveyed. Keep in mind that you are analyzing *how an advertisements or speech convinces an audience to accept a particular viewpoint that is advocated*. You are not arguing for or against this viewpoint; you are showing *how* the advertisement or speech conveys *its* argument.

For the purposes of this assignment, you will use strict APA document design and documentation style. This means that you will have sections in your essay. For an example of how APA sections are created, take a look at your handbook for how APA sets up an essay. Note that YOUR section titles will differ from these examples, and they may differ from your peers' sections, but you must use section headings of some kind. Here is one way, but not the only way, you might organize your analysis:

SECTION 1: This might be the introduction where you describe the advertisement or speech and what the main point is.

SECTION 2: This might contextualize the historical, social, or cultural elements that are pertinent to understanding the purpose of the advertisement or speech.

SECTION 3: This might be where you do the analysis of the rhetorical devices, explaining *what* the rhetorical devices are and *how* they work in the primary source. (Here is where your support will go.) You might have sub-sections here that divvy up the three components of the rhetorical triangle.

SECTION 4: This might be your concluding thoughts about the impact of the advertisement or speech.

Remember: You will go well beyond the five-paragraph essay format, for the five-paragraph essay limits the depth needed for this kind of analysis; however, the essay will still be organized in a logical way (smooth movement from one point to the next), and the development of your essay will be rich in analysis and explanation.

While there are no strictly "right" answers, you will need to support your interpretation of how the authors are using images and/or language in a particular way by quoting from the text, citing correctly in APA documentation style, and/or describing the text. You should also include secondary sources that inform the advertisement (perhaps looking at the company's website to see what they are trying to achieve by selling the product, service, or idea) or the speech (perhaps looking at when and where it was given).

Writer: _____ Readers: _____

PEER-REVIEW OF RHETORICAL ANALYSIS DRAFT 1

1. The controlling idea must be debatable. What is the paper saying is the meaning of the advertisement? Is this debatable?

2. Does the introductory section orientate readers to the advertisement/speech? What could be added?

3. *Logos*: Examine the section on *logos*.

   a. Locate an example the writer uses and verify it is *logos*.

   b. What other examples could be included in this section?

4. *Ethos*: Examine the section on *ethos*. What other elements could be included in this section?

   a. Locate an example the writer uses and verify it is *ethos*.

   b. What other examples could be included in this section?

5. *Pathos*: Examine the section on *pathos*.

   a. Locate an example the writer uses and verify it is *pathos*.

   b. What other examples could be included in this section?

6. Examine the links between the sections. To what extent does every section link back to the controlling idea?

7. Readers need to be able to see the advertisement or speech without having to actually have it in hand. What needs to be added to make the primary source "visible" for a reader? What might help a reader to "see" the primary source?

8. Where could the analysis be expanded upon? Why would this be important to do?

Name: _____ Date: _____

REFLECTIONS: RHETORICAL ANALYSIS WRITING

Describe your writing process for this rhetorical analysis. What strategies did you use? Why?

What did you find to be the hardest part about writing a rhetorical analysis?

What did you find to be the easiest part about writing a rhetorical analysis?

Compare your processes for writing a review and for writing a rhetorical analysis.

What similarities were there? Differences?

Why might that be the case?

What is your overall understanding of your writing process so far?

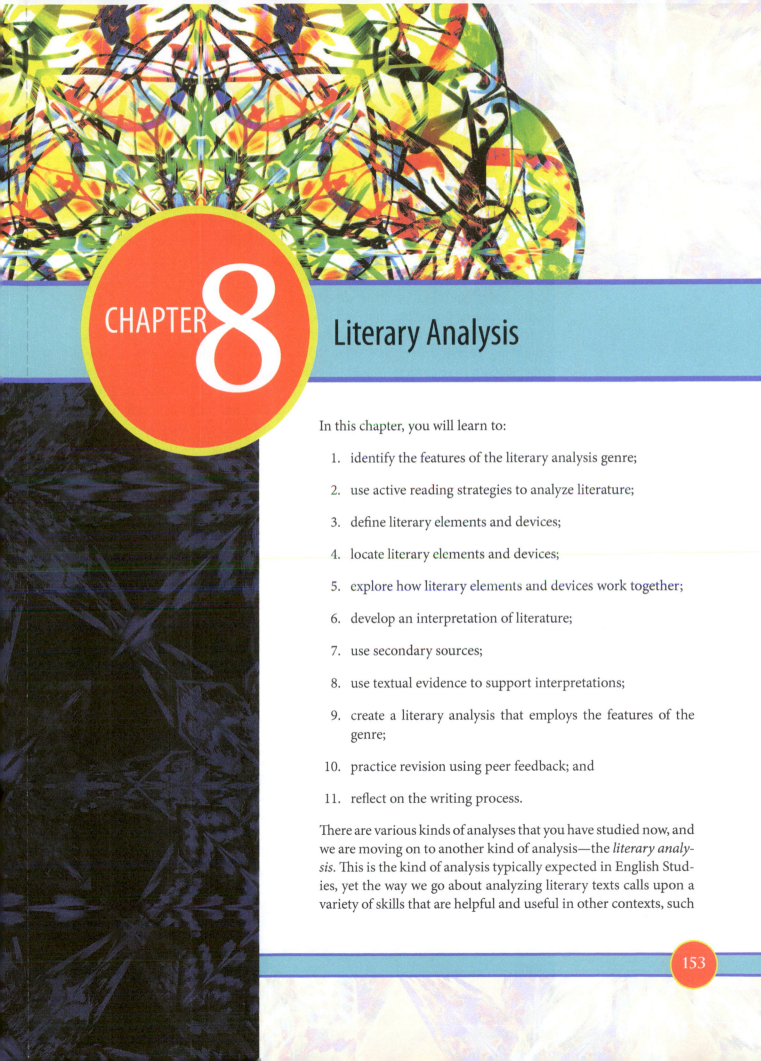

CHAPTER 8

Literary Analysis

In this chapter, you will learn to:

1. identify the features of the literary analysis genre;

2. use active reading strategies to analyze literature;

3. define literary elements and devices;

4. locate literary elements and devices;

5. explore how literary elements and devices work together;

6. develop an interpretation of literature;

7. use secondary sources;

8. use textual evidence to support interpretations;

9. create a literary analysis that employs the features of the genre;

10. practice revision using peer feedback; and

11. reflect on the writing process.

There are various kinds of analyses that you have studied now, and we are moving on to another kind of analysis—the *literary analysis*. This is the kind of analysis typically expected in English Studies, yet the way we go about analyzing literary texts calls upon a variety of skills that are helpful and useful in other contexts, such as marketing, history, and, yes, even the sciences! One of the ways literary analysis is helpful to writers outside of English is being able to describe processes or concepts that are highly specialized that only insiders (experts in the field) would understand. Hence, using analogies or vivid details, which are typical markers of literature, can help convey complex materials to persons outside of the field. Studying how language works in literature can help you convey ideas more effectively in other contexts where literature (e.g., short stories, poetry, drama, novels) is less prominent. Sometimes, there are assigned novels in History or Social Sciences that address a historical issue or social problem because literature can convey the emotional, human element that may be missing from facts or data that provide a more well-rounded understanding of the topic. Analyzing literature can provide insight into the human condition or what is valued in a culture. For example, reading Ernest Hemingway's novels, which are often set during WWII, can provide insight into how American culture views that war and its consequences. Studying women writers, like Aphra Behn who wrote in the late 1600s, shows us that women were participating in English culture and providing their view of the world around them. Examining some of the literature written by J. G. Ballard, who writes about the impact of science and technology on human activity in the twentieth and twenty-first centuries, can provide contemporary arguments for technological advancements and their consequences. In short, studying literature provides various viewpoints on controversial topics that are not readily available in other contexts.

Starred *thought*

The word "literature" has many meanings. In all disciplines, professors use the word "literature" to mean the body of knowledge in that field of study, so "literature" can mean case studies, reports, academic journals, and conference papers. In English studies, "literature" can have that meaning, and it also refers to the texts under study, such as novels, short stories, poems, and drama. The context is what provides the meaning for this term.

WHAT IS A LITERARY ANALYSIS?

Literary analyses are the most commonly assigned exercises in English. One of the main reasons for analyzing literature is to understand what is often referred to as "the deeper meaning." What this means is that there *are layers of meaning* in a text that have potential for various interpretations. You can think of studying literature as being a detective. The clues to understanding a story, for example, are found in the text itself, and your job is to ferret out the clues and make sense of how they lead you to a conclusion. As writers analyze those clues for meaning, they begin to see how there is a potential for current understanding of the contemporary world as literature often addresses such issues as love, war, family, identity, culture, values, religion, and so on. In short, literature often speaks to human nature and how we define what "human nature" is to begin with. Literature also provides another window out of which to look at the world and reconsider what is going on and why. We often learn something about ourselves, or human nature in general, when we study literary texts. Studying literature is simply another way of analyzing the world around us in a kaleidoscopic way.

In more practical terms, finding links between the specifics in a text to larger thematic issues is key to developing critical thinking. One of the main goals of a literary analysis is to deconstruct (take apart) a text to see how it works as a whole. Typically, writers of literary analyses examine themes, characters, and literary devices to discover how they function individually and then interact together to contribute to a meaning of the whole.

In literature, writers make claims—have an interpretation of a text—that is grounded in the text itself. The ability to make a claim is dependent upon how valid your argument is and the evidence (support from the text) you use. That argument is also contingent upon how well you are able to connect the clues other writers (other literary analysts) have found to your own and develop a logical conclusion about those connections. It is not enough to say that a literary text means "x." Your job as the writer is to show your reader how that is possible by taking the reader through a step-by-step analysis of how the individual parts depend upon the whole to create that meaning, and how others' works have helped you to make sense of those connections. In other words, you are creating a dialectic between your own thinking, the primary text, and the secondary texts—yet another turn of the kaleidoscope!

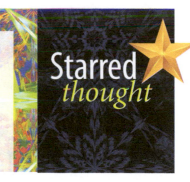

There are two kinds of texts. One is a primary text which is the one that you are analyzing, such as a poem or novel. The other one is a secondary text which is a text that others have written about that text. Secondary texts can be essays from journals, interviews with the author, or even historical information that provides context for the primary text. The strongest literary analyses are those that take information from various sources to support an interpretation of a primary text.

FEATURES OF THE LITERARY ANALYSIS

There are several important expectations or features of a literary analysis. They are what make this genre unique.

INTERPRETATION: After you have completed prewriting, you are ready to create a working interpretation or controlling idea. This is what you are saying is the point or possible meaning of the primary text or how some aspect of it can be read. You are not covering every possible interpretation, nor are you examining every single element in the primary text. Your job is to choose the most apt and supportive elements, passages, and ideas in the primary text to prove your interpretation to be accurate and plausible.

More sophisticated literary analyses approach the alternative views or alternative interpretations of a primary text. This is how you develop a stronger argument for your own view; by providing the counter-argument (the alternative interpretation), you bolster your own interpretation. Your instructor will direct you to how far you need to go with your literary analysis. As you move into higher-level courses, you may be asked to go this extra mile.

LITERARY ELEMENTS: Just as there are many interpretations, there are many literary elements that you could analyze, and depending upon the focus you have chosen (and what your instructor asks you to do), you will not be able to cover characters, themes, conflict, setting, language, and other elements in one essay. You will have to choose the elements that will help you to make your interpretation seem valid. It may be that characters and theme work together to support your interpretation of the primary text, and then you might choose two or three literary devices that show how that interpretation exists. In other words, these elements and devices work in tandem in your analysis.

THIRD-PERSON POINT OF VIEW: Literary analyses do not use "I" or other first-person pronouns. They are very "academic" and formal. The way you show your interpretation is not by saying "in my opinion" or "I think that…" Instead, you approach analysis of the primary text from an objective stance, and third person is one way to do that. Instead of "I think that the blanket means…," you state "the blanket means…." Notice how they are saying the same thing, but the second example is stronger, more forceful. The emphasis in the second example is an interpretation that you, obviously, are making! Therefore, you need to follow this statement with support from the text to show how the blanket means whatever you are saying it means.

STRUCTURE: In the first paragraph or two, you need to establish the text(s) you are analyzing along with the author(s). You also should briefly summarize the primary text in a few sentences. Think of the summary as what you find on the back of a DVD. It provides main characters and basic plot, and that is it. You will have a main focus, an interpretative stance, and this is typically found within the first paragraph or two, and the controlling idea should be more than a set of elements you will examine. You must tell your reader what the connection is between the elements and how they function to create a meaning of the primary text. The rest of the essay—the body paragraphs—is devoted to the interpretation of the primary text where you make a point that supports the interpretation and then provide the textual support for it. The conclusion is not simply a restating of the introduction. Instead, think of the conclusion as a final thought about what impact your analysis has on the interpretation of the primary text or what new insights your interpretation provides for the primary text. This is pushing beyond just a restatement of what you said you would do and acts more like a justification for why your interpretation is valid or valuable.

PRIMARY TEXT SUPPORT: You will quote directly from the novel, short story, poem, song, play, or whatever the primary text is, citing correctly and accurately. In English studies, MLA is used, so you should use strict MLA documentation style and document design. You also must go beyond simply quoting material; you must choose the most apt passages that will support the point you are making. If you say, for example, that the blanket means "love," where in the text is there proof of this? How would a reader read that quoted material to see "love" is a possible interpretation of that symbol?

SECONDARY SOURCES: Depending on the course you take, the purpose of the literary analysis, your instructor's directions, and required length, the number of secondary sources will vary. You must synthesize your ideas with those of others—engaging what others have already said—and connect your ideas and theirs to your overall point. You are not just using any passages. You must be strategic in choosing the passages that help to move your interpretation along, whether it be to support your own thinking or to provide an alternative reading. You also can use secondary sources about the historical time period or social or cultural conditions that the primary text was written in *if that information helps you to support your interpretation.*

LITERARY COMPONENTS

Literary analysts examine literature through a number of lenses and frameworks. For our purposes here, we will focus attention on literary elements, techniques, and devices, all of which can be used to interpret a piece of literature and make an argument for how that interpretation is possible and why it is important. There are fine distinctions between literary elements, techniques, and devices. The following lists are not exhaustive, but they provide us a starting point.

LITERARY ELEMENTS: Whether a poem, play, song, or short story, there are literary elements at work and that function as the backbone to literature. They include, but are not limited to:

- CHARACTERS: These are who or what is doing or receiving the action. Thus, characters can be human, inhuman, or animals. Sometimes, objects become characters, and because they have such an important role in what happens in the text, it is as if they are active participants. Pay attention to who is doing what to whom and look for any objects that function as actors in some way.

- SETTING: Where the action takes place has an impact on how we are supposed to read the text. Pay attention to locale, weather patterns, geography, climate, and rural or urban areas. Look for clues to time, too, to see if the past, present, or future is being addressed. Additionally, not all stories take place in real places; sometimes the action happens in the mind!

- **PLOT:** What is happening may not be limited to one action or even two. Sometimes the intersection of actions is the "plot" and what makes the text's story compelling. Pay attention to what is happening to individual characters and what is happening to all of the characters as a whole. Look for connections between individual actions and outside forces, which could include actions by weather or natural disasters or inanimate events like a stock market crash.

- **THEME:** The thread that runs through a text might be obvious or subtle, and there may be more than one thread that is at work. Sometimes one theme is coupled with another because the theme is actually the interaction between the two. Keep an eye out for these kinds of pairings and pay attention to which one seems to have more impact (if it does) on what is happening in the text.

- **TONE:** The sense you get from a text for it to be humorous, serious, sarcastic, or scary helps readers to interpret the actual meaning of the text. Pay attention to how you feel as you read, marking passages that suggest that feeling and why.

LITERARY TECHNIQUES OR DEVICES: These are the smaller units in a text that help to establish or develop literary elements. Dialogue, for example, is the literary device that helps to show characters, but the characterization, itself, is a literary element.

- **FIGURES OF SPEECH:** These attempt to compare or identify one idea/thing with another to help the reader make connections between ideas, yet there are several kinds of "figures of speech" with specific functions but which have subtle differences.

  - **Similes:** These are used to compare two things, using "like" or "as," that are obviously similar to each other to establish links between the two things being compared. Look for these to help establish characteristics of people or situations, for these devices help to show traits or conditions. Example: A person standing *like a statue* remained stoic and unmoving.

  - **Analogies:** A comparison of two things that seem to not be related, but when examined closely, both share similarities that make them alike significantly. They seem to be unlike but actually share qualities that are not obvious. Example: Think of a human life as you would a clock, with the first hour as birth and the last hour as death.

  - **Symbols:** A word, action, image, or event that stands for something else because of the associated qualities. For example, doves are symbolic of peace because doves are thought to be peaceful creatures; hawks, on the other hand, are birds of prey and are symbolic of war. Look for these to establish cultural relevancy, as in American politics when presidents are considered "dovish" or "hawkish."

- **Diction:** The choice of words are extremely important in any kind of writing, and in literature, the diction is even more insightful as it provides clues to how the author wants us to interpret the situation. If a writer says that a character is crying instead of the character is sobbing, what is the difference? Because people cry for different reasons—whether for joy or for pain—crying and sobbing have different tenors and may indicate different emotional states. Thus, looking very closely at the words (especially in poetry or songs) helps to interpret the possible meanings more accurately.

There are many, many more techniques or devices, and a Google search will provide sites you can use to find out just how many! Since literary analyses are just one of many kinds of writing, this list is not exhaustive and is meant only as a starting point. If you choose to examine other devices, great! The more you know, the more options you have for writing about literature.

Starred *thought*

ADDITIONAL TERMS AND CONCEPTS FOR ANALYZING LITERARY TEXTS

allegory A fictional work in which the setting, characters, plot, and other elements are all symbols, together conveying an abstract moral, religious, or social concept.

alliteration Repetition of identical consonants for effect. Example: Showers beat on broken blinds.

allusion A reference to a recognized literary work, person, historic event, artistic achievement, etc. that enhances the meaning of a detail in a literary work. Example: "Fred was a scrooge from the beginning," which is a reference to Ebenezer Scrooge in *A Christmas Carol* by Charles Dickens.

antagonist The individual or force that opposes the protagonist.

aphorism A pointed statement that expresses a principle or observation in a concise, memorable way. This statement by Ralph Waldo Emerson is an example: "Nothing great was ever achieved without enthusiasm."

Adapted from *Journey Into Literature* by R. Wayne Clugston. Copyright © 2014 by Bridgepoint Education. Reprinted by permission.

apostrophe A figure of speech in which something abstract or someone who is absent is addressed directly even though response is not possible. Example: "Death, be not proud, though some have called thee / Mighty and dreadful, for thou art not so," *Holy Sonnet X* by John Donne.

assonance A vowel sound repeated in nearby words. Example: the "o" sounds in smoky and broken.

carpe diem A Latin term that literally means "seize the day." In literature, it emphasizes the urgency for action and getting the most out of the present moment, given the brevity of life.

characterization The means a writer uses to reveal character: by outright description of an individual, by what an individual says and does, and by what others say about the individual.

climax The crisis or high point of tension that becomes the story's turning point—the point at which the outcome of the conflict is determined.

conceit A far-fetched comparison in which the similarity is exaggerated. The *Petrarchan conceit* is used in love poetry to make elaborate comparisons; the *metaphysical conceit* is used to make extended intellectual (sometimes witty) comparisons.

conflict The struggle that shapes the plot in a story. Conflict can rise from tension between main characters, from an internal struggle within a character, or from a battle with external forces such as nature, tradition, destiny, or even fate.

connotation The commonly known implications associated with a word.

consonance Occurs when the final consonants in words have a similar sound, but the vowels that come before them are different. Example: *dinner–downer.*

culture Common characteristics of a group or a region. Writers often reflect a particular culture through the setting of a story or the spirit of the characters' lives—providing insight, for example, into southern culture, post–World War I culture, or global culture.

denotation The exact, literal meaning of a word.

dramatic irony When the reader or audience knows more about the action than the character involved.

dynamic Changing, often as a result of conflicts and circumstances encountered.

enjambment Also called a run-on line, the continuation of a thought in a line of poetry into the succeeding line, uninterrupted by punctuation.

epiphany A profound and sudden personal discovery. Literary writers use epiphanies to reveal character and theme.

exposition Setting and essential background information presented at the beginning of a story or play.

falling action A reduction in intensity following the climax in a story or play, allowing the various complications to be worked out.

fate An outside source that determines human events.

first-person point of view Occurs when the narrator is a character in the story and tells the story from his or her perspective.

flashback The description of an event that occurred prior to the action in the story. By using this technique, a writer can give the reader background information relevant to the particular conflict the character is facing, thereby intensifying the dramatic tension in the story.

flat character Usually a static, minor character who is uncomplicated and does not change.

foil A character in a story or play presented in sharp contrast to another character, particularly to the main character.

foreshadowing A technique a writer uses to hint or suggest what the outcome of an important conflict or situation in a narrative will be.

hyperbole A figure of speech that deliberately exaggerates a description about something or somebody to create a desired effect.

internal rhyme Occurs when the rhyming words are not at the end of lines, but within the same line. Example: "For the moon never beams without bringing me dreams."

ironic purpose The development of characters or events to create insights or outcomes that are opposite of what is expected.

irony A contradiction in words or actions. There are three types of irony: verbal, situational, and dramatic.

legends Often traditions as well as stories, legends are rooted in history and have fewer supernatural aspects than myths.

limited omniscient point of view Occurs when a narrator has access to the thoughts and feelings of only one character in a story.

local color Writing that depicts the speech, dress, mannerisms, ways of thinking, and geographic features that are typical of a particular region.

metonymy A figure of speech, a kind of metaphor, formed when a characteristic of a thing is used to represent the whole thing. Example: "The pen [*inspiration/ thought*] is mightier than the sword [*battle*]."

minor character A character that serves mainly to move the plot forward. Example: a messenger.

mood The atmosphere, or emotional tone, created by a writer. The mood of a work may be joyful, eerie, foreboding, etc.

motif A recurring element in a literary work, often used to highlight the theme.

myths Anonymous, primitive stories that seek to explain the world, including the mysteries surrounding divinity, creation, truth, and death.

objective point of view A detached point of view, evident when an external narrator does not enter into the mind of any character in a story but takes an objective stance, often to create a dramatic effect.

omniscient point of view An all-knowing point of view, evident when an external narrator has access to the thoughts and feelings of all the characters in a story.

onomatopoeia A word whose sound suggests its meaning or sense. For example, sizzle or meow.

parable A brief story that illustrates a moral situation or lesson, with details of the story carefully paralleling those of the particular situation surrounding the moral.

paradox An apparent contradiction that actually reveals an underlying truth.

personification A figure of speech in which qualities normally associated with a person are attributed to abstract things or inanimate objects. Example: "Time creeps up on you."

point of view The perspective of the narrator who will present the action to the reader.

protagonist The main character, the most developed figure, upon whom the plot is centered and its outcome depends.

resolution The outcome of the action in a story or play.

rhyme Occurs when two words have the same sound following the last stressed vowel, as in mate–rate or flabby–shabby. Appears most commonly when end words in lines of poetry have the same sound.

rhyme scheme The sequence or pattern of end rhymes in a poem. Sequential letters of the alphabet, beginning with the letter "a," are used to identify the rhyming pattern.

rising action Conflicts and circumstances that build to a high point of tension in a story or play.

round character A dynamic, multidimensional character who has a major role in a story or drama. Like a real person, the round character is complex, most often exhibiting both positive and negative personality traits.

situational irony When the outcome in a situation is the opposite of what is expected.

static Uncomplicated or unchanging.

stock character A character who is readily recognized for exhibiting "role behavior," such as that of the mad scientist, the damsel in distress, the cruel stepmother, or the boy next door.

tale An anecdote about an event that is told in an uncomplicated manner.

third-person point of view Occurs when the narrator tells the story using third-person pronouns (he, she, they) to refer to the characters. Normally, the third-person narrator is external to the story, not a character in it. Third-person can take an omniscient, limited omniscient, or objective point of view.

verbal irony When words are used to convey a meaning that is opposite of their literal meaning.

HOW DO I DO A LITERARY ANALYSIS?

The best method for analyzing literature is to start with your own relationship with and interpretation of the primary text. In other words, read the text without doing any kind of research on it or the author. Engage the text on your own terms without getting bogged down in what everyone else has said. The exciting part of studying literature is that the you, the reader, are bringing to the text your own perspective, and this is what a literary analysis is trying to elicit from you. To read the text on your own terms without outside influence allows you to be clear about what interests you and why. Finding out what others have said—the research—will come later in the writing process. The research is very important, but you have to place it at the right time in your thinking.

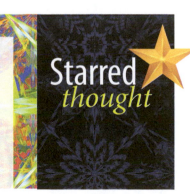

Although this seems obvious, too often students jump into researching the primary text to see what it is about or how others interpret it so that they get the "right" answer. It is true that there are multiple interpretations possible; however, this does not mean "anything goes." On the contrary, what you can say about a text must be grounded in the text itself. This is why close reading, also known as textual analysis, is the key to making your interpretation stand on its own and become a possible interpretation.

Starred *thought*

ANALYZING SHORT STORIES

There are many ways to go about an analysis of a literary text, and what you focus on is what determines what you need to pull from the text as support. For our purposes here, let us take a very close look at the use of *literary elements* called a *characters* and *setting* so that you have practice for how to read and think about a literary text. Using active reading strategies, follow the following three-part reading method so that you engage the text on your own terms without getting bogged down in what everyone else has said. To demonstrate this process and its usefulness, read the short story "There Will Come Soft Rains," by Ray Bradbury, using the following method for reading.

WHAT'S NEXT?

FIRST READ: The first reading should be done to orientate yourself to the content (who, where, when, what). Read the short story "There Will Come Soft Rains" to see what it is about. Use active reading strategies to mark important information related to the following: Who are the characters? Where are they? When does it take place? What has happened? What is happening?

[handwritten: gentle words] *[handwritten: –alliteration from nature]*

THERE WILL COME SOFT RAINS
By: Ray Bradbury

In the living room the voice-clock sang, *Tick-tock, seven o'clock, time to get up, time to get up, seven o 'clock!* as if it were afraid that nobody would. The morning house lay empty. The clock ticked on, repeating and repeating its sounds into the emptiness. *Seven-nine, breakfast time, seven-nine!*

In the kitchen the breakfast stove gave a hissing sigh and ejected from its warm interior eight pieces of perfectly browned toast, eight eggs sunny side up, sixteen slices of bacon, two coffees, and two cool glasses of milk.

"*Today is August 4, 2026*," said a second voice from the kitchen ceiling, "*in the city of Allendale, California.*" It repeated the date three times for memory's sake. "*Today is Mr. Featherstone's birthday. Today is the anniversary of Tilita's marriage. Insurance is payable, as are the water, gas, and light bills.*"

Somewhere in the walls, relays clicked, memory tapes glided under electric eyes.

Eight-one, tick-tock, eight-one o'clock, off to school, off to work, run, run, eight-one! But no doors slammed, no carpets took the soft tread of rubber heels. It was raining outside. The weather box on the front door sang quietly: "*Rain, rain, go away; umbrellas, raincoats for today...*" And the rain tapped on the empty house, echoing.

Outside, the garage chimed and lifted its door to reveal the waiting car. After a long wait the door swung down again.

[handwritten: – similie]

At eight-thirty the eggs were shrivelled and the toast was like stone. An aluminium wedge scraped them into the sink, where hot water whirled them down a metal throat which digested and flushed them away to the distant sea. The dirty dishes were dropped into a hot washer and emerged twinkling dry.

Nine-fifteen, sang the clock, *time to clean.* *[handwritten: rhyme & time notice]*

Out of warrens in the wall, tiny robot mice darted. The rooms were a crawl with the small cleaning animals, all rubber and metal. They thudded against chairs, whirling their moustached runners, kneading the rug nap, sucking gently at hidden dust. Then, like mysterious invaders, they popped into their burrows. Their pink electric eyes faded. The house was clean.

Ten o'clock. The sun came out from behind the rain. The house stood alone in a city of rubble and ashes. This was the one house left standing. At night the ruined city gave off a radioactive glow which could be seen for miles.

Ten-fifteen. The garden sprinklers whirled up in golden founts, filling the soft morning air with scatterings of brightness. The water pelted window panes, running

Reprinted by permission of Don Congdon Associates, Inc. Copyright © 1950 by the Crowell Collier Publishing Company, renewed 1977 by Ray Bradbury.

down the charred west side where the house had been burned, evenly free of its white paint. The entire west face of the house was black, save for five places. Here the silhouette in paint of a man mowing a lawn. Here, as in a photograph, a woman bent to pick flowers. Still farther over, their images burned on wood in one titanic instant, a small boy, hands flung into the air; higher up, the image of a thrown ball, and opposite him a girl, hands raised to catch a ball which never came down.

The five spots of paint - the man, the woman, the children, the ball - remained. The rest was a thin charcoaled layer.

The gentle sprinkler rain filled the garden with falling light.

Until this day, how well the house had kept its peace. How carefully it had inquired, "Who goes there? What's the password?" and, getting no answer from lonely foxes and whining cats, it had shut up its windows and drawn shades in an old-maidenly preoccupation with self-protection which bordered on a mechanical paranoia.

It quivered at each sound, the house did. If a sparrow brushed a window, the shade snapped up. The bird, startled, flew off! No, not even a bird must touch the house!

Twelve noon.

A dog whined, shivering, on the front porch.

The front door recognized the dog voice and opened. The dog, once huge and fleshy, but now gone to bone and covered with sores, moved in and through the house, tracking mud. Behind it whirred angry mice, angry at having to pick up mud, angry at inconvenience.

For not a leaf fragment blew under the door but what the wall panels flipped open and the copper scrap rats flashed swiftly out. The offending dust, hair, or paper, seized in miniature steel jaws, was raced back to the burrows. There, down tubes which fed into the cellar, it was dropped into the sighing vent of an incinerator which sat like evil Baal in a dark corner. — Similie

The dog ran upstairs, hysterically yelping to each door, at last realizing, as the house realized, that only silence was here.

It sniffed the air and scratched the kitchen door. Behind the door, the stove was making pancakes which filled the house with a rich baked odour and the scent of maple syrup.

The dog frothed at the mouth, lying at the door, sniffing, its eyes turned to fire. It ran wildly in circles, biting at its tail, spun in a frenzy, and died. It lay in the parlor for an hour.

Two o'clock, sang a voice.

Delicately sensing decay at last, the regiments of mice hummed out as softly as blown gray leaves in an electrical wind.

Two-fifteen.

The dog was gone.

In the cellar, the incinerator glowed suddenly and a whirl of sparks leaped up the chimney.

Two thirty-five.

Bridge tables sprouted from patio walls. Playing cards fluttered onto pads in a shower of pips. Martinis manifested on an oaken bench with egg-salad sandwiches. Music played. —house working

But the tables were silent and the cards untouched.

At four o'clock the tables folded like great butterflies back through the paneled walls. —similie

Four-thirty.

The nursery walls glowed.

Animals took shape: yellow giraffes, blue lions, pink antelopes, lilac panthers cavorting in crystal substance. The walls were glass. They looked out upon color and fantasy. Hidden films clocked through well-oiled sprockets, and the walls lived. The nursery floor was woven to resemble a crisp, cereal meadow. Over this ran aluminum roaches and iron crickets, and in the hot still air butterflies of delicate red tissue wavered among the sharp aroma of animal spoors! There was the sound like a great matted yellow hive of bees within a dark bellows, the lazy bumble of a purring lion. And there was the patter of okapi feet and the murmur of a fresh jungle rain, like other hoofs, falling upon the summer-starched grass. Now the walls dissolved into distances of parched grass, mile on mile, and warm endless sky. The animals drew away into thorn brakes and water holes. It was the children's hour.

Five o'clock. The bath filled with clear hot water. —house still working

Six, seven, eight o'clock. The dinner dishes manipulated like magic tricks, and in the study a click. In the metal stand opposite the hearth where a fire now blazed up warmly, a cigar popped out, half an inch of soft gray ash on it, smoking, waiting. —similie

Nine o'clock. The beds warmed their hidden circuits, for nights were cool here.

Nine-five. A voice spoke from the study ceiling: "*Mrs. McClellan, which poem would you like this evening?*" The house was silent.

The voice said at last, "*Since you express no preference, I shall select a poem at random.*" Quiet music rose to back the voice. "*Sara Teas dale. As I recall, your favourite . . .*

> *There will come soft rains and the smell of the ground,*
> *And swallows circling with their shimmering sound;*
>
> *And frogs in the pools singing at night,*
> *And wild plum trees in tremulous white;*
>
> *Robins will wear their feathery fire,*
> *Whistling their whims on a low fence-wire;*
>
> *And not one will know of the war, not one*
> *Will care at last when it is done.*
>
> *Not one would mind, neither bird nor tree,*
> *If mankind perished utterly;*
>
> *And Spring her s elf, when she woke at dawn*
> *Would scarcely know that we were gone.*"

[handwritten annotations: "clue?", "- just living life", "- animals wouldn't know if humans existed", "- nature continues"]

The fire burned on the stone hearth and the cigar fell away into a mound of quiet ash on its tray. The empty chairs faced each other between the silent walls, and the music played.

At ten o'clock the house began to die.

The wind blew. A falling tree bough crashed through the kitchen window. Cleaning solvent, bottled, shattered over the stove. The room was ablaze in an instant!

[handwritten: "\ fire"]

"*Fire!*" screamed a voice. The house lights flashed, water pumps shot water from the ceilings. But the solvent spread on the linoleum, licking, eating, under the kitchen door, while the voices took it up in chorus: "*Fire, fire, fire!*"

The house tried to save itself. Doors sprang tightly shut, but the windows were broken by the heat and the wind blew and sucked upon the fire.

The house gave ground as the fire in ten billion angry sparks moved with flaming ease from room to room and then up the stairs. While scurrying water rats squeaked from the walls, pistolled their water, and ran for more. And the wall sprays let down showers of mechanical rain.

But too late. Somewhere, sighing, a pump shrugged to a stop. The quenching rain ceased. The reserve water supply which had filled baths and washed dishes for many quiet days was gone.

The fire crackled up the stairs. It fed upon Picassos and Matisses in the upper halls, like delicacies, baking off the oily flesh, tenderly crisping the canvases into black shavings.

Now the fire lay in beds, stood in windows, changed the colors of drapes!

And then, reinforcements. From attic trapdoors, blind robot faces peered down with faucet mouths gushing green chemical.

— robots were killing the fire

The fire backed off, as even an elephant must at the sight of a dead snake.

Now there were twenty snakes whipping over the floor, killing the fire with a clear cold venom of green froth.

But the fire was clever. It had sent flame outside the house, up through the attic to the pumps there. An explosion! The attic brain which directed the pumps was shattered into bronze shrapnel on the beams.

The fire rushed back into every closet and felt of the clothes hung there.

The house shuddered, oak bone on bone, its bared skeleton cringing from the heat, its wire, its nerves revealed as if a surgeon had torn the skin off to let the red veins and capillaries quiver in the scalded air. *Help, help! Fire! Run, run!* Heat snapped mirrors like the first brittle winter ice. And the voices wailed. *Fire, fire, run, run*, like a tragic nursery rhyme, a dozen voices, high, low, like children dying in a forest, alone, alone. And the voices fading as the wires popped their sheathings like hot chestnuts. One, two, three, four, five voices died.

In the nursery the jungle burned. Blue lions roared, purple giraffes bounded off. The panthers ran in circles, changing color, and ten million animals, running before the fire, vanished off toward a distant steaming river.... Ten more voices died.

In the last instant under the fire avalanche, other choruses, oblivious, could be heard announcing the time, cutting the lawn by remote-control mower, or setting an umbrella frantically out and in, the slamming and opening front door, a thousand things happening, like a clock shop when each clock strikes the hour insanely before or after the other, a scene of maniac confusion, yet unity; singing, screaming, a few last cleaning mice darting bravely out to carry the horrid ashes away! And one voice, with sublime disregard for the situation, read poetry aloud in the fiery study, until all the film spools burned, until all the wires withered and the circuits cracked.

The fire burst the house and let it slam flat down, puffing out skirts of spark and smoke.

In the kitchen, an instant before the rain of fire and timber, the stove could be seen making breakfasts at a psychopathic rate, ten dozen eggs, six loaves of toast, twenty dozen bacon strips, which, eaten by fire, started the stove working again, hysterically hissing!

The crash. The attic smashing into kitchen and parlour. The parlour into cellar, cellar into sub-cellar. Deep freeze, armchair, film tapes, circuits, beds, and all like skeletons thrown in a cluttered mound deep under.

Smoke and silence. A great quantity of smoke.

Dawn showed faintly in the east. Among the ruins, one wall stood alone. Within the wall, a last voice said, over and over again and again, even as the sun rose to shine upon the heaped rubble and steam:

"Today is August 5, 2026, today is August 5, 2026, today is . . ."

WHAT'S NEXT?

SECOND READ: The second reading can be where you notice connections among the content, often requiring some kind of annotating. Choose three differently colored highlighters, and as you *re*read "There Will Come Soft Rains," use these colors to mark the following:

1. Yellow: Places in the text where you come across information that indicates *where* the short story is taking place.

2. Pink: To highlight the text where it provides clues about what *has happened*.

3. Green: To mark clues that indicate *who or what* qualifies as characters.

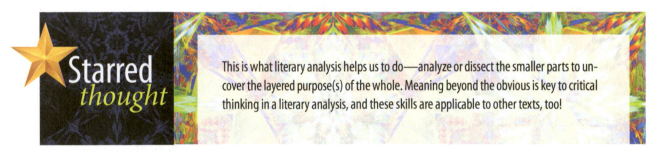

Starred *thought*

This is what literary analysis helps us to do—analyze or dissect the smaller parts to uncover the layered purpose(s) of the whole. Meaning beyond the obvious is key to critical thinking in a literary analysis, and these skills are applicable to other texts, too!

WHAT'S NEXT?

THIRD READ: The third reading is where you begin to see how the content is connected and to speculate about why. Out of this process come ideas for a controlling idea (an interpretation of the short story) and possible ways to support

After you have analyzed the connection(s) between the characters and the setting, step back and look at what seems to emerge from the analysis. Take some time to write out short answers to these following questions.

- What is the pattern that emerges for what has happened, is happening, and will happen?

- What does your analysis seem to suggest about the relationship between characters and setting?

- Why would reading the short story in this way (i.e., paying attention to characters and setting) help to make sense of the story overall? In other words, what does the author seem to be getting at?

After you examine a short story in this way, you might discover a potential overall meaning to the short story. The result can lead you to the basis for formulating a controlling idea about how to interpret literary elements for a literary analysis—a claim you are making about the meaning of the short story. The more complicated your controlling idea, the more literary elements you may have to examine to help you establish that claim as valid. Therefore, you might end up analyzing three or more elements in a short story to show how they work together to "prove" your interpretation.

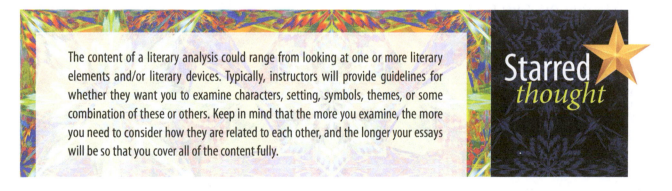

The content of a literary analysis could range from looking at one or more literary elements and/or literary devices. Typically, instructors will provide guidelines for whether they want you to examine characters, setting, symbols, themes, or some combination of these or others. Keep in mind that the more you examine, the more you need to consider how they are related to each other, and the longer your essays will be so that you cover all of the content fully.

Starred *thought*

WHAT'S NEXT?

Now that you have some experience with reading one short story, go to the ancillary website www.grtep.com for the second. It is a short story by Daniel Keyes called "Flowers for Algernon." For your analysis of this story, focus on characters and theme.

FIRST READ: The first reading should be done to orientate yourself to the content (who, where, when, what). Read the short story, "Flowers for Algernon" to see what it is about. Use active reading strategies to mark important information related to the following: Who are the characters? Where are they? What happens? When does it take place? What seems to be the theme?

WHAT'S NEXT?

SECOND READ: As you *reread* "Flowers for Algernon," mark the text when you notice significant changes in how Charlie writes and thinks. Use a dialectical notebook (as in the table below) to keep track of these instances. What do the changes in Charlie's writing and thinking suggest about his character development? When do these changes occur? Who or what is responsible for these changes?

What changes are there in Charlie's character? (Include page numbers)	How do you know? (Examples from the text that show that change)	What is the context for these changes?
friendly (pg 5) charlie was always very excited. to learn & happy (oblivious)	"a nice young man was in a room & he had some white cards w/ ink spilled all over them"	
he always laughed & was curious whet ppl said to him		
he then started to analyize his surroundings & started to become smarter		
no longer enthusiatic his intelligence drew everyone away & realized the fraud he once had for all of them		
he starts to get irritated and starts to forget things (getting depressed) pg (24)	"why can't I remember?" "Then it all comes to me in a flash. Figures of amnesia!" (pg. 24)	The symptoms of the experiment/surgery is now failing & decreasing his brain knowledge

WHAT'S NEXT?

THIRD READ: The third reading is where you begin to see how the individual elements of character development are connected and to speculate about how that connects to the theme. Out of this process come ideas for a controlling idea (an interpretation of the character as it relates to the theme) and possible ways to support it, which functions as prewriting for how we might interpret the character of Charlie. How do the changes connect to the theme of the story? *Reconsider Charlie's changing characterization and what that means for how we might interpret the short story's meaning.*

Characterization (p. #)	Possible Meaning(s)

Questions to ask about the notes you have taken:

1. What patterns emerge?

2. When you compare and contrast different characterizations of Charlie, what do you notice?

3. Who or what might Charlie represent in general?

4. What theme does his characterizations suggest?

5. What possible links between the character and the theme are there to the short story's title?

Take some time to write out short answers to these questions. Take one example from your dialectical notebook and write about the pattern you see. Then, do this again with the next example. Now, link them. Again, as you are doing this kind of prewriting, you are working toward seeing possible foci for your literary analysis that work out how characters and themes are linked, and any one of these can become a working, controlling idea. The more complicated your controlling idea, remember, the more literary elements you may have to examine to help you establish that claim as valid.

Starred *thought*

Keep in mind that you could write several literary analyses on a single primary text, so what you choose to focus on in one analysis is just one of many options. Thus, you need to work out what you want your focus to be for the analysis you are working on presently. Save other ideas for later!

WRITING YOUR OWN LITERARY ANALYSIS ABOUT A SHORT STORY

In your literature courses, you will often have a selection of primary texts that your instructor assigns. Sometimes the literature under study is in an anthology, a book that includes several different writers and their writings, and sometimes you will have several novels written by different writers or a collection of writings by a given author. Either way, instructors will often assign the primary text they want you to analyze or they will provide you a choice.

For our purposes, you will choose a short story for your literary analysis. Your job is to compose a literary analysis that shows your reader a possible interpretation of that short story. You will need to choose the *literary element*, or *elements*, that you will use to examine the interpretation in addition to examining how the *literary devices* help to shape that interpretation. Like other genres you have studied in this textbook , you are looking at the parts to discover the whole. Ask yourself, "How do the literary elements and devices contribute to the interpretation I see in the short story?" You will not be able to cover everything, so you will need to choose deliberately.

After you have chosen the short story you want to work on (or the one that your instructor has assigned), use the same method as we did for the analysis of "There Will Come Soft Rains" and "Flowers for Algernon" In other words, *apply the strategies* for reading to discover what you want to work on. If you wish to work on theme instead of characters, then you will need to modify the exercises to address that focus, but the principle is the same: What are you looking at? Where is it in the text? What does it mean? How do you know?

WHAT'S NEXT

After your prewriting, you will need to develop a draft. Typically, a literary analysis is structured in the following way:

INTRODUCTION: Typically, the writer will provide the author, the title of the short story, and a short summary of the plot. The literary analysis summary is similar to a review summary. The summary provides the "gist" or main idea of the story, something that might be found on the back of the book cover. You are not providing any more than that. You also need to provide your controlling idea: What meaning is there in the short story that you are going to persuade your reader to see?

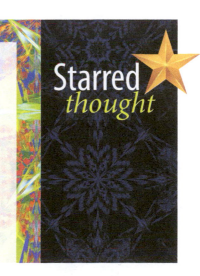

Given the concept of "audience" we have been examining in this textbook, you should now see that you should not assume that your reader has read the story you are analyzing, yet you should not assume that you need to provide a moment-by-moment account of everything that goes on in the story, either! There is a balance that you will strike through practice. Even if your instructor says that you should assume your reader has read the story, you still should not assume that he or she has read it the same way as you have. You are presenting an interpretation based upon how you have read the story and its meaning. Therefore, your goal is to provide just enough basic information (main plot, characters, problem or conflict) to orientate your reader, and then provide a LOT of analysis of the text to show how your interpretation is valid or at least plausible.

Starred *thought*

BODY: There are several paragraphs in the body (well beyond five!) where you take your reader through a systematic analysis of how to read the short story in a particular way to discover the possible meaning of it. While there are no strictly "right" ways to interpret literature, there are more persuasive interpretations, and these are grounded firmly in the primary text. If the text does not say it directly or you cannot explain how it is implied, then your interpretation will fall flat. Therefore, you must be a diligent reader. Close reading and analysis are essential in creating a persuasive interpretation. You will also include secondary sources from published literary critics who have also studied the short story in-depth. Therefore, you will have quoted material from both the primary and the secondary sources, but the emphasis is always on the primary.

CONCLUSION: Typically, the final paragraph or two will round out your interpretation. You bring together all of the analysis you have compiled in the body paragraphs (the parts) into a cohesive final interpretation (the whole). You are not simply restating your controlling idea, but you are bookending your analysis. You are making a final observation about the short story that you want to drive home for your reader.

As for document design and documentation style, literary analyses are typically assigned in English courses, so you should follow strict MLA.

ANALYZING POETRY

Poems can be interpreted just as short stories (or other kinds of literature) can, and the only differences are 1. the way you quote and cite examples and 2. the nuances you need to pay attention to in the text. In other words, poems also have *literary elements*, such as characters, themes, and settings that need to be examined, but poetry analysis will also include looking at *literary devices*, such as figures of speech and diction. (See p. 159–163 for a list of literary elements and devices.)

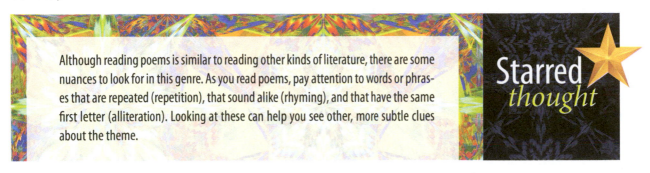

Although reading poems is similar to reading other kinds of literature, there are some nuances to look for in this genre. As you read poems, pay attention to words or phrases that are repeated (repetition), that sound alike (rhyming), and that have the same first letter (alliteration). Looking at these can help you see other, more subtle clues about the theme.

Starred *thought*

WHAT'S NEXT?

Use the same kind of reading and analyzing you used for short stories for reading and analyzing poetry. Apply the three-stage reading strategies for the following poems: Sara Teasdale's "There Will Come Soft Rains" (found within Bradbury's short story) and for John Grey's "To Artificial Living."

FIRST READ: The first reading should be done to orientate yourself to the content (who, where, when, what). Use active reading strategies to mark important information related to: Who are the characters? Where are they? When does it take place? What happens?

"THERE WILL COME SOFT RAINS"

by Sara Teasdale (1918)

Sara Teasdale - 1884-1933
(War Time)

There will come soft rains and the smell of the ground,
And swallows circling with their shimmering sound;

And frogs in the pools singing at night,
And wild plum trees in tremulous white,

Robins will wear their feathery fire
Whistling their whims on a low fence-wire;

And not one will know of the war, not one
Will care at last when it is done.

Not one would mind, neither bird nor tree
If mankind perished utterly;

And Spring herself, when she woke at dawn,
Would scarcely know that we were gone.

"TO ARTIFICIAL LIVING"

by John Grey (2014)

TO ARTIFICIAL LIVING

My body is not the hostile environment
it once was.
It's more than ready to accept
synthetic bone material,
a pig's heart,
some artificial skin.
Once, like an earthling
battling an alien invader,
my left arm
almost ripped my prosthetic right
from its metal cooker.
My glass eye
couldn't believe
what it wasn't seeing.
And my blood,
for the longest time,
flat our would flow anywhere
but down those plastic blood vessels.
But now, there's a truce
in the body ware.
My gold teeth chew side by side
with my real ones.
My computerised leg
jogs happily in harmony

"To Artificial Living" From *Stars Like Sand: Australian Speculative Poetry* by Tim Jones and P.S. Cottier, Eds.
Copyright © 2014 by Interactive Publications Pty Ltd. Reprinted by permission.

with the flesh and bone other.
My knee-cap gets on so well
with its stainless steel
anterior cruciate ligament
it doesn't know how it ever rotated
without it.
Besides, my original bite
are now in the minority,
and have come to the conclusion
that for them it's either adjust
to the newcomers
or join the obsolete.
My microchips
couldn't have said it better.

SECOND READ: As you re-read "There Will Come Soft Rains" and "To Artificial Living," look for possible themes. Mark and label the lines that address the theme (or themes). Use a dialectical notebook to keep track of the lines that suggest the theme(s) that are appearing and explain how they work toward establishing that theme.

"THERE WILL COME SOFT RAINS"

by Sara Teasdale

Lines (include the line number)	What is the theme?	Explanation

"TO ARTIFICIAL LIVING"

by John Grey

Lines (include the line number)	What is the theme?	Explanation

THIRD READ: The third reading is where you begin to see what literary elements and devices are used and how to interpret them. Out of this process come ideas for a controlling idea (an interpretation of the poem and its theme) and possible ways to support it, which function as prewriting. How might we interpret the lines, words, and ideas?

"THERE WILL COME SOFT RAINS"

by Sara Teasdale

Words/Phrases from the poem (include line number)	Possible meaning(s)

"TO ARTIFICIAL LIVING"

by John Grey

Words/Phrases from the poem (include line number)	Possible meaning(s)

Questions to ask about the notes you have taken about each of the poems:

1. What theme or themes are there?

   a. Teasdale's poem:

   b. Grey's poem:

2. How do the lines support your claim that the theme is what you say it is?

   a. Teasdale's poem:

b.   Grey's poem:

3.   What literary devices help to establish the theme or themes?

a.   Teasdale's poem:

b.   Grey's poem:

4.   What is the overall message of the poem?

a.   Teasdale's poem:

b.   Grey's poem:

WHAT'S NEXT?

After you have analyzed the specific literary components in a poem, then you are ready to make connections to how these shape an understanding of what message or overall take-away there is. Step back and look at your prewriting work. Ask:

- What theme(s) emerge(s) in each poem?

- Which lines provide the strongest support for the theme?

- What does your analysis seem to say about what we, as readers, should see as the message in the theme?

Take some time to write out short answers to these questions. Take one example from your dialectical notebook and write about the theme and literary devices you see. Then, do this again with the next example. Continue to do this until you have some paragraphs that you can link together to show your analysis of the parts, which are demonstrating to your reader how the parts can be read to show a theme.

After you examine the development of the theme, you might discover that this leads to some overall meaning to the poem. This examination, then, lends itself to an analysis of the other literary elements and devices in the poem. The result of this kind of analysis is that you will have the basis for formulating a controlling idea for the literary analysis. The more complicated your controlling idea, the more literary elements you may have to examine to help you establish that claim as valid. Therefore, you might end up analyzing three or more elements in a literary analysis to show how they work together to "prove" your interpretation.

WRITING YOUR OWN LITERARY ANALYSIS ABOUT A POEM

Poems are often assigned in literature courses alongside other kinds of literature. Sometimes, there are whole courses devoted to just poetry and the various poetic sub-genres (e.g., sonnets, haikus, emblematic poems). Either way, a literary analysis of a poem is still putting forth an interpretation of the primary source that is based upon the words on the page.

For our purposes, you will choose a poem for your literary analysis. Your job is to compose a literary analysis that shows your reader a possible interpretation of that poem and its theme. You will need to choose the literary element, or elements, that you will use to examine the interpretation in addition to examining how the literary devices help to shape that interpretation. Like other genres you have studied in this textbook, you are looking at the parts to discover the whole. Ask yourself, "How do the literary elements and devices contribute to the interpretation I see in the poem?" You will not be able to cover everything, so you will need to choose deliberately.

After you have chosen the poem you want to work on (or the one that your instructor has assigned), use the same method as we did for the analysis of "There Will Come Rains" or "To Artificial Living." In other words, *apply the strategies* for reading to discover what you want to work on. If you wish to work on imagery instead of theme, then you will need to modify the exercises to address that focus, but the principle is the same: What are you looking at? Where is it in the text? What does it mean? How do you know?

WHAT'S NEXT?

After your prewriting, you will need to develop a draft. Typically, a literary analysis is structured in the following way:

INTRODUCTION: Typically, the writer will provide the author, the title of the poem and often the genre, and a short summary. The literary analysis summary is similar to a review summary. The summary provides the main idea the poet is addressing or the action he or she is describing. Again, think of the summary as something found on the back of a DVD. See if you can reduce the summary to no more than two or three sentences. The writer will also provide the overall interpretation that he or she is seeing the text, which must be debatable. That is, there may be many ways to read the primary text, and you are advocating and arguing for one of them.

BODY: There are several paragraphs in the body (well beyond five!) where you take your reader through a systematic analysis of how to read the poem in a particular way to discover the possible meaning of it. While there are no strictly "right" ways to interpret literature, there are more persuasive interpretations, and these are grounded firmly in the primary text. If the text does not say it directly or you can not explain how it is implied, then your interpretation will fall flat. Therefore, you must be a diligent reader. Close reading and analysis are essential in creating a persuasive interpretation. You will also include secondary sources from published literary critics who have also studied the poem in-depth. Therefore, you will have quoted material from both the primary and the secondary sources, but the emphasis is always on the primary.

CONCLUSION: Typically, the final paragraph or two will round out your interpretation. You bring together all of the analysis you have compiled in the body paragraphs (the parts) into a cohesive final interpretation (the whole). You are not simply restating your controlling idea, but you are bookending your analysis. You are making a final observation about the poem that you want to drive home for your reader.

As for document design and documentation style, literary analysis are typically assigned in English courses, so you should follow strict MLA.

Writer: _____ Reader: _____

PEER-REVIEW FOR LITERARY ANALYSIS (SHORT FICTION) DRAFT 1

1. Locate the writer's controlling idea. Highlight it. To verify it is a debatable interpretation, what would an alternative interpretation be?

2. What literary element(s) is the writer interpreting? What does the writer say is the meaning of that element?

3. What literary devices not already used could be incorporated into the analysis? Why?

4. Annotate the writer's essay. Does each paragraph contribute to the controlling idea? If not, explain what the writer needs to do to revise this.

5. After reading the literary analysis, what one question are you left pondering? Why would the writer need to answer that?

6. Look at where the writer is using the primary and secondary texts. Does the writer QuAC appropriately? If not, suggest how to do so more fully.

7. Suggest two passages from the primary text that could be included in the paper and explain what these will help the writer do in the paper.

Writer: _____ Reader: _____

PEER-REVIEW FOR LITERARY ANALYSIS (POETRY) DRAFT 1

1. Locate the writer's controlling idea. Highlight it. To verify it is a debatable interpretation, what would an alternative interpretation be?

2. What literary element(s) is the writer interpreting? What does the writer say is the meaning of that element?

3. What literary devices not already used could be incorporated into the analysis? Why?

4. Annotate the writer's essay. Does each paragraph contribute to the controlling idea? If not, explain what the writer needs to do to revise this.

5. After reading the literary analysis, what one question are you left pondering? Why would the writer need to answer that?

6. Look at where the writer is using the primary and secondary texts. Does the writer QuAC appropriately? If not, suggest how to do so more fully.

7. Suggest two passages from the primary text that could be included in the paper and explain what these will help the writer do in the paper.

REFLECTIONS: LITERARY ANALYSIS WRITING

WRITING ABOUT A POEM

Describe your writing process for writing about a poem. What strategies did you use?

Compare the strategies you used for writing about poems to writing about short stories. What differences were there?

Which strategies would you like to try next time? Why?

What did you find to be the hardest part about writing about a poem? Why?

What did you find to be the easiest part about writing about a poem? Why?

CHAPTER 9

Visual Analysis and Artwork

In this chapter, you will learn to:

1. identify the features of the visual analysis genre;

2. use active viewing strategies to analyze visuals;

3. define visual elements and devices;

4. locate visual elements and devices;

5. explore how visual elements and devices work together;

6. develop an interpretation of a visual text;

7. use textual evidence to support interpretations;

8. create a visual analysis that employs the features of the genre;

10. practice revision using peer feedback; and

11. reflect on the writing process.

The next genre we are studying is called a *visual analysis*. This is a specialized kind of analysis where writers examine a visual text. Most people will immediately imagine that a visual text is a painting or sculpture, but theater performances, rock concerts, advertisements, posters, and even book covers are considered visual texts, too, because much of what these texts are saying is being said *visually* rather than through words. Consider the following and identify the visual aspects of each:

Rock Concert:

A Parade:

Play:

Birthday Cake:

- What are the differences in *what* we look at in each of the examples above? What terms do we use?

- What are the similarities in what we look at in each of the examples above? What terms do we use?

- What do these differences and similarities suggest about how we examine something that is visual?

Seeing an original painting at a museum or art show will give you the opportunity to see exactly what the artist intended for you to see, which includes an up-close look at the materials used: the paint, the brushstrokes, and the framing; this is quite a different experience from seeing a reproduction online or in a book. Going to a live performance of a play, hearing actors project their voices and hearing the audience react to the stage performance, rather than watching a film version, offers quite a different experience. Seeing a film at the movie theater with surround sound and a massive screen is very different from seeing it on DVD at home. In other words, a visual text, in all of its manifestations (e.g., painting, photograph, film, play, music, sculpture), is really meant to be experienced first-hand, in person, in a particular environment. Unfortunately, we are not always able to see artwork in its original format or venue, so when we analyze a visual text, we have to take into consideration how we are seeing them and adjust the way we analyze to those conditions. Additionally, because of the *variety of visual texts*, writers need to be able to identify the genre of the visual text so that they examine the rhetorical situation of that visual text, which provides the context for what they can say about it.

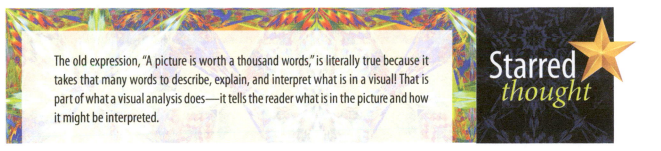

If paintings have brushstrokes that can not be seen in an online reproduction, then a visual analyst must recognize that there is a limitation; however, this does not mean that the painting cannot be analyzed meaningfully. If you have the opportunity to see a visual text in its intended environment, do it! Then, you will include analysis of those aspects that are available, and this added element will make your analysis even more interesting!

Starred *thought*

WHAT IS A VISUAL ANALYSIS?

What is unique about visual texts is that they can communicate beliefs, culture, values, and worldviews through the use of images that viewers *interpret*. Because visual texts are imbedded with many potential interpretations, they are powerful forms of communication. When we look at visuals, we have a reaction: This is beautiful; this makes me sad; this makes me laugh. The question for the visual analyst is: What does the artist intend for the viewer to see beyond what is literally there? How does the artist achieve this? Why does the artist want the viewer to see this? Just as with other forms of analysis, the visual analyst examines the smaller parts to see how they work together to create a larger meaning of the whole.

The old expression, "A picture is worth a thousand words," is literally true because it takes that many words to describe, explain, and interpret what is in a visual! That is part of what a visual analysis does—it tells the reader what is in the picture and how it might be interpreted.

Starred *thought*

Although visual artists have in mind a particular idea of what they want their viewers to see and hope they will feel, the viewer is left to decipher the meaning on his or her own. Therefore, artists rely upon *assumptions* to convey meanings in their art. Consider, for example, colors. When you think of an angel, do you not typically see a fair-haired, winged creature with a human face dressed in white? When you imagine a bouquet of red roses, do you not also think of love? These associations that we make with colors also extend to age, gender, and location.

Youth are viewed as naïve and reckless while elders are considered to be wise and responsible.

Women are mothers and are associated with kindness, compassion, and caretaking.

Cities are considered to be busy and loud; rural areas are considered to be idle and quiet.

Of course, we must be cautious about making assumptions so that we do not fall into stereotyping; however, cultural assumptions often aid interpretation, and artists may use them to guide us toward an interpretation, <u>or</u> they may manipulate these to force us to reconsider these assumptions.

Because there are so many kinds of visual texts, there is flexibility in how you analyze them, yet there are common elements that will allow you to analyze any kind of visual text. You have to *choose which elements are appropriate* for the visual you are analyzing and under the conditions that you are viewing it.

VISUAL COMPONENTS

For our purposes here, we will focus attention on some introductory-level visual elements that will allow you to engage in a visual text whether it is online or in a museum, a digital image or a painting. Out of this engagement will come an opportunity to consider what meanings or interpretations there are and how the artist has conveyed them.

VISUAL ELEMENTS: Like a work of literature, there are some fundamental elements that serve as the starting point for analysis. They include, but are not limited to:

- CHARACTERS: In visual texts, who or what is there contributes to the overall meaning of the work. Therefore, you have to identify people, things, objects, and animals that are part of what you are seeing and speculate about what the relationship is (if there is one) between them. If there are no animate beings, this might give you a clue to what the artist is trying to get you to consider as important in that particular visual text.

- SETTING: Some visual texts capture landscapes, a moment in time, a past or future event, or a famous event, person, or people. The "setting," then, is *where* the visual is taking place, *what* action might be occurring, and *when* the action is occurring, all of which could be part of what the setting is.

- TONE: The sense you get from visual text that elicits an emotional response, whether it is joy, sadness, fear, or celebration, is what helps viewers to interpret the actual meaning of the visual.

VISUAL TECHNIQUES OR DEVICES: These are the methods that an artist uses to show viewers what the meaning might be and gives clues to how to view the characters, the setting, and tone. These are the smaller units that bring the entire text together. When you can isolate the techniques/devices and see how they function, then you can speculate about how all of them are working together to provide an overall meaning that you can interpret.

- **LINE:** The "line" of a work of art can include actual lines, but more important is the way your eyes are guided to look at "x" point before moving on to "y" point. In other words, the line is the way you actually view the artwork. The movement of your eyes from top to bottom, bottom to top, left to right, right to left are part of the line. Artists will use color, size, and shapes to manipulate their viewers to see one part of the visual before the other. Pay attention, then, to how you are pulled in a particular direction, often referred to as *movement* in visual analyses, and see if you can identify how the artist has achieved this.

- **PLACEMENT/SPACE:** Examining where the artist has placed objects and people in the visual art provides insights into what is important. Pay attention to who or what is the foreground (what appears closest to you) and the background (what appears farthest away). Additionally, what is placed at the top of a painting, or at the bottom, sides, or middle, also suggests something important about that image. Consider, too, the use of space and what part of the image is empty, if at all. Where the artists places images will give rise to *balance*. If a visual text seems "busy," consider how that is conveyed. If a visual text seems simple or calm, consider how the use of images and their placement convey this.

- **SIZE AND SHAPE:** Artists will manipulate the size of images to encourage a viewer to see relationships and importance. The larger the size of an image, the closer it will seem, and this may suggest its importance. The smaller the size, the farther away, and this may suggest its unimportance. Also, shapes have meaning. Circles, for example, suggest continuity or lack of beginning or end; triangles suggest hierarchy. When you examine the shape and size together, there is a sense of *scale*.

There are several visual devices that can be used for this kind of writing because they help us to engage in the text in a specific way. One of the most obvious ways to analyze visual texts is through *color*. However, color is a complex device and deserves extra attention. Jeffery Hoover provides information about this component and its complexities, which can aid us in analyzing why artists use colors the way they do.

ART*

- Two- and three-dimensional art—painting, drawing, photography, and sculpture are often emphasized—using things seen and touched

* From *Arts and Society* by Jeffrey Hoover. Copyright © 2016 by Kendall Hunt Publishing Company. Reprinted by permission.

Literally, ranging from the "writing on the wall" to the three-dimensional presence in front of us, the visual arts are considered by some to be the most valuable arts discipline in society because of its relatively permanent and consistent presentation. *We can see what we are talking about, and we can agree upon what we see, even if we don't agree on the interpretation.* The visual arts have long been produced by mankind, and document and interpret life throughout history as well as contemporary ideals. Changes in technology have expanded an artist's ability to realize ideas, including use of digital technology to create what previous generations could produce only with physical materials.

Elements of Art	Principles of Art
Color (as hue, intensity, and value)	Balance
Line	Complexity
Shape-Volume	Simplicity
Space (as an element of sculpture)	Repetition
Texture (as an element—visual, tactile, auditory)	Rhythm
	Gradation
	Contrast
	Space

COLOR THEORY

One important aspect of the visual arts is color. As an element, its intellectual impact can be the same as other elements; however, people focus on color very quickly when seeing an artwork, and therefore color merits extra attention at this point.

The history of color theory is quite lengthy, and aspects of color are tied to both cultural and religious beliefs, as well as visual-aesthetic concerns. Shapes have also been associated with color. Color is also used symbolically in the creation of art, to give us more information or perspective on what is being shown. For example, the color blue is associated with the Heavens, and one sees the interior of some Islamic mosque domes set in blue, like the sky. Another historic association, in Christianity, is the use of the color blue in garments worn by Mary, the mother of Jesus, the Christ. Color can also have different meanings in different cultures. The color yellow is associated with knowledge, and the shape of the triangle is association with this color.

To better understand color, it's useful to consider some fundamentals that are taught in the traditional art school training of Western artists. *The discussion here pertains to the mixing and interaction of pigments. Colors achieved through the mixing of light itself, as in theatrical lighting, works differently.*

Color theory is often presented as a **triadic theory**, where three **primary** colors (red, yellow, and blue) are the foundation. The basic quality of a color is its **hue**— that is, its "redness" or "blueness" in its pure form. In the illustration, they are shown with their "family" connections as a triangle with solid-line sides. When two adjacent pigments are mixed together, it creates a new color, a **secondary** color. These are orange, green, and violet. These are seen in the illustration with a dotted line.

There are many associated characteristics, in addition to hue, that shape how we perceive color. How colors are manipulated determine part of our response to an artwork. Another class of colors are known as **achromatic**. These are neutral colors, such as tan and brown, and at the extreme are white and black. They do not possess the visual energy of the colors derived from triadic color mixing, but can create a harmony between objects or even an accent by creating a visual accent. **Value** is another aspect of color—how black, white, or gray a color is, on a scale of 0 (completely black) to 10 (the brightest white possible), with a balanced neutral gray being 5. **Tint** (light) *and* **shade** (dark) variations of colors are achieved by mixing different levels of these achromatic colors with triadic color hues. **Complimentary colors** are when two colors directly across from each other on the color wheel are shown at the same time, creating a visual interaction, or a vibrancy. Red and green, or yellow and blue, are two common complimentary color combinations. As pigments, they possesses a polarity, to the extent that when two complementary colors are mixed, rather than placed side by side, they neutralize each other and create gray. This is a property that artists are able to exploit to achieve subtle and remarkable effects. A **split compliment** is created when one of the two colors is one position adjacent to the true compliment, for example, red and yellow-green. The vibrancy is still present, but the adjustment in this relationship begins to push the relationship in a new direction. While complimentary colors create a vibrancy, split compliments create a softer sense of "glow" or **luminosity**. The **warm colors** are those associated with physical warmth, such as red, orange, and yellow, as seen on the right side of the illustration. **Cool colors**, such as blue, green, and violet, are seen on the left side of the illustration. Acommon perception is that warm colors are near to us or approach us, whereas cool colors are farther away or recede from us. This can help create a sense of perspective or distance.

As one can see, there are a multitude of aspects that impact color (otherwise known as hue). Artists are able to adjust all of these aspects to create a blend, or harmony, between colored objects; or contrast, to make the objects stand out.

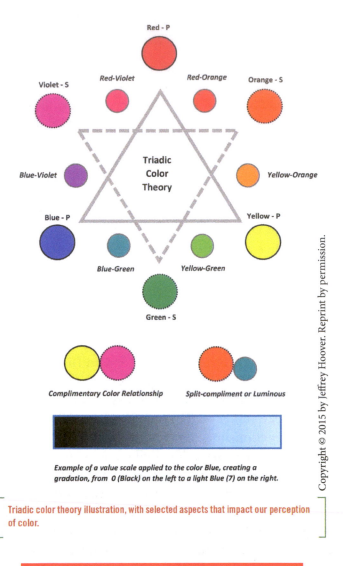

Copyright © 2015 by Jeffrey Hoover. Reprint by permission.

Triadic color theory illustration, with selected aspects that impact our perception of color.

Starred *thought*

Notice that you already know several rhetorical devices and literary devices, and you are now expanding your repertoire to include visual devices. In other words, you are building upon what you already know with new information that sounds familiar but is being used in a new way. You are engaging in another turn of the kaleidoscope!

HOW DO I DO A VISUAL ANALYSIS?

Approach a visual text as you would a work of literature by viewing it several times with a different purpose each time. Once you get comfortable with the process for viewing visuals, you will then become more comfortable with how to write about them. To start, there are some basic questions to ask that can be modified later to meet the specific needs of the visual text you are analyzing. If you don't have an answer for them, then consider if that is part of what the artist is trying to convey. If not, then move on, but if so, then dig a bit deeper into why.

CHARACTERS: Who or what is depicted? Are they alone or with others? How many are there? What is the gender, age, race/ethnicity, cultural background? Are there people, animals, objects, a combination? Are there more of some than others? Are they animate or inanimate, alive or dead?

SETTING: Can you tell where they are? If not, what might that suggest? If so, what might that suggest? Are they in a place/location that is easily identifiable? Why might this be the case? What is happening? Why might it be happening? Does the image capture a moment in time or an ongoing activity? A future, present, or past event? Is it a famous place or a common one?

TONE: How does the visual text make you feel? Why do you feel that way? What other possible emotions are there? Does one outweigh the other? How so? Do the characters, location, or a combination of the two suggest a feeling? How so?

WHAT'S NEXT?

Let us examine two different images, practicing how to read a visual and applying the tools for analyzing visual texts.

FIRST VIEWING: The first time you take a look at a visual, your goal should be to orientate yourself to the content (who, where, when, what). View the image here

Gordana Sermek / Shutterstock.com

Image 1: Cyberwoman Removing Make-up

to see, literally, what it is about. Use the modified and specific questions that follow the visual text to guide you in an initial engagement with what could be called a digital work of art.

Who/What is depicted?

Where is she?

What is she doing?

What is your initial reaction? Why?

WHAT'S NEXT?

SECOND VIEWING: The second viewing is when you begin to identify the visual elements at work in a more directed way. Consider the following questions as a way to engage in a preliminary analysis of the image. Try using a dialectical notebook, like the one here, for each of the *visual elements*.

Characters If it is possible to do so, identify:	What assumptions might be embedded? Why?
Gender	
Age	
Race/Ethnicity	
Culture	
Eye and Hair Color	

Setting If it is possible to do so, identify:	What assumptions might be embedded? Why?
Where she is	
What she is doing	
Why she is doing it	
Who is seeing her doing it	

Tone	What assumptions might be embedded? Why?
How does she make you feel?	
What emotions does she show?	
Is there a conflict between the two?	

WHAT'S NEXT?

THIRD VIEWING: The third viewing is when you begin to identify the visual devices at work and how they work in concert with the visual elements to suggest an interpretation. Try using a dialectical notebook, like the one here, for each of the *visual devices*.

LINE AND MOVEMENT

Describe the line of the image. Is it straight? Curved? Angular? Rounded? Combination? Something else?

Where do your eyes go first? Second? Third? Why?

How does the line affect the movement?

How does line and movement help shape your viewing of the image? What visual elements are most affected? Why?

PLACEMENT/SPACE AND BALANCE

Describe the placement and pace of the image. What is where?

What is emphasized?

How does placement suggest that emphasis?

How balanced would you say is the image? What does this suggest about the meaning?

SIZE/SHAPE AND SCALE

What shapes are there? Circles? Squares? Triangles? Abstract shapes?

How does shape suggest importance?

How does shape create scale in this image?

COLOR

What colors are being used? Primary? Black and white? Pastels?

What meanings and symbolism are there?

What associations or special significance comes to mind?

How does color help you to interpret the possible meaning?

WHAT'S NEXT?

CONNECTING ELEMENTS, DEVICES, AND POTENTIAL MEANING

Fastwrite: For 3 minutes, write what you think the image is saying. To put it another way, what do you think the visual text is about, and what is the artist saying about it? Identify one element and one device that supports this idea.

WHAT'S NEXT?

Let's continue to practice analyzing a visual by examining another image, using the same method.

FIRST VIEWING: The first time you look at a visual, your goal should be to orientate yourself to the content (who, where, when, what). View the next image to see, literally, what it is about. Use the modified and specific questions that follow the visual text to guide you in an initial engagement with what could be called a digital work of art.

Who/What is depicted?

Where are they?

What are they doing?

What is your initial reaction? Why?

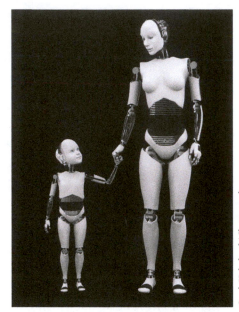

Image 2: Cyberwoman and Cyberchild Holding Hands

Sarah Holmlund / Shutterstock.com

WHAT'S NEXT?

SECOND VIEWING: Consider the following questions as a way to engage in a preliminary analysis of the image. Try using a dialectical notebook, like the one here, for each of the *visual elements*.

Characters If it is possible to do so, identify:	What assumptions might be embedded? Why?
Gender	
Age	
Race/Ethnicity	
Culture	
Eye and Hair Color	

Setting If it is possible to do so, identify:	What assumptions might be embedded? Why?
Where they are	
What they are doing	
Why they are doing it	
Who is seeing them doing it	

Tone	What assumptions might be embedded? Why?
How do they make you feel?	
What emotions do they show?	
Is there a conflict between how you feel and the emotions depicted?	

WHAT'S NEXT?

THIRD VIEWING: The third viewing is when you begin to identify the visual devices at work and how they work in concert with the visual elements to suggest an interpretation. Try using a dialectical notebook, like the one here, for each of the *visual devices*.

LINE AND MOVEMENT

Describe the line of the image. Is it straight? Curved? Angular? Rounded? Combination? Something else?

Where do your eyes go first? Second? Third? Why?

How does the line affect the movement?

How does line and movement help shape your viewing of the image? What visual elements are most affected? Why?

PLACEMENT/SPACE AND BALANCE

Describe the placement and pace of the image. What is where?

What is emphasized?

How does placement suggest that emphasis?

How balanced would you say is the image? What does this suggest about the meaning?

SIZE/SHAPE AND SCALE

What shapes are there? Circles? Squares? Triangles? Abstract shapes?

How does shape suggest importance?

How does shape create scale in this image?

COLOR

What colors are being used? Primary? Black and white? Pastels?

What meanings and symbolism are there?

What associations or special significance comes to mind?

How does color help you to interpret the possible meaning?

WHAT'S NEXT?

CONNECTING ELEMENTS, DEVICES, AND POTENTIAL MEANING

FASTWRITE: For 3 minutes, write what you think the image is saying. Identify one element and one device that supports this idea.

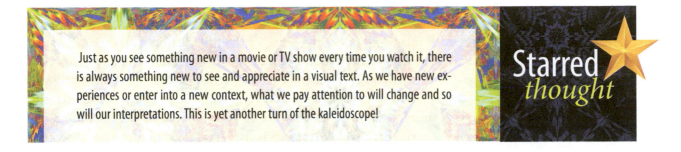

Just as you see something new in a movie or TV show every time you watch it, there is always something new to see and appreciate in a visual text. As we have new experiences or enter into a new context, what we pay attention to will change and so will our interpretations. This is yet another turn of the kaleidoscope!

Starred *thought*

FEATURES OF THE VISUAL ANALYSIS

There are several important expectations or features of a visual analysis. They are what make this genre unique.

VISUAL TEXT: A visual analyst must keep in mind that in writing, the reader is not present nor should be expected to have access to the visual text. This means, then, that the writer must describe in detail what the image is before any kind of analysis is attempted. It is helpful to a reader to have a copy of the image, so writers will not only provide the name of the artist (if known) and the title of the work (if there is one), but they will also provide either a link to an online site where the image can be seen, or they can provide an "Appendix," a section of a paper that comes *after* the bibliography that provides a copy of the image. In the introduction of a visual analysis, the writer will describe the image, provide context, and direct the reader to that appendix in a parenthetical citation (see Appendix A) immediately following the identification of the image. Visual texts should also appear as an entry in the bibliography, for they are the primary sources you are using for your analysis.

INTERPRETATION: Artists are deliberate in what they choose to show their audience, and they leave clues to how to interpret the work. Your job, as the visual analyst, is to decipher what the intended meaning might be and explain to the reader how that is possible. In other words, art can have many meanings, but they are all grounded in the text under analysis and in the context that surrounds it. Your interpretation, then, is the explanation of what that work of art could be saying and how it is saying it, and this becomes your controlling idea.

EVIDENCE: Visual analysts describe what the work of art contains as a means of guiding the reader through an analysis of what the possible interpretation might be. Honing in on the visual elements and visual devices allows the visual analyst to identify concrete aspects of a visual which function as evidence. Additionally, visual analysts are careful to identify and explain what cultural assumptions are imbedded in those elements that help to make a case for how to interpret the work of art. Thus, the writer uses the tools available and the logical connection between them to show what that visual might be saying. Like other kinds of analyses, the smaller parts work together to make a larger statement about the whole.

Secondary Sources: You do not have to be an expert in art or know a lot about the history of art in order to appreciate it and conduct an analysis of it. Conducting research on a work of art, the artist, or the time period it was created surely offers an even richer understanding of what the work of art might mean. However, the goal of this chapter is to get you to use what you already know about how to "read a text" and apply this to a visual text. The first stage in visual analysis is to ground an interpretation of the artwork in your analysis of the image and not on what "experts" have said. If research is used, you must not let what others say overshadow your own view. Additionally, any insights or context you glean from research must be properly cited.

Third-person Point of View: Although art tends to be viewed as having an effect on the viewer that is personal and individual, formal writing about art requires objectivity. This is achieved, in part, through the use of third person. Instead of writing about the personal reaction you have to a work of art, you examine what the artist's work might mean and how the artist conveys this meaning. The reader will be left with a possible interpretation that he or she might agree is present or modify her or his own understanding through yours. In other words, you are attempting to persuade your reader to see the possible meaning that exists, and this contributes to a richer experience with artwork and how a variety of perspectives sheds light on the multiple meanings possible.

WRITING YOUR OWN VISUAL ANALYSIS

Choose a visual text for your visual analysis that is not a famous work of art. Avoid famous works of art as you may be tempted to rely on what experts have said rather than being confident in using the tools you have learned about here to do your own analysis. You might consider:

One of the images in this chapter
The cover of your favorite book or graphic novel
A work of art at an art show or local museum
A movie poster
A calendar
A post card
DVD cover

Your goal is to analyze the visual text and, using a critical lens, analyze how that work conveys meaning(s), and this will become your controlling idea for the analysis. Keep in mind that this will emerge after you do the analysis, and the essential goal is to *argue for an interpretation of the text based upon your analysis of the parts*. This kind of writing is not asking you to take a stand for or against an issue that may be presented; it is asking you to interpret what the artist seems to be conveying and how the artist does this.

Here are some considerations for structuring your visual analysis.

INTRODUCTION: Typically, visual analysts will introduce the visual by providing the name of the artist, if known, and the title of the work, if known. In some cases, like the images in this chapter, the visual text may be untitled or lack an author; in such cases, you will need to provide some kind of description for what the image is depicting. This is simply a way to orientate your reader to the what of your essay. You also might try being creative by introducing a possible story that the image tells, which will bring your reader into your essay who will be curious about it. Try different introductions:

1. Suggest a story that the image is telling.

2. Provide a more academic introduction where you give the name and title of the image along with your controlling idea upfront.

3. Describe the way the image makes a viewer feel that is exactly opposite of what it does.

4. Provide a possible context for the image and its meaning.

BODY PARAGRAPHS: The body paragraphs take the reader through an analysis of the image where the visual elements are described and interpreted. The writer must ensure that the analysis of the parts is linking to the whole. In other words, each paragraph needs to show how the parts as individuals are working together to account for the overall meaning that you are seeing in the image. Also, using visual devices is key in this analysis since the devices are what will help you to make your case for the interpretation.

CONCLUSION: Depending upon how you started your essay, your conclusion will need to bookend appropriately. You might suggest what importance the image has for some larger issue or what the image might help viewers to reconsider. After all, art is more than just something to look at; it is intended to make people feel something or to consider something. Identifying that will remind the reader about the importance of art.

Writer: _____ Reader: _____

PEER-REVIEW OF VISUAL ANALYSIS DRAFT 1

1. Rate the strength of this paper's controlling idea (i.e., interpretation of the artwork).

5	4	3	2	1
Wow! Very insightful				*Boo! Lacks a controlling idea.*

2. At which point did you feel most interested in my visual analysis? Why?

3. At which point did you feel least interested? Explain.

4. Rate this paper's overall depth of analysis.

5	4	3	2	1
20,000 leagues deep!				Shallow, surface.

5. To what extent does this paper rely on evidence or on opinion/intuition? If the latter, cite examples where I slip into personal opinion and intuition and give suggestions as to how I can write more objectively.

6. I have attempted to argue for an interpretation of this artwork. How convinced are you?

7. Is the argument reasonable? Do I provide enough links between the parts of the argument (paragraphs) and the overall, controlling idea ("thesis")? Why or why not?

8. How clearly do I express my ideas?

5	4	3	2	1
Crystal Clear.				Muddy.

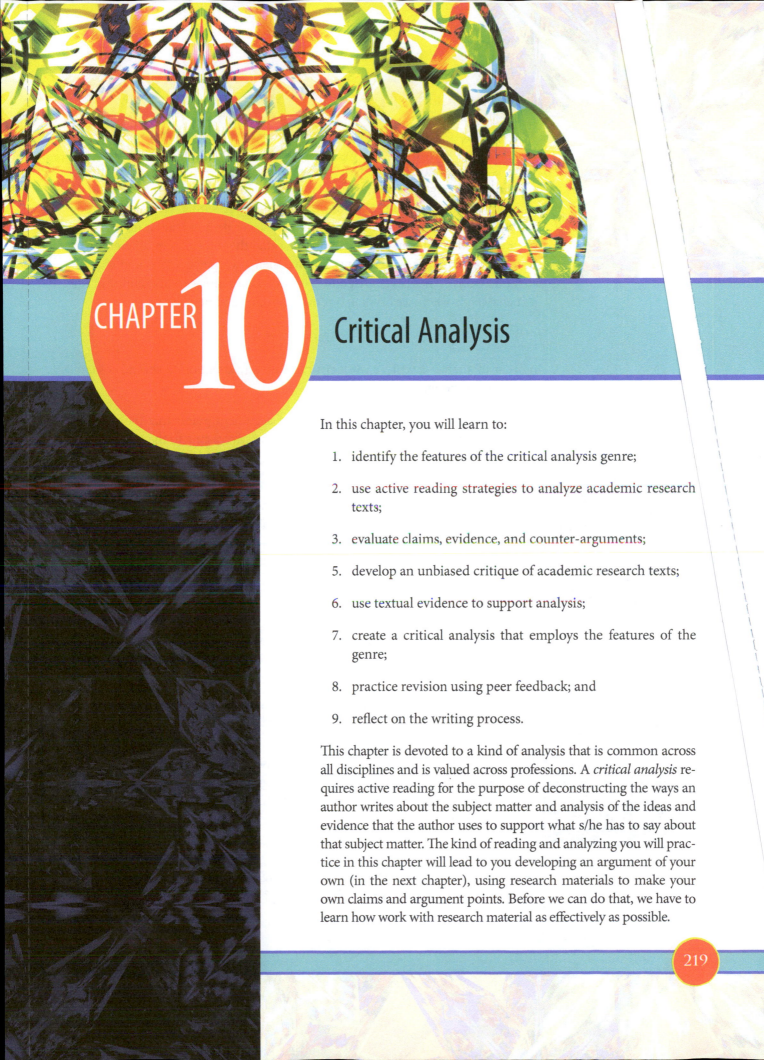

CHAPTER 10

Critical Analysis

In this chapter, you will learn to:

1. identify the features of the critical analysis genre;

2. use active reading strategies to analyze academic research texts;

3. evaluate claims, evidence, and counter-arguments;

5. develop an unbiased critique of academic research texts;

6. use textual evidence to support analysis;

7. create a critical analysis that employs the features of the genre;

8. practice revision using peer feedback; and

9. reflect on the writing process.

This chapter is devoted to a kind of analysis that is common across all disciplines and is valued across professions. A *critical analysis* requires active reading for the purpose of deconstructing the ways an author writes about the subject matter and analysis of the ideas and evidence that the author uses to support what s/he has to say about that subject matter. The kind of reading and analyzing you will practice in this chapter will lead to you developing an argument of your own (in the next chapter), using research materials to make your own claims and argument points. Before we can do that, we have to learn how work with research material as effectively as possible.

WHAT IS A CRITICAL ANALYSIS?

The point of a critical analysis is to *critique* a text based on what it says and not necessarily on whether or not we agree with it. We might agree with what the writer is saying, but what the writer is saying may not be true. In fact, both we and the writer might be basing our claims on incomplete, incorrect, or outdated information. On the other hand, we might disagree with a writer and his/her claims, but the information may be absolutely accurate and true. It may be that we interpret that information differently or value the information differently. In short, critical analysis writers must remove their own perspectives and analyze what is in front of them as is. (Argument-synthesis, a genre we will examine in the next chapter, is where we bring in our own thinking and perspective.)

COMPONENTS OF A CRITICAL ANALYSIS

In order to analyze a writer's work critically, we pay attention to several components of the writing:

- The claims: What are the main ideas or argument points that the writer is using? How are they connected to each other, according to the writer?

We must first be able to identify accurately what the main ideas are before we can scrutinize them. If we misidentify the main ideas, then we may be misreading the text, which undermines our own analysis. Once we identify the issues, ideas, and claims, then we can try to see from the author's point of view how they are connected and why.

- Evidence: What evidence does the write use to support his/her thinking about the claims? Are they valid? Current? Reliable? Authentic? Appropriate to the topic/subject matter?

Recall your study of the rhetorical analysis and the use of *logos*. In a critical analysis, we must be able to identify accurately the writer's logic, use of common sense, statistics, facts, and/or cultural values. Then, we can analyze them and check for accuracy, validity, and usability.

- Counter-arguments: Does the writer address the weaknesses within his/her own argument and respond appropriately? If not, why not?

Starred *thought*

As we analyze the writer's thinking, we might discover that the writer has not adequately explained away the ideas that undermine his/her own argument or has not addressed the ways in which the argument is flawed. We can attempt to figure out how strong or weak these counterarguments are or why the writer ignores them, if s/he does.

Starred *thought*

You are in some ways making an interpretation of the text and the approach the author is taking, so you might be drawn to those elements in the text that support your own beliefs; however, *critical analysis* requires that you put personal biases aside, that you step back from personal reactions, and focus, instead, on the author's perspective and why that perspective, from his/her point of view, is valid or not. This kind of writing is not asking you to take a stand for or against the issue at hand; it is asking you to concern yourself solely with how the author is presenting and interpreting the issue or subject matter.

WHAT'S NEXT?

In Chapters 8 and 9, we examined literary texts and visual images that were linked by a common theme: The relationship between humans and technology. Now, we will examine how non-fiction texts, written by experts in the field of biotechnology and bioethics, and tackle these issues from an academic, rather than creative, point of view. We will examine the ways in which the authors make their arguments and why they do.

FIRST READ: Read the following non-fiction article by Leon R. Kass called "Biotechnology and Our Human Future: Some General Reflections." As you read the following article, pay attention to the following elements in the writing, marking them as you read:

The three aspects of the rhetorical triangle

Starred *thought*

Remember that the rhetorical triangle not only helps us to write our own texts but also helps us to read others' works. Considering who an author is, what s/he is writing about (and how), and who s/he sees as the potential reader helps to shape how we read the work and interpret it for our purposes.

The topic or issues the author is addressing

Writers may initially approach a topic or issue from a very broad stance, but they will then hone in on specifics. Notice that Kass provides "some general reflections"; however, he is very specific about what those are and the impact of technology on humanity.

The main argument point or controlling idea about that topic or issue

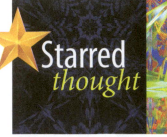

Writers do not just write to inform or to entertain. Writers attempt to persuade their readers to consider the importance or implications of the subject matter. More specifically, writers develop a thesis, an argument, a controlling idea, and persuade the reader to consider its validity and importance.

The kinds of research (e.g., examples, texts, cultural references) used as support

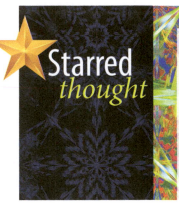

Research helps writers in two significant ways. The first is to provide a context for what has already been said, providing an abundance of information that can be used *as support,* and the second is to reveal to a writer what has not been addressed so that the writer can hone in on that specific element, allowing the writer to contribute to the conversation already in progress. Questions that come up for you after reading a text may be the catalyst for your own research project and may help you develop a possible controlling idea.

BIOTECHNOLOGY AND OUR HUMAN FUTURE

Some General Reflections

Leon R. Kass

As nearly everyone appreciates, we live near the beginning of the golden age of biomedical science and technology. For the most part, we should be mightily glad that we do. We and our friends and loved ones are many times over the beneficiaries of its cures for diseases, prolongation of life, and amelioration of suffering, psychic and somatic. We should be deeply grateful for the gifts of human ingenuity and for the devoted efforts of scientists, physicians, and entrepreneurs who have used these gifts to make those benefits possible. And, mindful that modern biology is just entering puberty, we suspect that "ya' ain't seen nothin' yet."

Yet, notwithstanding these blessings, present and projected, we have also seen more than enough to make us concerned. For we recognize that the powers made possible by biomedical science can be used for nontherapeutic purposes, serving ends that range from the frivolous and disquieting to the offensive and pernicious. Biotechnologies are available as instruments of bioterrorism (for example, genetically engineered drug-resistant bacteria, or drugs that obliterate memory); as agents of social control (for example, drugs to tame rowdies and dissenters or fertility-blockers for welfare recipients); and as means of trying to improve or perfect our bodies and minds or those of our children (for example, genetically engineered "super-muscles," or drugs to improve memory or academic performance). Anticipating possible threats to our security, freedom, and even our very humanity, many people are increasingly worried about where biotechnology may be taking us. We are concerned not only about what others might do to us, but also about what we might do to ourselves. We are concerned that our society might be harmed and that we ourselves might be diminished, indeed, in ways that could undermine the highest and richest possibilities of human life.

In this essay I will consider only the last and most seductive of these disquieting prospects—the use of biotechnical powers to improve upon human nature or to pursue "perfection," both of body and of mind. I select this subject for several reasons. First, although it is the most neglected topic in public bioethics, it is I believe the deepest source of public anxiety about biotechnology and the human future, represented in concerns expressed about "man playing God" or about the arrival of the Brave New World or a "post-human future." Second, it raises the weightiest questions—questions about the ends and goals of the biomedical enterprise, the nature and meaning of human flourishing, and the intrinsic threat of dehumanization (or the promise of super-humanization). It therefore, third, compels attention to what it means to *be* a human being and to be active *as* a human being. Finally, it gets us beyond our narrow preoccupation with the "life issues" of abortion or embryo destruction, important though they are, to deal with what is genuinely novel in the biotechnical revolution: not the old, crude power to kill the creature made in God's image, but science-based sophisticated powers to remake him after our own fantasies.

What exactly are the powers that I am talking about? What sorts of ends are they likely to serve? How soon are they available? They are powers that affect the capacities and activities of the human body, powers that affect the capacities and activities of the mind or soul, and powers that affect the shape of the human life cycle, at both ends and in between. We already have powers to prevent fertility and to promote it; to initiate life in the laboratory; to screen our genes, both as adults and as embryos, and to select (or reject) nascent life based on genetic criteria; to insert new genes into various parts of the adult body and someday soon also into gametes and embryos; to enhance muscle performance and endurance; to replace body parts with natural or mechanical organs, and perhaps soon, to wire ourselves using computer chips implanted into the body and brain; to alter memory, mood, desire, temperament, and attention though psychoactive drugs; and to prolong not just the average but also the maximum human life expectancy. The technologies for altering our native capacities and activities are mainly those of genetic screening and genetic engineering; drugs, especially psychoactive ones; and the ability to replace body parts or to insert novel ones. The availability of some of these capacities, using these techniques, has been demonstrated only with animals; but others are already in use in humans.

It bears emphasis that these powers have not been developed for the purpose of producing perfect or post-human beings. To the contrary, they have been produced largely for the purpose of preventing and curing disease and of reversing disabilities. Even the bizarre prospects of machine-brain interaction and implanted nanotechnological devices start with therapeutic efforts to enable the blind to see and the deaf to hear. Yet the "dual use" aspects of most of these powers, encouraged by the ineradicable human urge toward "improvement" and the commercial interests that see market opportunities for such nontherapeutic uses, means that we must not be lulled to sleep by the fact that the originators of these powers were no friends to the Brave New World. Once here, techniques and powers can produce desires where none existed before, and things often go where no one ever intended—not least because each technological success in combating disease and disability seems only to increase popular demand for evermore-effective means of overcoming any and all remaining obstacles to satisfying our desires and working our wills.

How to organize our reflections? One should resist the temptation to begin with the new techniques or even with the capacities for intervention that they make possible. To do so runs the risk of losing the human import and significance of the undertakings. Better to begin with the human desires and goals that these powers and techniques are destined to serve, among them, the desires for better children, superior performance, ageless bodies, happy souls, and a more peaceful and cooperative society.[1] In this essay, I will concentrate mainly on the strictly personal goals of self-improvement and self-enhancement, and especially on those efforts to preserve and augment the vitality of the body and to increase the happiness of the soul. These goals are, arguably, the least controversial, the most continuous with the aims of modern medicine and psychiatry (better health, peace of mind), and the most attractive to most potential consumers—probably indeed to most of us. Indeed, these were the very goals, now at last in the realm of possibility, that animated the great founders of modern science, Francis Bacon and René Descartes: flawlessly healthy bodies, unconflicted and contented souls, and freedom from the infirmities of age, perhaps indefinitely.

Although our discussion here will not be driven by the biotechnologies themselves, it may be useful to keep in mind some of the technological approaches and innovations that, in varying degrees, can serve these purposes. For example, in pursuit of "ageless bodies," (1) we can replace worn-out parts, by means of organ transplantation or, in the future, by regenerative medicine where decayed tissues are replaced with new ones produced from stem cells; (2) we can improve upon normal and healthy parts, for example, via precise genetic modification of muscles, through injections of growth factor genes that keep the transformed muscles whole, vigorous, and free of age-related decline;[2] and (3) most radically, we can try to retard or stop the entire process of biological senescence. Especially noteworthy for this last possibility are recent discoveries in the genetics of aging that have shown how the *maximum* species lifespan of worms and flies can be increased two- and threefold by alterations in a *single* gene, a gene now known to be present also in mammals, including humans.

In pursuit of "happy souls," we can eliminate psychic distress, we can produce states of transient euphoria, and we can engineer more permanent conditions of good cheer, optimism, self-esteem, and contentment. Accordingly, please keep in mind the existence of drugs now available that, administered promptly at the time of memory formation, blunt markedly the painful emotional content of the newly formed memories of traumatic events (so-called memory blunting or erasure, a remedy being sought to prevent posttraumatic stress disorder). Keep in mind, second, the existence of euphoriants, like Ecstasy, the forerunner of Huxley's "soma," widely used on college campuses; and, finally, powerful yet seemingly safe antidepressants and mood brighteners like Prozac, wonderful for the treatment of major depression yet also capable in some people of utterly changing their outlook on life from that of Eeyore to that of Mary Poppins.

PROBLEMS OF DESCRIPTION: THE DISTINCTION BETWEEN THERAPY AND ENHANCEMENT

People who have tried to address our topic have usually approached it through a distinction between "therapy" and "enhancement": "therapy," the treatment of individuals with known diseases or disabilities; "enhancement," the directed uses of biotechnical power to alter, by direct intervention, not diseased processes but the "normal" workings of the human body and psyche. Those who introduced this distinction hoped by this means to distinguish between the acceptable and the dubious or unacceptable uses of biomedical technology: therapy is always ethically fine, enhancement is, at least *prima facie*, ethically suspect. Gene therapy for cystic fibrosis or Prozac for psychotic depression is fine; insertion of genes to enhance intelligence or steroids for Olympic athletes is not.[3]

This distinction is useful as a point of departure: restoring to normal does differ from going beyond the normal. But it proves finally inadequate to the moral analysis. Enhancement is, even as a term, highly problematic. Does it mean "more" or "better," and, if "better," by what standards? Can both improved memory and selective erasure of memory both be "enhancements"? If "enhancement" is defined in opposition to "therapy," one faces further difficulties with the definitions of "healthy" and "impaired," "normal" and "abnormal" (and hence, "super-normal"), especially in the area of "behavioral" or "psychic" functions and activities. Some psychiatric diagnoses are notoriously vague, and their boundaries indistinct: how does "social anxiety disorder" differ from shyness, "hyperactivity disorder" from spiritedness, "oppositional disorder" from the love of independence? Furthermore, in the many human qualities (for example, height or IQ) that distribute themselves "normally," does the average also function as a norm, or is the norm itself appropriately subject to alteration? Is it therapy to give growth hormone to a genetic dwarf but not to an equally short fellow who is just unhappy to be short? And if the short are brought up to the average, the average, now having become short, will have precedent for a claim to growth hormone injections. Needless arguments about whether or not something is or is not an "enhancement" get in the way of the proper questions: What are the good and bad uses of biotechnical power? What makes a use "good," or even (merely) "acceptable"? It does not follow from the fact that a drug is being taken solely to satisfy one's desires— for example, to sleep less or to concentrate more—that its use is objectionable. Conversely, certain interventions to restore natural functioning wholeness—for example, to enable postmenopausal women to bear children or sixty-year-old men to keep playing professional ice hockey—might well be dubious uses of biotechnical power.

This last observation points to the deepest reason why the distinction between healing and enhancing is finally insufficient, both in theory and in practice. For the human whole whose healing is sought or accomplished by biomedical therapy is finite and frail, medicine or no medicine. The healthy body declines and its parts wear out. The sound mind slows down and has trouble remembering things. The soul has aspirations beyond what even a healthy body can realize, and it becomes weary from frustration. Even at its fittest, the fatigable and limited human body rarely carries out flawlessly even the ordinary desires of the soul. Moreover, there is wide variation in the natural gifts with which each of us is endowed: some are born with perfect pitch, others are born tone-deaf; some have flypaper memories, others forget immediately what they have just learned. And as with talents, so too with the desires and temperaments: some crave immortal fame, others merely comfortable preservation. Some are sanguine, others phlegmatic, still others bilious or melancholic. When nature deals her cards, some receive only from the bottom of the deck.[4]

As a result of these infirmities, human beings have long dreamed of overcoming limitations of body and soul, in particular the limitations of bodily decay, psychic distress, and the frustration of human aspiration. Until now these dreams have been pure fantasies, and those who pursued them came crashing down in disaster. But the stupendous successes over the past century in all areas of technology, and especially in medicine, have revived the ancient dreams of human perfection. We major beneficiaries of modern medicine are less content than we are worried, less grateful for the gifts of longer life and better health and more anxious about losing what we have. Accordingly, we regard our remaining limitations with less equanimity, even to the point that dreams of getting rid of them can be turned into moral imperatives. For these reasons, thanks to biomedical technology, people will be increasingly tempted to pursue these dreams, at least to some extent: ageless and ever-vigorous bodies, happy (or at least not unhappy) souls, and excellent human achievement (with diminished effort or toil).

Why should anyone be bothered by these prospects? What could be wrong with efforts to improve upon human nature, to try, with the help of biomedical technology, to gain ageless bodies and happy souls? I begin with some familiar sources of concern.

FAMILIAR SOURCES OF CONCERN

Not surprisingly, the objections usually raised to the "beyond therapy" uses of biomedical technologies reflect the dominant values of modern America: health, equality, and liberty.

1. *Health: issues of safety and bodily harm.* In our health-obsessed culture, the first reason given to worry about any new biological intervention is safety, and that is true also here. Athletes who take steroids will later suffer premature heart disease. College students who take Ecstasy will damage dopamine receptors in their basal ganglia and suffer early Parkinson's disease. To generalize: no biological agent used for purposes of self-perfection will be entirely

safe. This is good conservative medical sense: anything powerful enough to enhance system A is likely to be powerful enough to harm system B. Yet many good things in life are filled with risks, and free people if properly informed may choose to run them, if they care enough about what is to be gained thereby. If the interventions are shown to be *highly* dangerous, many people will (later if not sooner) avoid them, and the Food and Drug Administration and/ or tort liability will constrain many a legitimate purveyor. It surely makes sense, as an ethical matter, that one should not risk basic health pursuing a condition of "better than well." But, on the other hand, if the interventions work well and are indeed highly desired, people may freely accept, in trade-off, even considerable risk of later bodily harm. But in any case, the big issues have nothing to do with safety; as in the case of cloning children, the real questions concern not the safety of the procedures but what to think about the perfected powers, assuming that they may be safely used.

2. *Equality: issues of unfairness and distributive justice.* An obvious objection to the use of personal enhancers by participants in competitive activities is that they give those who use them an unfair advantage: blood doping or steroids in athletes, stimulants in students taking the SATs. The objection has merit, but it does not reach to the heart of the matter. For even if *everyone* had *equal* access to brain implants or genetic improvement of muscle strength or mind-enhancing drugs, a deeper disquiet would still remain. Even were steroid or growth hormone use by athletes to be legalized, most athletes would be ashamed to be seen injecting themselves before coming to bat. Besides, not all activities of life are competitive: it would matter to me if she says she loves me only because she is high on "erotogenin," a new brain stimulant that mimics perfectly the feeling of falling in love. It matters to me when I go to a seminar that the people with whom I am conversing are not drugged out of their right minds.

The distributive justice question is less easily set aside than the unfairness question, especially if there are systematic disparities between who will and who will not have access to the powers of biotechnical "improvement." The case can be made yet more powerful to the extent that we regard the expenditure of money and energy on such niceties as a misallocation of limited resources in a world in which the basic health needs of millions go unaddressed. It is embarrassing, to say the least, to discover that in 2002, for example, Americans spent one billion dollars on baldness, roughly ten times the amount spent worldwide for research on malaria. But, once again, the inequality of access does not remove our disquiet to the thing itself. And it is to say the least paradoxical, in discussions of the dehumanizing dangers of, say, eugenic choice, when people complain that the poor will be denied equal access to the danger: "The food is contaminated, but why are my portions so small?" Check it out: yes, Huxley's *Brave New World* runs on a deplorable and impermeably rigid class system, but would you want to live in that world if offered the chance to enjoy it as an alpha (one of the privileged caste)? Even an elite can be dehumanized, can dehumanize itself. The central matter is not equality of access, but the goodness or badness of the thing being offered.

3. *Liberty: issues of freedom and coercion, overt and subtle.* This comes closer to the mark, especially with uses of biotechnical power exercised by some people upon other people, whether for social control—say in, the pacification of a classroom of Tom Sawyers—or for their own putative improvement—say, with genetic selection of the sex or sexual orientation of a child-to-be. This problem will of course be worse in tyrannical regimes. But there are always dangers of despotism within families, as parents already work their wills on their children with insufficient regard to a child's independence or long-term needs or the "freedom to be a child." To the extent that even partial control over genotype—say, to take a relatively innocent example, musician parents selecting a child with genes for perfect pitch—adds to existing social instruments of parental control and its risks of despotic rule, this matter will need to be attended to.

There are also more subtle limitations of freedom, say, through peer pressure. What is permitted and widely used may become mandatory. If most children are receiving memory enhancement or stimulant drugs to enable them to "get ahead," failure to provide them for your child might come to be seen as a form of child neglect. If all the defensive linemen are on steroids, you risk mayhem if you go against them chemically pure. And, a point subtler still, some critics complain that, as with cosmetic surgery, Botox, and breast implants, the enhancement technologies of the future will likely be used in slavish adherence to certain socially defined and merely fashionable notions of "excellence" or improvement, very likely shallow, almost certainly conformist.

This special kind of restriction of freedom—let's call it the problem of conformity or homogenization—is in fact quite serious. We are right to worry that the self-selected nontherapeutic uses of the new powers, especially where they become widespread, will be put in the service of the most common human desires, moving us toward still greater homogenization of human society—perhaps raising the floor but greatly lowering the ceiling of human possibility, and reducing the likelihood of genuine freedom, individuality, and greatness. Indeed, such homogenization may be the most important society-wide concern, if we consider the aggregated effects of the likely individual choices for biotechnical "self-improvement," each of which might be defended or at least not objected to on a case-by-case basis (the problem of what the economists call "negative externalities"). For example, it would be difficult to object to a personal choice for a life-extending technology that would extend the user's life by three healthy decades or a mood-brightened way of life that would make the individual more cheerful and untroubled by the world around him. Yet the aggregated social effects of such choices, widely made, could lead to a Tragedy of the Commons, where genuine and sought for satisfactions for individuals are nullified or worse, owing to the social consequences of granting them to everyone.[5] And, as Aldous Huxley strongly suggests in *Brave New World*, the use of biotechnical powers to produce contentment in accordance with democratic tastes threatens the character of human striving and diminishes the possibility of human excellence; perhaps the best thing to be hoped for is preservation of pockets of difference (as on the remote islands in *Brave New World*) where the desire for high achievement has not been entirely submerged in the culture of "the last man."

But, once again, important though this surely is as a social and political issue, it does not settle the question regarding individuals. What if anything can we say to justify our disquiet over the individual uses of performance-enhancing genetic engineering or mood-brightening drugs for other than medical necessity? For even the safe, equally available, non-coerced and non-faddish uses of these technologies for "self-improvement" raise ethical questions, questions that are at the heart of the matter: the disquiet must have something to do with the essence of the activity itself, the use of technological means to intervene into the human body and mind not to ameliorate disease but to change and improve their normal workings. Why, if at all, are we bothered by the voluntary *self*-administration of agents that would change our bodies or alter our minds? What is disquieting about our freely chosen attempts to improve upon human nature, or even our own particular instance of it?

It will be difficult, I acknowledge at the outset, to put this disquiet into words. Initial repugnances are hard to translate into sound moral arguments. We are probably repelled by the idea of drugs that would erase memories or change personalities, or interventions that might enable seventy-year-olds to bear children or play professional sports, or, to engage in some wilder imaginings, the prospect of mechanical implants that would enable men to nurse infants or computer/body hookups that would enable us to download the *Oxford English Dictionary*. But is there wisdom in this repugnance? Taken one person at a time, with a properly prepared set of conditions and qualifications, it is going to be hard to say what is wrong with any biotechnical intervention that could give us (more) ageless bodies or superior performances or could make it possible for us to have happier souls.

If there are essential reasons to be concerned about these activities and where they may lead us, we sense that they must have something to do with challenges to what is naturally human, to what is humanly dignified, or to attitudes that show proper respect for what is naturally and dignifiedly human. In reverse order, I will make three arguments, one on each of these three themes: respect for "the naturally given," threatened by hubris; the dignity of unadulterated human activity, threatened by "unnatural" means; and the nature of full human flourishing, threatened by spurious, partial, or shallow substitutes.

HUBRIS OR HUMILITY? RESPECT FOR "THE GIVEN"

A common man-on-the-street reaction to these prospects is the complaint of "men playing God." If properly unpacked, this worry is in fact shared by people holding various theological beliefs and by people holding none at all. Sometimes the charge means the sheer prideful presumption of trying to alter what God has ordained or nature has produced, or what should, for whatever reason, not be fiddled with. Sometimes the charge means not so much usurping godlike powers, but doing so in the absence of godlike knowledge: the mere playing at being God, the hubris of acting with insufficient wisdom.

Over the past few decades, environmentalists, forcefully making the case for respecting Mother Nature, have urged upon us a "precautionary principle" regarding our interventions into the natural world. Go slowly, they say, you can ruin everything. The point is certainly well taken in the present context. The human body and mind, highly complex and delicately balanced as a result of eons of gradual and exacting evolution, are almost certainly at risk from any ill-considered attempt at "improvement." There is not only the matter of unintended consequences, a concern present even with interventions aimed at therapy. There is also the matter of uncertain goals and absent natural standards, once one proceeds "beyond therapy." When a physician intervenes therapeutically to correct some deficiency or deviation from a patient's natural wholeness, he acts as a servant to the goal of health and as an assistant to nature's own powers of self-healing, themselves wondrous products of evolutionary selection. But when a bioengineer intervenes to "improve upon nature," he stands not as nature's servant but as her aspiring master, guided by nothing but his own will and serving ends of his own devising. It is far from clear that our delicately integrated natural bodily powers will take kindly to such impositions, however desirable the sought-for change may seem to the overconfident intervener. And there is the further question of the goodness of the goals being sought, a matter to which I will return.

One revealing way to formulate the problem of hubris is what Michael Sandel has called the temptation to "hyper-agency," a Promethean aspiration to remake nature, including human nature, to serve our purposes and to satisfy our desires. This attitude is to be faulted not only because it can lead to bad, unintended consequences; more fundamentally, it also represents a false understanding of, and an improper disposition toward, the naturally given world. The root of the difficulty, according to Sandel, seems to be both cognitive and moral: the failure properly to appreciate and respect the "giftedness" of the world.

To acknowledge the giftedness of life is to recognize that our talents and powers are not wholly our own doing, nor even fully ours, despite the efforts we expend to develop and to exercise them. It is also to recognize that not everything in the world is open to any use we may desire or devise. An appreciation of the giftedness of life constrains the Promethean project and conduces to a certain humility. It is, in part, a religious sensibility. But its resonance reaches beyond religion.[6]

The point is well taken, as far as it goes, for the matter of our attitude toward nature is surely crucial. Human beings have long manifested both wondering appreciation for nature's beauty and grandeur and reverent awe before nature's sublime and mysterious power. From the elegance of an orchid to the splendor of the Grand Canyon, from the magnificence of embryological development to the miracle of sight or consciousness, the works of nature can still inspire in most human beings an attitude of respect, even in this age of technology. Nonetheless, the absence of a respectful attitude is today a growing problem in many quarters of our high-tech world. It is worrisome when people act toward, or even talk about, our bodies and minds—or human nature itself—as if they were mere raw material to be molded according to human will. It is worrisome when people speak as if they were wise enough to redesign human beings, improve the human brain, or reshape the human life cycle. In the face of such hubristic temptations, appreciating that the given world—including our natural powers to alter it—is not of our own making could induce a welcome attitude of modesty, restraint, and humility. Such an attitude is surely recommended for anyone inclined to modify human beings or human nature for purposes beyond therapy.

Yet the respectful attitude toward the "given," while both necessary and desirable as a restraint, is not by itself sufficient as a guide. The "giftedness of nature" also includes smallpox and malaria, cancer and Alzheimer's disease, decline and decay. Moreover, nature is not equally generous with her gifts, even to human beings, the most gifted of her creatures. Modesty born of gratitude for the world's "givenness" may enable us to recognize that not everything in the world is open to any use we may desire or devise, but it will not *by itself* teach us *which* things can be tinkered with and *which* should be left inviolate. Respect for the "giftedness" of things cannot tell us which gifts are to be accepted as is, which are to be improved through use or training, which are to be housebroken through self-command or medication, and which opposed like the plague.

The word "given" has two relevant meanings, the second of which Sandel's account omits: "given," meaning "bestowed as a gift," and "given" (as in mathematical proofs), something "granted," definitely fixed and specified. Most of the given bestowals of nature have their given species-specified *natures*: they are each and all of a given *sort*. Cockroaches and humans are equally bestowed but differently natured. To turn a man into a cockroach would be dehumanizing. To try to turn a man into more than a man might be so as well. To avoid this, we need more than generalized appreciation for nature's gifts. We need a particular regard and respect for the special gift that is our own given nature.

In short, only if there is a human "givenness," or a given "humanness," that is also *good and worth respecting*, either as we find it or as *it could be perfected without ceasing to be itself*, will the "given" serve as a *positive* guide for choosing what to alter and what to leave alone. Only if there is something precious *in our given human nature*—beyond the mere fact of its giftedness—can what is given guide us in resisting efforts that would degrade it. When it comes to human biotechnical engineering beyond therapy, only if there is something inherently good or dignified about, say, natural procreation, the human life cycle (with its rhythm of rise and fall), and human erotic longing and striving; only if there is something inherently good or dignified about the ways in which we engage the world as spectators and appreciators, as teachers and learners, leaders and followers, agents and makers, lovers and friends, parents and children, citizens and worshippers, and as seekers of our own special excellence and flourishing in whatever arena to which we are called, only then can we begin to see why those aspects of our nature need to be defended against our deliberate redesign.

We must move, therefore, from the danger of hubris in the powerful designer to the danger of degradation in the designed, considering how any proposed improvements might impinge upon the nature of the one being improved. With the question of human nature and human dignity in mind, we move to questions of means and ends.

"UNNATURAL" MEANS: THE DIGNITY OF HUMAN ACTIVITY

Until only yesterday, teaching and learning or practice and training exhausted the alternatives for acquiring human excellence, perfecting our natural gift through our own efforts. But perhaps no longer: biotechnology may be able to do nature one better, even to the point of requiring no teaching and less training or practice to permit an improved nature to shine forth. The insertion of the growth factor gene into the muscles of rats and mice bulks them up and keeps them strong and sound without the need for nearly as much exertion. Drugs to improve memory, alertness, and amiability could greatly relieve the need for exertion to acquire these powers, leaving time and effort for better things. What, if anything, is disquieting about such means of gaining improvement?

The problem cannot be that they are artificial, unnatural, in the sense of having man-made *origins*. Beginning with the needle and the fig leaf, man has from the start been the animal that uses art to improve his lot. By our very nature, we are constantly looking for ways to better our lives through artful means and devices, for we humans are creatures with what Rousseau called "perfectibility." Ordinary medicine makes extensive use of artificial means, from drugs to surgery to mechanical implants, in order to treat disease. If the use of artificial means is absolutely welcome in the activity of healing, it cannot be their unnaturalness alone that makes us uneasy when they are used to make people "better than well."

Still, in those areas of human life in which excellence has until now been achieved only by discipline and effort, the attainment of those achievements by means of drugs, genetic engineering, or implanted devices looks to many people to be "cheating" or "cheap." Many people believe that each person should work hard for his achievements. Even if one prefers the grace of the natural athlete or the quickness of the natural mathematician—people whose performance deceptively appears to be effortless—we admire also those who overcome obstacles and struggle to try to achieve the excellence of the former. This matter of character— the merit of disciplined and dedicated striving—though *not* the deepest basis of one's objection to biotechnological shortcuts, is surely pertinent. For character is not only the source of our deeds, but also their product. Healthy children whose disruptive behavior is "remedied" by pacifying drugs rather than by their own efforts are not learning self-control; if anything, they are learning to think it unnecessary. People who take pills to block out from memory the painful or hateful aspects of a new experience will not learn how to deal with suffering or sorrow. A drug to induce fearlessness does not produce courage.

Yet things are not so simple. Some biotechnical interventions may assist in the pursuit of excellence without cheapening its attainment. And many of life's excellences have nothing to do with competition or adversity. Drugs to decrease drowsiness or increase alertness, sharpen memory, or reduce distraction may actually help people to pursue their natural goals of learning or painting or performing their civic duty. Drugs to steady the hand of a neurosurgeon or to prevent sweaty palms in a concert pianist cannot be regarded as "cheating," for they are not the source of the excellent activity or achievement. And, for people dealt a meager hand in the dispensing of nature's gifts, it should not be called cheating or cheap if biotechnology could assist them in becoming better equipped—whether in body or in mind.

Nevertheless, there is a sense here where the issue of "naturalness" of means matters. It lies not in the fact that the assisting drugs and devices are artifacts, but in the danger that they will violate or distort human agency and undermine the dignity of the naturally human way of being-at-work in the world. Here, in my opinion, is one of the more profound ways in which the use of at least some of these biotechnological means of seeking perfection— those that work on the brain—come under grave suspicion. In most of our ordinary efforts at self-improvement, whether by practice or training or study, we sense the relation between our doings and the resulting improvement, between the means used and the end sought. There is an experiential and intelligible connection between means and ends; we can see how confronting fearful things might eventually enable us to cope with our fears. We can see how curbing our appetites produces self-command. The capacity to be improved is improved by using it; the deed to be perfected is perfected by doing it.

In contrast, biomedical interventions act directly on the human body and mind to bring about their effects on a subject who is not merely passive but who plays no role at all. He can at best *feel* their effects *without understanding their meaning in human terms.*[7] Thus, a drug that brightened our mood would alter us without our understanding how and why it did so—whereas a mood brightened as a fitting response to the arrival of a loved one or an achievement in one's work is perfectly, because humanly, intelligible. And not only would this be true about our states of mind. *All* of our encounters with the world, both natural and interpersonal, would be mediated, filtered, and altered. Human experience under biological intervention becomes increasingly mediated by unintelligible forces and vehicles, separated from the human significance of the activities so altered. The relations between the knowing subject and his activities, and between his activities and their fulfillments and pleasures, are disrupted. The importance of human effort in human achievement is here properly acknowledged: the point is not the exertions of good character against hardship, but rather the humanity of an alert and self-experiencing agent making his deeds flow intentionally from his willing, knowing, and embodied soul.[8]

To be sure, an increasing portion of modern life is mediated life: the way we encounter space and time, the way we "reach out and touch somebody" via the telephone or internet. And one can make a case that there are changes in our souls and dehumanizing losses that accompany the great triumphs of modern technology. Life becomes easier, but, at the same time, it becomes less "real" and less immediate, as all our encounters with each other and the world are increasingly filtered through the distorting lenses of our clever devices and crude images. But so long as these technologies do not write themselves directly into our bodies and minds, we are in principle able to see them working on us, and free (again, in principle) to walk away from their use (albeit sometimes only with great effort). Once they work on us in ways beyond our ken, we are, as it were, passive subjects of what might as well be "magic." We become, in a sense, more and more like artifacts, creatures of our chemists and bioengineers.

The same point can perhaps be made about enhanced achievements as about altered mental states: to the extent that an achievement is the result of some extraneous intervention, it is detachable from the agent whose achievement it purports to be. That I can use a calculator to do my arithmetic does not make me a knower of arithmetic; if computer chips in my brain were to "download" a textbook of physics, would that make me a knower of physics? Admittedly, this is not always an obvious point to make: if I make myself more alert through Ritalin or coffee, or if drugs can make up for lack of sleep, I may be able to learn more using my unimpeded native powers and in ways to which I can existentially attest that it is *I* who is doing the learning. Still, if human flourishing means not just the accumulation of external achievements and a full curriculum vitae but a lifelong *being-at-work* exercising one's *human* powers *well* and without great impediment, our genuine happiness requires that there be little gap, if any, between the dancer and the dance.

Like dancing, most of life's activities are, to repeat, noncompetitive; most of the best of them—loving and working and savoring and learning—are self-fulfilling beyond the need for praise and blame or any other external reward. Indeed, in these activities, there is at best no goal beyond the activity itself. Such for-itself human-being-at-work-in-the-world, unimpeded and wholehearted, is what we are eager to preserve against dilution and distortion.

In a word: one major trouble with biotechnical (especially mental) "improvers" is that they produce changes in us by disrupting the normal character of human being-at-work-in-the-world, what Aristotle called *energeia psyches*, activity of soul, which, when fine and full constitutes human flourishing. With biotechnical interventions that skip the realm of intelligible meaning, we cannot really own the transformations nor experience them *as genuinely ours*. And we cannot know whether the resulting conditions and activities of our bodies and our minds are, in the fullest sense, our own *as human*.

PARTIAL ENDS, FULL FLOURISHING

In taking up first the matter of questionable means for pursuing excellence and happiness, we have put the cart before the horse: we have neglected to speak about the goals. The issue of good and bad means must yield to the question about good and bad ends.

What do we think about the goals of ageless bodies and happy souls? Would their attainment in fact improve or perfect our lives *as* human beings? These are very big questions, too long to be properly treated here. But the following considerations seem to merit attention.

The case for ageless bodies seems at first glance to look pretty good. The prevention of decay, decline, and disability, the avoidance of blindness, deafness, and debility, the elimination of feebleness, frailty, and fatigue all seem to be conducive to living fully as a human being at the top of one's powers—of having a good "quality of life" from beginning to end. We have come to expect organ transplantation for our worn-out parts. We will surely welcome stem-cell-based therapies for regenerative medicine, reversing by replacement the damaged tissues of Parkinson's disease, spinal cord injury, and many other degenerative disorders. It is hard to see any objection to obtaining in our youth a genetic enhancement of all of our muscles that would not only prevent the muscular feebleness of old age but would empower us to do any physical task with much greater strength and facility throughout our lives. And, should aging research deliver on its promise of adding not only extra life to years but also extra years to life, who would refuse it? Even if you might consider turning down an ageless body for yourself, would you not want it for your beloved? Why should she not remain to you as she was back then when she first stole your heart? Why should her body suffer the ravages of time?

To say no to this offer seems perverse, but I would suggest that it is not. Indeed, the deepest human goods may be ours only because we live our lives in aging bodies, made mindful of our living in time and inseparable from the natural life cycle through which each generation gives way to the one that follows it. Yet because this argument is so counterintuitive, we need to begin not with the individual choice for an ageless body, but to look first at what the individual's life might look like in a world in which everyone made the same choice. We need to make the choice universal, and see the meaning of that choice in the mirror of its becoming the norm.

What if everybody lived life to the hilt, even as they approached an ever-receding age of death in a body that looked and functioned—let's not be too greedy—like that of a thirty year old? Would it be good if each and all of us lived like light bulbs, burning as brightly from beginning to end, but then popping off without warning, leaving those around us suddenly in the dark? Or is it perhaps better that there be a shape to life, everything in its due season, the shape also written, as it were, into the wrinkles of our bodies that live it? What would the relations between the generations be like if there never came a point at which a son surpassed his father in strength or vigor? What incentive would there be for the old to make way for the young, if the old slowed down but little and had no reason to think of retiring—if Michael could play until he were not forty but eighty or if most members of Congress could serve for more than sixty years? And might not even a moderate prolongation of life span with vigor lead to a prolongation in the young of functional immaturity—of the sort that has arguably already accompanied the great increase in average life expectancy experienced in the past century? One cannot think of enhancing the vitality of the old without retarding the maturation of the young.

Going against both common intuition and my own love of life, I have tried elsewhere to make a rational case for the blessings of mortality. In an essay entitled "*L'Chaim* and Its Limits: Why Not Immortality?"[9] I suggest that living self-consciously with our finitude is the condition of the possibility of many of the best things in human life: engagement, seriousness, a taste for beauty, the possibility of virtue, the ties born of procreation, the quest for meaning. Though the arguments are made against the case for immortality, they have weight also against even more modest prolongations of the maximum life span, especially in good health, that would permit us to live as if there were always tomorrow. For it is, I submit, only our ability to number our days that enables us to make them count.

Although human beings are understandably reluctant to grow old and die, and although many religions offer us the promise of a better life hereafter, I contend that the human desire for immortality is in fact a desire not so much for deathlessness as for something transcendent and perfect. It is therefore not a desire that the biomedical conquest of aging or the possession of an ageless body can satisfy. No amount of prolonging earthly life—not even a limitless period of "more of the same"—will answer our deepest longings, namely, longings for wholeness, wisdom, goodness, or godliness. Indeed, our relentless pursuit of perfect bodies and further life extension will deflect us—may indeed already be deflecting us—from realizing more fully the aspirations to which our lives naturally point, and from living well rather than merely staying alive.

A preoccupation with personal agelessness is finally incompatible with accepting the need for procreation and human renewal. Both for individuals and for a whole society, to covet a prolonged life span for ourselves is both a sign and a cause of our failure to open ourselves to procreation and to any higher purpose. It is probably no accident that it is a generation whose intelligentsia proclaims the death of God and the meaninglessness of life that embarks on life's indefinite prolongation and that seeks to cure the emptiness of life by extending it forever. For the desire to prolong youthfulness is not only a childish desire to eat one's life and keep it; it is also an expression of a childish and narcissistic wish incompatible with devotion to posterity. It seeks an endless present, isolated from anything truly eternal and severed from any true continuity with past and future. It is in principle hostile to children, because children, those who come after, are those who will take one's place; *they* are life's answer to mortality, and their presence in one's house is a constant reminder that one no longer belongs to the frontier generation. One cannot pursue agelessness for oneself and remain faithful to the spirit and meaning of perpetuation.

Those who think that having an ageless body would solve the problems of growing old ignore the psychological effects simply of the passage of time—of experiencing and learning about the way things are. After a while, no matter how healthy we are, no matter how respected and well placed we are socially, most of us cease to look upon the world with fresh eyes. Little surprises us, nothing shocks us, righteous indignation at injustice dies out. We have seen it all already, seen it all. We have often been deceived; we have made many mistakes of our own. Many of us become small-souled, having been humbled not by bodily decline or the loss of loved ones but by life itself. So our ambition also begins to flag, or at least our noblest ambitions. As we grow older, Aristotle already noted, we "aspire to nothing great and exalted and crave the mere necessities and comforts of existence." At some point, most of us turn and say to our intimates, "Is this all there is?" We settle, we accept our situation—if we are lucky enough to be able to accept it. In many ways, perhaps in the most profound ways, most of us go to sleep long before our deaths—and we might even do so earlier in life if awareness of our finitude no longer spurred us to make something of ourselves.

Finally, a world devoted to ageless bodies paradoxically would not lead us to appreciate life or celebrate the health we have. On the contrary, as we have seen in recent decades, it would likely be a world increasingly dominated by anxiety over health and fear of death, intolerant of all remaining infirmity and disability and absolutely outraged by the necessity of dying, now that each of us is, like Achilles, seemingly but a heel short of immortality.

Assume for the sake of the argument that some of these consequences would follow from a world of greatly increased longevity and vigor: would it be simply good to have an ageless body? Is there not wisdom and goodness in the natural human life cycle, roughly three multiples of a generation: a time of coming of age; a time of flourishing, ruling, and replacing of self; and a time of savoring and understanding, but still sufficiently and intimately linked to one's descendants to care about their future and to take a guiding, supporting, and cheering role?

And what about pharmacologically assisted happy souls? Painful and shameful memories are disquieting; guilty consciences disturb sleep; low self-esteem, melancholy and world-weariness besmirch the waking hours. Why not memory blockers for the former, mood brighteners for the latter, and a good euphoriant—without risks of hangovers or cirrhosis—when celebratory occasions fail to be jolly? For let us be clear: if it is imbalances of neurotransmitters—a modern equivalent of the medieval doctrine of the four humors— that are responsible for our state of soul, it would be sheer priggishness to refuse the help of pharmacology for our happiness, when we accept it guiltlessly to correct for an absence of insulin or thyroid hormone.

The problem with pursuing a happy soul differs from the problem with pursuing an ageless body. An ageless body, I have argued, is a goal incompatible with preserving our full humanity. Being happy, however, would seem to be precisely a proper, even *the* proper, goal of human life. Still, seeking happiness through pharmacology is dubious on two grounds, each having to do with the shrunken view of "happiness" that informs such a quest and the limited (and limiting) sort of happiness that is obtainable with the aid of drugs. Regarding the removal of psychic troubles, it turns out that some suffering and unhappiness are probably good for us; regarding the creation of psychic satisfactions, it turns out that the mere fragrance of happiness gets mistaken for its real flowering.

Notwithstanding the reality of serious mental illness and the urgent need to treat it (with drugs, of course, if necessary), a little reflection makes clear that there is something misguided about the pursuit of *utter* psychic tranquility or the attempt to eliminate shame, guilt, and all painful memories. Traumatic memories, shame, and guilt, are, it is true, psychic pains. In extreme doses, they can be crippling. Yet short of the extreme, they can also be helpful and fitting. They are appropriate responses to horror, disgraceful conduct, and sin, and as such help us to avoid or fight against them in the future. Witnessing a murder *should* be remembered as horrible; doing a beastly deed *should* trouble one's soul. Righteous indignation at injustice depends on being able to feel injustice's sting. An untroubled soul in a troubling world is a shrunken human being. Moreover, to deprive oneself of one's true memories—in their truthfulness also of feeling—is to deprive oneself of one's own life and identity.

The positive feeling-states of soul (especially those inducible by drugs), though perhaps accompaniments of human flourishing, are not its essence. Ersatz pleasure or feelings of self-esteem are not the real McCoy. They are at most but shadows divorced from *the underlying human activities that are the essence of human flourishing*. Not even the most doctrinaire hedonist wants to have the pleasure that comes from playing baseball without swinging the bat or catching the ball. No music lover would be satisfied with getting from a pill the pleasure of listening to Mozart without ever hearing the music. Most people want both to feel good and to feel good about themselves, but only as a result of being good and doing good.

At the same time, there appears to be a connection between the possibility of feeling deep unhappiness and the prospects for genuine happiness. If one cannot grieve, one has not loved.[10] And to be capable of aspiration, one must know and feel lack. As Wallace Stevens put it, "Not to have is the beginning of desire." In short, if human fulfillment depends on our being creatures of need and finitude and therewith of longing and attachment, there may be a double-barreled error in the pursuit of ageless bodies and factitiously happy souls: far from bringing us what we really need, pursuing these partial goods could deprive us of the urge and energy to seek a richer and more genuine flourishing.

It is, indeed, the peculiar gift of our humanity to recognize the linkage between our unavoidable finitude and our higher possibilities. As Plato's Socrates observed long ago (in the *Symposium*), the heart of the human soul is *eros*, an animating power born of lack but pointed upward. At bottom, human *eros* is the fruit of the peculiar conjunction of and competition between two competing aspirations conjoined in a single living body, both tied to our finitude: the impulse to self-preservation and the urge to reproduce. The first is a self-regarding concern for our own personal permanence and satisfaction; the second is a self-denying aspiration for something that transcends our own finite existence, and for the sake of which we spend and even give our lives. Other animals, of course, live with these twin and opposing drives. But only the human animal is conscious of their existence and is driven to devise a life based in part on the tension between them. In consequence, only the human animal has explicit and conscious longings for something higher, something whole, something eternal, longings that we would not have were we not the conjunction of this bodily "doubleness," elevated and directed upward through conscious self-awareness. Nothing humanly fine, let alone great, will come out of a society that has crushed the source of human aspiration, the germ of which is to be found in the meaning of the sexually complementary "two" that seek unity and wholeness, and willingly devote themselves to the well-being of their offspring. Nothing humanly fine, let alone great, will come out of a society that is willing to sacrifice all other goods to keep the present generation alive and intact. Nothing humanly fine, let alone great, will come from the desire to pursue bodily immortality or pharmacological happiness for ourselves.

Looking into the future at goals pursuable with the aid of new biotechnologies, we can turn a reflective glance at our present human condition and the prospects now available to us to live a flourishing human life. For us today, assuming that we are blessed with good health and a sound mind, a flourishing human life is not a life lived with an ageless body or an untroubled soul, but rather a life lived in rhythmed time, mindful of time's limits, appreciative of each season and filled first of all with those intimate human relations that are ours only because we are born, age, replace ourselves, decline, and die— and know it. It is a life of aspiration, made possible by and borne of experienced lack, of the disproportion between the transcendent longings of the soul and the limited capacities of our bodies and minds. It is a life that stretches toward some fulfillment to which our natural human soul has been oriented, and, unless we extirpate the source, will always be oriented. It is a life not of better genes and enhancing chemicals but of love and friendship, song and dance, speech and deed, working and learning, revering and worshipping.

If this is true, then the pursuit of an ageless body may prove finally to be a distraction and a deformation. The pursuit of an untroubled and self-satisfied soul may prove to be deadly to desire, if finitude recognized spurs aspiration and fine aspiration acted upon *is itself* the core of happiness. Not the agelessness of the body, not the contentment of the soul, and not even the list of external achievements and accomplishments of life, but the engaged and energetic being-at-work of what nature uniquely gave to us is what we need to treasure and defend. All other "perfections" may turn out to be at best but passing illusions, at worst a Faustian bargain that could cost us our full and flourishing humanity.

NOTES

1. The 2003 report of the President's Council on Bioethics on this topic, *Beyond Therapy: Biotechnology and the Pursuit of Happiness*, is organized around the first four of these themes. The complete text is available online at www.bioethics.gov or in two commercially reprinted editions published by ReganBooks (HarperCollins) and the Dana Press. This essay, in many places, draws on the council's report.

2. These powers, already used to produce "mighty mouse" and "super rat," will soon be available for treatment of muscular dystrophy and muscle weakness in the elderly. They will also be of interest to football and wrestling coaches and to the hordes of people who spend several hours daily pumping iron or sculpting their bodies.

3. Health-care providers and insurance companies have for now bought into this distinction, paying for treatment of disease and disability but not for enhancements.

4. Curiously—but, on reflection, not surprisingly—it is often the most gifted and ambitious who most resent their limitations: Achilles was willing to destroy everything around him, so little could he stomach that he was but a heel short of immortality.

5. I myself will later argue such a case with respect to the goal of increasing longevity with ageless bodies.

6. See his "What's Wrong with Enhancement?" a working paper prepared for the President's Council on Bioethics (http://www.bioethics.gov/background/sandelpaper.html). See also his "The Case against Perfection" in the April 2004 issue of *The Atlantic*.

7. So do alcohol and caffeine and nicotine, though, it should be pointed out, we use these agents not as pure chemicals but in forms and social contexts that, arguably, give them a meaning different from what they would have were we to take them as pills. Besides, our acceptance of these "drugs" cannot, without extensive further argument, serve as precedent or moral justification for accepting newer psychoactive enhancers. On the contrary, concerns about the newer possibilities may rightly serve to clarify and intensify our misgivings about these age-old "uppers" and "downers."

8. The lack of "authenticity" sometimes complained of in these discussions is not so much a matter of "playing false" or of not expressing one's "true self," as it is a departure from "genuine," unmediated, and (in principle) self-transparent human activity.

9. It appears as the penultimate chapter of my book, *Life, Liberty and the Defense of Dignity: The Challenge for Bioethics* (Encounter Books, 2002). The discussion in the next few paragraphs borrows heavily from that essay.

10. As C. S. Lewis observed profoundly, speaking about his grief, "The pain I feel now is the happiness I had before. That's the deal."

WHAT'S NEXT?

SECOND READ: *Re*read the article, and pay close attention to the major claims Kass makes, the evidence that he uses, and any counter-arguments, and his response to them, that he includes. Mark these in different ways so that you can easily identify them later.

WHAT'S NEXT

THIRD READ: *Re*read the article a third time. You are now going to use the following guiding questions to really "dig" into the article and analyze it for the kinds of elements we look for in a critical analysis. As you reread, write out your answers to these questions.

CRITICAL ANALYSIS QUESTIONS FOR "BIOTECHNOLOGY AND OUR HUMAN FUTURE: SOME GENERAL REFLECTIONS"

1. What do you think inspired Kass to write about this subject? To put it another way, why might this subject be important to examine?

2. Whom do you think Kass imagined his audience to be? What evidence is there in the text to support your answer?

3. How does Kass present the topic? What is the tone he uses? Why has he taken this tone?

4. What is Kass' argument or controlling idea?

5. What are the strongest points that support his argument? What evidence does he use for his strongest points?

6. What are his weakest points in support of this? What evidence does he use to for his strongest point?

7. What do you notice about the kinds of evidence he uses and how you determined if it was "strong" or "weak"?

8. What counter-arguments does he include, and how does he deal with them? (If he doesn't provide counter-arguments, speculate about why he doesn't.)

9. Identify the kinds of research he incorporates. Into what categories do they fall?

10. Why might he have included these instead of other kinds?

11. Why has Kass not included in-text citations?

12. What do his "Notes" at the end of his essay provide readers?

13. Regarding the subject matter, what questions does he not address?

Notice that the questions you just answered serve to help you critically consider not only the topic/issue, but also the source itself. This kind of *critical analysis* allow you to see how research operates in a non-fiction, academic work as well as what kinds of research you will likely need to consider for your own work.

WHAT'S NEXT

As we read about subject matter and explore the ways in which experts in the field deal with issues that arise in it, it is important to read broadly. That is, we need to read more than one source so that we get a better view of the issues so that we can better understand why the issues exist and what the options are for dealing with them.

Starred *thought*

Keep in mind that the number of sources you will need to read and critically analyze for a project will depend on a number of factors: the time you have, the length of the paper, and how much you already know or don't know about it. Instructors will typically give you the number of sources required, so be sure to take this into account when it is time to work with sources!

FIRST READ: Read the following non-fiction article by Raymond Kurzweil called "Live Forever" and consider not only what he is writing about but also how this article complements the previous one. Use the same active reading strategies as you used above.

The three aspects of the rhetorical triangle

The topic or issues he is addressing

The main argument point or controlling idea about that topic or issue

The kinds of research (e.g., examples, texts, cultural references) he uses to support it

LIVE FOREVER

By Raymond Kurzweil

For a link to this article, go to the ancillary website www.grtep.com.

WHAT'S NEXT?

SECOND READ: *Re*read the article, and pay close attention to the major claims Kurzweil makes, the evidence that he uses, and any counter-arguments, and his response to them, that he includes. Mark these in different ways so that you can easily identify them later.

WHAT'S NEXT

THIRD READ: *Re*read the article a third time. You are now going to use the following guiding questions to really "dig" into the article and analyze it for the kinds of elements we look for in a critical analysis. As you reread, write out your answers to these questions.

CRITICAL ANALYSIS QUESTIONS FOR "LIVE FOREVER"

1. Why might Kurzweil have written this article? Is the purpose different from or the same as Kass'? Explain.

2. Who do you think Kurzweil imagined his audience to be? What evidence is there in the text to support your answer?

3. This article was originally published in 2000 on *Psychology Today*'s website with the same name. How does this publication information shape how we might view it as a source? (In other words, why would an article like this appear in this format?)

4. What is Kurzweil's argument or controlling idea?

5. What are the strongest points that support his argument? What evidence does he use for his strongest points?

6. What are his weakest points in support of this? What evidence does he use to for his strongest point?

7. What do you notice about the kinds of evidence he uses and how you determined if it was "strong" or "weak"?

8. Identify the kinds of research he incorporates. Are these different from or the same as the kinds he used in the previous article?

9. Why might he have included these instead of other kinds?

10. Regarding the subject matter, what sources does he use that you might need to locate and read? Why?

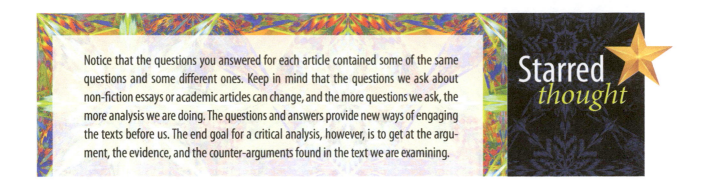

Notice that the questions you answered for each article contained some of the same questions and some different ones. Keep in mind that the questions we ask about non-fiction essays or academic articles can change, and the more questions we ask, the more analysis we are doing. The questions and answers provide new ways of engaging the texts before us. The end goal for a critical analysis, however, is to get at the argument, the evidence, and the counter-arguments found in the text we are examining.

Starred *thought*

WHAT'S NEXT?

Now that you have critically analyzed two different texts, you can choose one (or one that your instructor has assigned) and begin to draft a critical analysis essay of it. Below are the features of this genre.

FEATURES OF A RHETORICAL ANALYSIS

Controlling Idea: After you have completed the analysis by using critical analysis questions to guide your reading, you will have a good idea of what the text's author's main idea is and why. You will provide your readers with a controlling idea about what that argument or main idea is and explain how the primary text holds up to scrutiny. You might point out that the overall take-away of the primary text is either soundly argued and persuasive or has flaws that make the author's overall argument weak.

Textual Support: You will identify major supporting ideas and the evidence used to support them. This requires you to quote from the text (citing ethically), analyze what is being argued, and then connect that to the overall argument the author is making. (Review QuACing in Appendix A.) In addition, you will need to explain how those supporting ideas link to the main argument the author laid out in his/her text. Not only are you examining the kinds of evidence the author is using, but you are also using that as evidence for how you are doing the critical analysis.

Additional Sources: While not necessarily required, you can use other sources to help you analyze the validity of your critique. For example, if you notice that the evidence the author uses is out-of-date, you might point this out and then refer the reader to a current source that provides up-to-date information. This becomes strong evidence for you to say that the source you are using has flaws.

Third-person point of view: Critical analyses do not use "I" or other first person pronouns because the focus is on the primary text's argument and claims and not your personal stake in the subject matter.

WHAT'S NEXT?

WRITING YOUR OWN CRITICAL ANALYSIS

Here are some structural suggestions for how to set-up your critical analysis.

INTRODUCTION: It is a good idea to establish the author(s), the text, and the context. Identify the subject matter and what the author(s) say(s) is the importance of it. Explain how the text holds up to scrutiny or whether or not the author's main argument is sound.

BODY: The body is where you will show your reader why *your* analysis is sound. This means you will have multiple paragraphs laying out how the author's text is structured by laying out how the author makes his/her argument. You will identify the main points s/he makes, what evidence is used, whether or not this is convincing or not. (This is what is meant by "strongest points" and "weakest" points in the guiding questions.) You will need to imbed direct quotes from the text, analyze those quotes, and explain how they are flawed or not. Counter-arguments and responses to them by the author should also be analyzed and included as part of the persuasiveness of the text.

CONCLUSION: The conclusion will reaffirm why the text is persuasive or flawed. If there are both strong and weak points, then you can evaluate whether or not the text *overall* is sound or problematic. You can also address what issues the author does not address but could to make the author's overall argument more complete.

Writer: _____ Reader: _____

PEER-REVIEW OF CRITICAL ANALYSIS DRAFT 1

1. What is the main idea, major point, or central claim that the writer is making in his/her essay about the text s/he is critiquing?

2. The writer's job is NOT to weigh in on the topic being examined. His/Her job is to analyze the strength and weakness of the arguments made in the text in an attempt to understand soundness or persuasiveness of the text's author's overall argument. To what extent has the writer been able to stay grounded in an analysis of the texts?

3. As a reader, do you find the writer's analysis illuminating? If not, explain what the writer needs to do to make it so. If so, explain where in the essay the writer has done this well and why you think so.

4. Based upon the writer's analysis, what does the writer seem to be saying about the text's overall argument?

5. Consider the soundness, validity, and justification of the writer's analysis about the text. What alternative inferences, judgments, and conclusions are just as reasonable? How might the writer address these in his/her final draft?

6. Review the conclusion of this paper. To what extent does the conclusion convincingly draw from the analysis of the texts in the body paragraphs? Explain how the writer might improve it.

REFLECTIONS: CRITICAL ANALYSIS WRITING

Describe your writing process for this critical analysis. What strategies did you use? Why?

What did you find to be the hardest part about writing a critical analysis?

What did you find to be the easiest part about writing a critical analysis?

Describe how your process for writing this essay was different from or similar to writing a literary analysis.

Why might that be the case?

If you had more time, what would you want to work on further, and why?

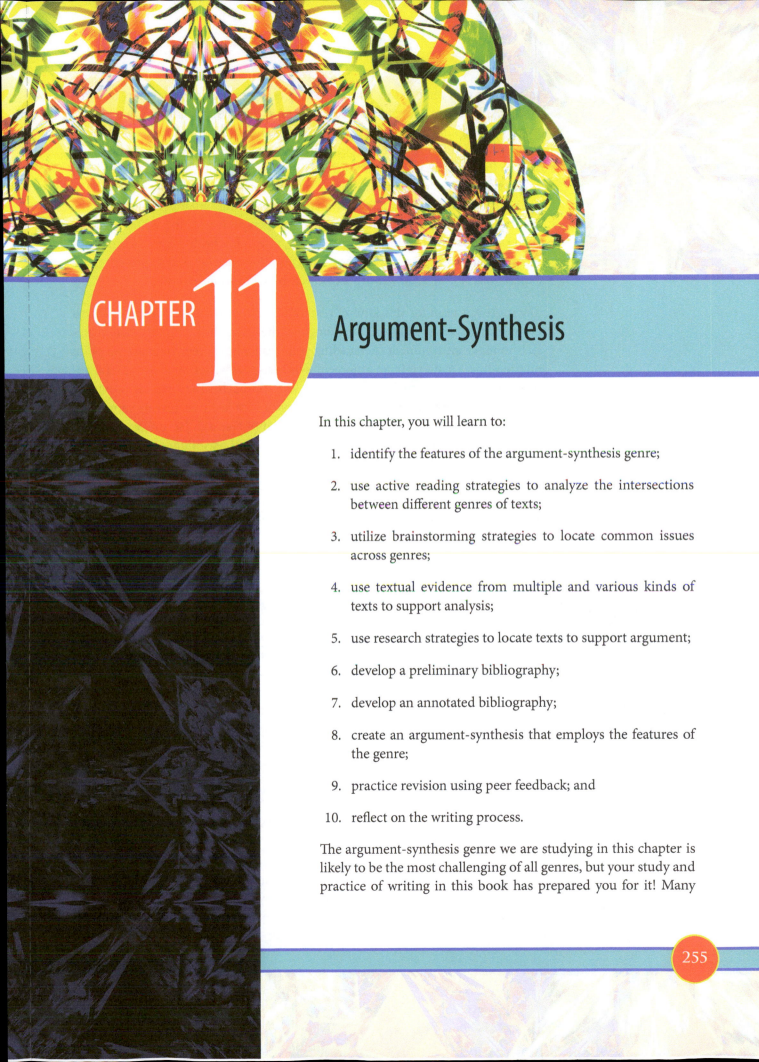

CHAPTER 11

Argument-Synthesis

In this chapter, you will learn to:

1. identify the features of the argument-synthesis genre;

2. use active reading strategies to analyze the intersections between different genres of texts;

3. utilize brainstorming strategies to locate common issues across genres;

4. use textual evidence from multiple and various kinds of texts to support analysis;

5. use research strategies to locate texts to support argument;

6. develop a preliminary bibliography;

7. develop an annotated bibliography;

8. create an argument-synthesis that employs the features of the genre;

9. practice revision using peer feedback; and

10. reflect on the writing process.

The argument-synthesis genre we are studying in this chapter is likely to be the most challenging of all genres, but your study and practice of writing in this book has prepared you for it! Many instructors may refer to this kind of writing as a "research project" or a "research essay." As you have come to see, most writing at university includes some kind of research. The kind and number of sources differ, but the importance of research is the same: To frame your own thinking in what has already been thought and said so that you can extend the conversation. Whether you include a professional review of a "thing" in a review essay or a literary critic's ideas about the theme in "Flowers for Algernon" in a literary analysis, all writings attempt to persuade the reader to consider, if not outright adopt, the perspective of the writer. Because such expertise is valued in academic writing, research is both the *activity* for finding pertinent and appropriate sources and also the *material* used to present those expert voices. Hence, all writing is research-based to some extent.

The more apt term for this kind of research-based writing is *argument-synthesis* because it describes what you are doing: Synthesizing (bringing together) materials to make an argument (persuading your readers to accept your overall point on the subject matter). In an argument-synthesis, the writer must use several approaches and texts to make her/his point. The approaches may include providing analysis of a work of literature or art (primary sources) that reveals some kind of insight into an issue as well as incorporation of research (secondary sources) on that issue. As you have learned, writers use logical reasoning, common sense, emotions, facts, primary and secondary sources, and many other available means to get the reader to see the overall point that they are making. In other words, an argument-synthesis *synthesizes* multiple texts, and often multiple genres of texts, and various components of research to make the strongest argument that will persuade a reader to accept the controlling idea proposed.

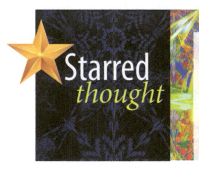

Other kinds of writing you have studied in this book contain *argumentative* elements. That is, writers want their readers to believe something, think something, or consider something, so writers are always arguing for an interpretation, belief, or idea they believe to be true or at least valid. Depending upon the subject matter and in what context, the ways a writer uses argument strategies will take different forms.

HOW IS AN ARGUMENT-SYNTHESIS USING MULTIPLE KINDS OF TEXTS?

You have had experience in the past using secondary sources and working with how they relate to primary ones. The argument-synthesis goes a step further, however, to include different *genres* of texts. To make this point clearer, let us examine how the work you did in Chapters 8, 9, and 10 work together and can be recombined for an argument-synthesis.

The readings contained in Chapters 8-10 all are connected by the common subject or theme of humans/technology. The literature, visuals, and academic articles all address this theme, but they do so in different ways. If we now consider a specific question—how does technology impact the human world?—we can build an argument that answers that question. We can utilize literature, visual texts, and academic texts to build a complex and thought-provoking argument. Bringing these texts together, and adding on further research, becomes a dynamic path for examining an issue even more in-depth, and this allows us to bring in our own arguments about how to view the topic and the issues that arise.

WHAT'S NEXT?

VISUAL TEXTS

Consider how the critical essays and the critical analyses you completed in Chapter 10 can reshape how you view the visuals in chapter 9.

1. Referring to Leon R. Kass' article, "Biotechnology and Our Human Future: Some General Reflections,":

    a. What questions arise about the image of the "Cyberwoman Removing Make-up" (see p. 203)?

OR

    b. What questions arise about the image of "Cyberwoman and Cyberchild Holding Hands" (see p. 208)?

2. Referring to Raymond Kurzweil's article, "Live Forever,":

    a. What questions arise about the image of the "Cyberwoman Removing Make-up" (see p. 203)?

OR

    b. What questions arise about the image of "Cyberwoman and Cyberchild Holding Hands" (see p. 208)?

3. How might we interpret the image (whichever you chose) differently now that we have *contextualized* it within the subject matter of "humans and technology" as discussed in the critical essays?

4. If you were to include a visual analysis of this image, what questions arise that could be answered by the readings?

5. What further questions might you need to explore? Why?

WHAT'S NEXT?

LITERARY TEXTS

Consider how the critical essays and the critical analyses you completed in Chapter 10 can reshape how you view the literature in Chapter 8.

1. Referring to Leon R. Kass' article, "Biotechnology and Our Human Future: Some General Reflections.":

    a. What questions arise about the short story "There Will Come Soft Rains" (see p. 165–170)?

    OR

    b. What questions arise about the short story "Flowers for Algernon" (See ancillary site: www.grtep.com.)?

    OR

    c. What questions arise about the poem "There Will Come Soft Rains" (see p. 179–180)?

    OR

d. What questions arise about the poem "To Artificial Living" (see p. 180–181)?

2. Referring to Raymond Kurzweil's article, "Live Forever,":

   a. What questions arise about the short story "There Will Come Soft Rains" (see p. 165–170)?

OR

   b. What questions arise about the short story "Flowers for Algernon" (See ancillary site: www.grtep.com.)?

OR

   c. What questions arise about the poem "There Will Come Soft Rains" (see p. 179–180)?

OR

    d.   What questions arise about the poem "To Artificial Living" (see p. 180–181)?

3.   How might we interpret the literary texts (whichever you chose) differently now that we have *contextualized* it within the subject matter of "humans and technology" as discussed in the critical essays?

4.   If you were to include one of the literary texts, what questions arise that could be answered by the readings?

5.   What further questions might you need to explore? Why?

In terms of synthesizing sources, these questions show you the possibilities there are in taking different kinds of texts and examining them in relation to each other. This, in turn, may lead to writing about a topic or issue from different perspectives. Hence, you are synthesizing on two levels: between texts and between the texts and your own thinking.

DEVELOPING WAYS TO EXPLORE FURTHER

Let's consider how synthesizing texts in various combinations leads to further exploration. Imagine you are writing an essay on humans and technology and *the effect that technology has on human conception of mortality*. (This is a very specific focus, and it is just an example).

1. What do the images suggest is the problem? Solution?

2. What do the short stories suggest is the problem? Solution?

3. What do the articles say is the problem? Solution?

3. When juxtaposed, how do the images (and short stories or poems) shape what the articles are saying?

4. When juxtaposed, how do the articles shape what the images (and short stories or poems) are saying?

5. How might you synthesize one of the images, one of the short stories or poems, and one of the critical essays?

6. What possible controlling ideas might exist for such an essay that synthesizes these texts?

7. What might an outline look like if you were to synthesize analyses of these texts into an essay on human conception of mortality?

8. What other genres of texts might be helpful in examining the subject matter? Why?

9. What further research do you need to do? Why?

FEATURES OF AN ARGUMENT-SYNTHESIS

As the above activities have demonstrated, argument-synthesis brings together several texts, and different *kinds* of texts, into a dialogue or dialectic. Out of that dialogue come possible foci for a paper that will make an argument about a specific, narrow topic or issue found in the subject matter that initially drives the research. The controlling idea is presented and argued for through an analysis of the texts, synthesis of the texts, and the ideas that emerge from this dialectic.

The nature of an argument-synthesis, then, includes several interlocking components. The first element, the argument, is traditionally understood as the writer taking a position, perspective, or stance on a particular subject and persuading the reader to take it on, too. The writer uses claims to make a point, addresses counter-arguments that weaken that position, and then diffuses them to make the overall point—the writers' argument or controlling idea—hold up to scrutiny. The writer uses several texts and kinds of texts to make her/his point resonate on different levels with the reader. The end goal is to get the reader to consider the argument to be valid and important and perhaps to even spark further consideration.

Here is what this genre of writing includes.

THIRD-PERSON: Like the other genres you studied, the argument-synthesis is not about personal feelings or opinions, although these might drive our purpose for writing. Instead, we need to keep a level head and an unbiased tone when we are trying to persuade others. If we appear too emotional or too fanatical, then our readers will not be inclined to consider the issue. Remember, too, that some topics/subjects are fraught with emotion, so if we can approach the issue calmly, from a stance of facts, honesty, and compassion for alternative views, then we are more likely to be heard and even more likely to persuade others to adopt the view we are advocating.

ARGUMENT: As in other kinds of writing, the argument (a.k.a., thesis, controlling idea, main claim, main argument) is what the purpose is for the writing. After doing research, you will come to some conclusion about the subject matter you studied, and you will persuade your reader to understand what that is. The argument will likely be a multifaceted one that may take two or three sentences to articulate. For example, if a writer were interested in the relationship between humans and technology, the writer would then have to examine several different aspects of this. First, what kind of technology are we talking about? What kind of relationship? Which humans? All of them? Specific people? Under what conditions? Finally, the writer would then have to make a connection to why this is important. What is at stake? Why does the topic matter?

Out of the process of researching and critically thinking about the issues, the writer will then be able to develop some kind of working argument. It might include examining how different texts, such as artwork or digital images, depict that relationship in conjunction with how modern medical science also addresses it. Out of analysis of different texts, the writer can develop different controlling ideas. Here are two that are possible:

> Technological advances, although helpful in making life easier and more efficient, has ultimately undermined any great progress in human relationships. In fact, technology has destroyed the sense of "humanity" that once united people.

> OR

> The relationship everyday people have with technology in the home has blurred the lines between what a human should do and what

technology can do more efficiently. These blurred lines are revealed in digital images, film, and popular readings, resulting in the power of technology changing what is meant by "humanity."

Notice how these controlling ideas are long, complex, and debatable! Not everyone will agree with them nor see how these ideas are even possible. Therefore, your job, as the writer, would be to show how they are, in fact, possible, valid, and important.

COUNTER-ARGUMENTS: Good arguments make a strong case in defense of the controlling idea, yet writers must acknowledge alternative points of view and critique of the controlling idea. Therefore, writers must address the arguments against the controlling idea, which are called *counter-arguments*. Some counter-arguments will be easy to identify and articulate; others will be found while researching what the alternatives views, positions, or critiques are. Once identified, then the writer can address them, making the writer seem informed and reasonable. If the counter-arguments are particularly strong and hard to argue against, the writer can address these early in the essay, leaving the writer's strongest and most compelling arguments for last.

SYNTHESIS: Synthesis is the incorporation of several texts, which can include different kinds of texts, that blend together to make a cohesive and coherent whole. In some ways, you can think of this kind of writing as taking parts (ideas, argument points, texts, research materials) and bringing them together into a whole as well as bringing together the different texts you have into a dialectic.

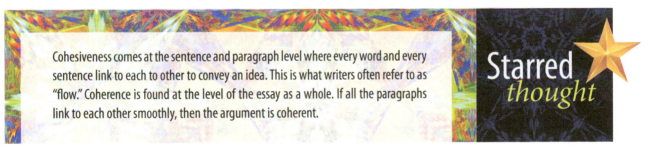

Cohesiveness comes at the sentence and paragraph level where every word and every sentence link to each to other to convey an idea. This is what writers often refer to as "flow." Coherence is found at the level of the essay as a whole. If all the paragraphs link to each other smoothly, then the argument is coherent.

Starred *thought*

STRUCTURE: Argument-synthesis essays are lengthy because the nature of a research at this level is to examine the subject matter in-depth and from multiple sides. Therefore, writers typically provide background information about the issue or subject matter, establishing well-known facts or contextual information, early in the essay. The writer also establishes her/his argument (controlling idea) early in the essay so that the reader knows what the argument is.

RESEARCH: The kind of research needed will depend upon the subject matter, but the best kinds of argument-syntheses are the ones that bring in information from various sources and various kinds of sources. In other words, you are not going to use just books or journals. You might need to look at quantitative data from polling or surveys that provide information about trends, such as what the Gallup Poll provides. You might bring in case-studies or first-hand accounts, such as published interviews, that relate to the subject matter. You might need to bring in historical or social contexts because they shape how we view the subject matter. Whatever the research, you need to use authentic, reliable, and appropriate sources, and they need to be academic.

In other words, research is not just about finding sources that agree with you. Research is used to provide background information, insights into the various viewpoints, counter-arguments, and cultural insights that only the research will reveal. Therefore, you will need to read widely and try to capture the scope of the subject and the issues that arise so that you will be an informed writer who will be *able to persuade* the reader.

Starred *thought*

The argument-synthesis is highly academic, so you will need to do library research using online library databases. Googling for information or using commercial websites is not valued in this genre, for you need have peer-reviewed sources, those that are vetted by experts in the field from which you get your sources.

RESEARCHING FOR YOUR OWN ARGUMENT-SYNTHESIS

After you have decided on what texts you will synthesize, you will need to conduct further research regarding the issue that arises out of that synthesis. As you see connections between texts of various kinds, you will begin to develop questions that you need to explore. Research becomes the tool for you to build up your knowledge about the issues. You will need to locate academic research sources to help you shape the context for the issue for yourself and for your reader.

There are several stages to writing an argument-synthesis. Because researching is integral to this kind of writing, what follows is a detailed strategy for you to use to build up to the actual final project you are composing.

Starred *thought*

The information you find in one source and the questions that arise for you as a reader will direct your research. In other words, research is more than just locating sources for your own argument. Research is *how you go about discovering* what you want to write about in the first place! Research, then, is a tool as much as a product.

SELECT A TOPIC

Selecting a topic can be achieved once you decide on what literature and visuals you want to work with. When you combine the texts, there will be a topic or issue that they address. You can use any of the brainstorming strategies you learned about to help you identify a topic if one does not naturally emerge. Once you have selected the topic, then you are poised to begin researching because the entire researching process is based upon *what the topic is*.

Now consider what Myrtle S. Bolner, et al, suggest for helping you to choose a topic (Figure 11.4).

WRITING A RESEARCH PAPER

The research paper is a formal essay based on an accumulation of facts and ideas gathered in the research process. The research paper offers the researcher an opportunity to examine issues, locate material relevant to an issue, digest, analyze, evaluate, and present the information with conclusions and interpretations. In preparing a research paper, you will search for appropriate resources in the library or on the Internet.

Although research may differ by discipline, there are two basic types of research: argumentative and analytical. According to the Purdue Online Writing Lab (owl.english.purdue.edu):

- The purpose of argumentative research, in which an author takes a stance (a thesis statement) on a controversial or debatable topic then cites and discusses sources that support the thesis, is *to persuade*.

- The purpose of analytical research, in which a researcher asks questions or explores a topic in an objective manner, is *to produce original research*.

No matter what type of paper or report is required, it is important to know what resources are available and how to use those resources appropriately and effectively.

STEPS IN PREPARING A(N ARGUMENTATIVE) PAPER

It is helpful to approach an argumentative paper assignment as a series of stages or steps. Some rather obvious steps are:

1. Selecting a topic
2. Formulating a thesis
3. Preparing an outline
4. Finding information

5. Evaluating sources
6. Taking notes
7. Writing the text of the paper
8. Documenting the sources

SELECTING A TOPIC

Sometimes the initial step in the preparation of a research paper is the most challenging one. The selection of a topic is also the most crucial step in determining the success of the research paper. If your instructor assigns a topic, you need only determine how to proceed with the research. In most cases, however, you must choose your own topic. While this might tend to increase your apprehensions about the research paper, it also affords some exciting and rewarding possibilities. After all, research is about acquiring new knowledge and looking at information in new ways. The trick is to focus on a topic that interests you and to discover all the aspects that you want to work with. The best way to do this is to examine several possibilities systematically. Several overriding principles that should be considered in selecting a research topic are shown in Figure 11.1.

PRELIMINARY RESEARCH AND BIBLIOGRAPHY

Figure out what you know (K), do not know (NK), and want to find out (W). Using the KNKW chart, keep track so that you can see your progress! As you do preliminary research, keep track of what sources look promising and why. Keep a list of sources with citation information.

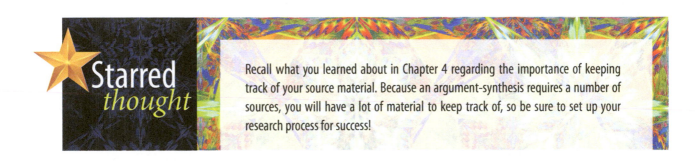

Starred thought

Recall what you learned about in Chapter 4 regarding the importance of keeping track of your source material. Because an argument-synthesis requires a number of sources, you will have a lot of material to keep track of, so be sure to set up your research process for success!

FIGURE 11.1   Selecting a topic

Selecting a Topic

Initial consideration	Beware of topics that may be too
· conforms to the instructor's assignment	· recent
· your prior understanding of topic	· regional
· manageability of topic	· emotional
· length of assignment/project	· complex
· due date of assignment/project	· broad
· your interest in the topic	· narrow
· availability of information on the topic	

KNKW Chart

What I Know	What I Do Not Know	What I Want to Find Out

After figuring out what information you need to look up, begin to locate possible sources. Develop a *preliminary bibliography* that provides an alphabetized (by author's last name) list of sources that you have found. As you continue to do your research, include and remove sources from that list, paying close attention to why you want to keep or remove them. Once you have completed the preliminary research process, you will have a list of sources that you will then turn to for closer reading and scrutiny. Once you decide what sources you absolutely will need and why you need them, the preliminary bibliography will turn into a finalized list of sources that will appear in your essay and on your bibliography page.

DEVELOP POSSIBLE CONTROLLING IDEA

After preliminary research is done, you will have a greater sense of what the landscape is and what your position is on some aspect of it. This will function as your controlling idea for now. Keep in mind that this controlling idea can change after you have done more research, but you will now have a goal in mind, an end to work toward, and this will help you sift through the research and find what you need. Consider what Bolner, et al, suggest for helping you to develop a possible controlling idea.

 **FIGURE 11.2** Formulating a Controlling Idea

Formulating a Controlling Idea

Developing a Controlling Idea
- Begin with a question—not an opinion. Do not just give the purpose of the paper.
- Conduct preliminary research to look for points that will help you shape or form an opinion.
- Prepare a final statement that indicates that the thesis is supported by evidence. (A thesis statement should be brief—no more than three sentences.)

Sample Topic
Effect of Television Advertising on Children

Initial Question
Are children under the age of eight adversely affected by advertising they see on TV?

After Further Research
What is the purpose of TV advertising that is directed toward children?
Do advertisers use tricks or unfair practices to influence children?
What are some of the parental concerns relative to TV advertising directed toward children?
Is there evidence to show that children and families are adversely affected by TV advertising?
Should there be an outright ban of advertising on children's TV programs?
Should the government regulate TV advertising on children's programs?

FINAL Controlling Idea
Numerous studies have found that TV advertising directed toward children can adversely affect their mental and physical health. The two most advertised products on children's TV, toys and food, place undue emphasis on consumerism and result in poor eating habits. Although there have been attempts to regulate TV advertising directed toward children, parental intervention seems to offer the best solution for countering the adverse effects of TV advertising on children.

DEVELOP WORKING OUTLINE

A working outline is used to provide some early control over the material you find. You will find more information than you will need, so a working outline helps you to decide what is needed and what can be put aside. Keep in mind that the outline can change as you do research. In fact, if it doesn't change, then you are probably reading about information you already know. The whole point of reading widely is to find answers for what you do not know and then figure out how that fits into your purpose for the essay. Consider what Bolner, et al, suggest for helping you to develop a working outline.

PREPARING AN OUTLINE FOR ARGUMENTATIVE PAPER

The third step in the research process is to prepare a working outline. The outline serves as a tool that organizes your information into a pattern you can understand and follow. In the initial stage, it is important to the search strategy, since the search should be directed to the relevant points in the outline. After you have completed your research, it serves as the skeleton for writing the final paper.

- It should be based on the controlling idea and should include all the facets of the topic to be investigated.

- To be useful, the outline should divide your controlling idea into the sections that will address the major points; each of the points should be further divided until you can visualize the outline as a guide for research.

- The outline should follow a logical sequence with related points grouped together.

- In the process of locating information, it is probable that other aspects of the topic not included in the working outline will be discovered and that the final outline will be revised and improved.

CHOOSING AN OUTLINE STYLE

Your instructor may ask that you use an outline style which is *informal* or one that is *formal*, or you may choose the style that suits you best.

- An *informal outline* lists the major points by sections. Subcategories are listed below the main headings. Specific facts and phrases gathered in the course of your research are listed below the major points (see Figure 11.3).

CHOOSE APPROPRIATE SOURCES

Consider what Bolner, et al, suggest for helping you to choose the right kinds of sources.

FIGURE 11.3   Example of an informal outline for argumentative research

Topic: Children and Television Advertising
Purpose
Statistics
    Viewing time by children
    Advertising directed toward children
Adverse effects
    Research findings
    Products
    Toys
    Food
Regulations
    U.S.
    Other countries
Parental intervention

STEPS IN PREPARING AN OBJECTIVE/ANALYTICAL RESEARCH PAPER

What is objective or analytical research? This type of research has been defined as "a systematic process of collecting, analyzing, and interpreting information (data) in order to increase understanding of the phenomenon about which we are interested or concerned" (Leedy and Ormrod, 2004, 2). Typically, analytical research requires development of a research proposal for approval before conducting the research.

There are two basic types of analytical research:

1. Qualitative research is related to the social sciences, is grounded in social science theory, and seeks to understand phenomena (data are gathered then analyzed for recurring themes; the focus of the study may shift or evolve in this process). Examples include case studies and historical studies. Typically, descriptive statistics (percentages) are used to report results.

2. Quantitative research is related to the hard sciences, is based on the scientific method in which hypotheses are developed and tested (once developed, the focus and hypotheses do not change; the data either support or do not support each hypothesis). Examples include surveys and experimental research. Typically, inferential statistics (probability) is used to draw inferences from a random sample to a more generalized population.

STEPS IN OBJECTIVE/ANALYTICAL RESEARCH PAPER

1. Begin with a general focus or topic to investigate

2. Decide on a research methodology

3. Search the scholarly peer-reviewed literature for previous research related to the topic and the methodology

4. Develop general problem statement and more specific sub-problems

5. Develop research questions or hypotheses that address each sub-problem

6. Identify limitations and critical assumptions of the research methodology

7. Write a research proposal, which includes background information, a statement of the research problem and sub-problems, specific research questions or hypotheses, relevant definitions, limitations and assumptions of the research, review of relevant scholarly literature, and methodology (If the research involves humans, apply for approval from the Internal Review Board (approval for human research by an IRB is required by law for institutions that accept federal funding)

8. If the proposal is approved, conduct the research and write the research report (the proposal should state what research will be conducted and how it will be conducted; once approved, data are gathered and analyzed and the research results are reported).

Five D's of Research: A Brief Summary of the Research Process

1. Define the problem

2. Design research methodology

3. Do the research

4. Describe results

5. Discuss implications

FINDING INFORMATION

Once you have settled on the type of research (argumentative or objective/analytical) and a) decided on a topic and have written a controlling idea

FIGURE 11.4 Example of Outline for Objective/Analytical Research

I. Introduction
   A. Background information (cite reference sources to introduce the reader to the topic)
   B. Importance of the study
   C. Statement of the general problem and more specific sub-problems
   D. Research questions or hypotheses (should be related to the sub-problems)
   E. Operational definitions and acronyms
   F. Limitations and delimitations of the study (what will the study exclude and include)
   G. Assumptions (assumptions embedded in the methodology; for instance, if it is a survey, it is assumed that respondents will answer the questions truthfully)

II. Review of the Literature

Research builds upon previous research so review similar, previous studies that are related to the topic and methodology. The reviews should be in narrative format and include the purpose, methodology, and major results.

III. Methodology
   A. Description: source of data, what data are collected, data collection procedures
   B. Data analysis: how data are compiled and analyzed

IV. Results
   A. Restate each research question and answer OR restate each hypothesis and state whether data support or do not support it
   B. Use tables and figures to display or illustrate results

V. Discussion, Conclusion
   A. Summarize results and discuss possible implications
   B. Relate to previous research results, whether the results are similar or different
   C. End with recommendation for further research in the future

along with a working outline for an argumentative paper or b) developed a research problem and methodology for an objective study, you are ready for what many consider to be the most interesting part of the research process: finding relevant information. In this phase you will be looking for information in a variety of sources: books, periodicals, and the Internet. Before you begin your search, it is essential that you know how to recognize sources and to analyze them with respect to the type of source and the depth and extent of coverage appropriate for your research.

- For argumentative research, you will search for information that supports the controlling idea.

- For objective/analytical research, you will search for background information on the topic for the introduction section and previous, similar research for the review of the literature section.

UNDERSTANDING THE SOURCES

As you plan your research and locate information, you must be able to identify whether a source is **primary**, **secondary**, or **tertiary** and to understand the level of scholarship—whether the treatment of the topic is *popular* or *scholarly*. These concepts are critical to determining the appropriateness of a source.

PRIMARY SOURCES

A *primary* source is a firsthand or eyewitness account of an event. It includes events in which the author is an active participant or an observer, raw data (such as census data), information gathered in surveys, and research reports. Objects such as maps, works of art, and historical artifacts are also considered primary sources. The test of whether or not something is a primary source is whether it is actually firsthand evidence without any interpretation beyond that which the observer or participant provided, whether the raw data are from a reliable source such as the Census Bureau, or whether the research is original and peer-reviewed.

SECONDARY SOURCES

A *secondary* source provides an interpretation, analysis, explanation, or a restatement of a primary source. The author of a secondary source is not present at an actual event being described; rather, he/she reports on the events by interpreting or conveying the facts and opinions of others who were direct witnesses or participants. There is usually a lapse of time between the initial happening of an event or the original creation of a source and the time other authors begin to write or talk about the event. In fact, authors of secondary sources can also be one or more steps removed from the original event. Primary sources are frequently included in secondary sources to prove a point or to try to persuade the reader to hold a certain opinion.

TERTIARY SOURCES

A *tertiary* source selects, compiles, and indexes primary and secondary sources. Tertiary sources point to and make it possible to find and use primary and secondary sources. It is sometimes difficult to distinguish between secondary and tertiary sources. Think of them as sources which are once removed in the timeline from secondary sources. Sources which provide summaries or chronologies are considered to be tertiary sources. Some almanacs and encyclopedias fall into this category if they are merely compilations of the primary and secondary sources.

Figure 11.5 lists some examples of primary, secondary and tertiary sources.

FIGURE **11.5**   Examples of primary, secondary, and tertiary sources

Primary Sources	Secondary Sources	Tertiary Sources
eyewitness accounts of an event (e.g., newspaper articles)	biographies	bibliographies
research reports	journal articles	indexes and abstracts
diaries, journals, letters, family records	magazine articles	online databases (not full-text)
statistics (original, e.g., 2010 Census)	dictionaries (long articles based on primary sources)	library catalogs
surveys	encyclopedias (long articles, signed, documented)	directories
speeches	textbooks	literature surveys
interviews	monographs (non-fiction, e.g., histories)	book reviews (brief)
autobiographies	bibliographical essays	almanacs (brief facts)
maps	textbooks	dictionaries (no analyses, brief definitions or explanations)
poems, novels, short stories, films, works of art	dissertations and theses (may also be primary)	encyclopedias (brief survey type articles)
dissertations and theses (may also be secondary)		
historical artifacts		
public documents, laws, treaties, court records		

INFORMATION TIMELINES

The distinction between *primary*, *secondary*, and *tertiary* sources can be understood by examining the timeline during which the information is created. An author presents an eyewitness account of an event in a newspaper; an architect designs a building; a researcher conducts a study of a disease; an artist creates a painting; Congress passes a law. These are the first stages of the information cycle—the primary sources. Following these firsthand accounts, secondary sources begin to appear in various media. The third phase in the information cycle occurs when information from both sources is indexed in bibliographies, online databases or other indexing services or is reviewed by various reviewing media.

Figure 11.6 illustrates the timeline for an important event.

Information Timeline

Event: Three Mile Island Nuclear Accident

On March 28, 1979, an incident described as a minor malfunction of a piece of equipment at the Three Mile Island nuclear reactor at Harrisburg, Pennsylvania, resulted in the worst nuclear accident in U.S. history.

↓ **PRIMARY:**

Within hours news reporters converged on the site and reports providing eyewitness accounts appeared in various media (newspaper, radio, and television).

EXAMPLE: Newspaper Article
Meltdown most feared of accidents. (1979, March 3). *The Patriot* (Harrisburg, PA), p. 1.

Videotapes and photographs taken at the time of the event are available from a number of places including Pennsylvania State University Library at Harrisburg, PA.

Transcripts of television and radio broadcasts can be located through an Internet search.

↓ **SECONDARY**

After a lapse of time, articles interpreting the event were published in periodicals, books, special reports and on the Internet.

EXAMPLE: Book
Gray, M. & Rosen, I. (1982). *The warning*. London: Norton.

EXAMPLE: Periodical Article:
Erikson, K. (1991, March). Radiation's lingering dread. *Bulletin of the Atomic Scientists*, 47 (2), 34–39.

↓ **TERTIARY**

Listings of publications dealing with the event and its aftermath can be found in numerous indexes, abstracts, databases and on the Internet.

EXAMPLE: Indexes and Databases
New York Times Index, *LexisNexis Academic*, Internet (For newspaper articles)

Applied Science and Technology Index (For technical articles in journals)

Engineering Index (print) or *Compendex* (electronic) (For scholarly articles, conference papers, and research reports)

Reader's Guide to Periodical Literature and *EBSCOhosts* (For popular articles aimed at a general audience)

Energy Citations Database (http://www.osti.gov/energycitations/) (For government reports)

POPULAR AND SCHOLARLY SOURCES

Books and periodical publications found in libraries vary as to the level of scholarship. Knowing something about the characteristics of each level—*popular* or *scholarly*—will help you identify the level of scholarship that is appropriate for your research.

Scholarly information is usually produced by scholars for education or research purposes. It is often peer reviewed before it is published. It is intended for scholars and students in special fields.

Popular material has been written in a language and format suitable for the general public as opposed to academics.

If you are looking for an analytical treatment of the topic "effects of television violence on viewers," you are more likely to find the information you need in the scholarly journal, *Psychological Bulletin*, rather than in the popular magazine, *Time*. In addition to popular magazines and scholarly journals, periodical literature also includes *trade/professional journals* that cover news and information about specific businesses or industries, usually published by a trade association or a business. Chapter 8 gives more detail about the types of periodical literature and the indexes and databases used to locate specific articles.

Popular and scholarly sources are not limited to periodical literature. Reference books, books that you locate in the library's catalog, and Internet sources may also be popular or scholarly. *World Book Encyclopedia*, for example, is a general encyclopedia intended for a wide audience; the *Encyclopedia of Psychology* is a specialized subject encyclopedia written by authors selected for their expertise in the field. The comparisons listed in Figure 11.7 will help you understand the differences between popular and scholarly literature.

THE SEARCH STRATEGY

As you begin your search for sources of information, it is easy to feel confused considering the vast amount and the different types of information available. Where do you start? A better question is, "How do you start?" The first thing you need to do is develop a search strategy, a plan of research. This is a three-step process:

1. determine appropriate search terms that will guide your research,

2. analyze the type of information sources you need, and

3. locate the sources.

DETERMINING APPROPRIATE SEARCH TERMS

The key to locating information in any of the library or Internet tools is the use of appropriate search terms. The more focused and specific your search, the more successful you will be in retrieving appropriate information.

- Compile a list of key terms based on your thesis statement and outline.

- Add any related terms that might lead to more information.

FIGURE **11.7**   Popular and scholarly literature: a comparison

	Popular	*Scholarly*
Purpose	To inform or entertain	To communicate research and scholarly ideas to the academic and professional communities
Intended audience	General public	Scholars, researchers, practitioners, or students in a particular field or discipline
Content	Covers a wide variety of public interest topics Brief articles—usually 1-5 pages.	Highly specialized topics Technical or analytical articles Long articles—often over 5 pages
Authors	Usually professional journalists or freelance writers	Experts or scholars (e.g., professors, researchers, specialists in their field)
Publishers	Commercial publishers	Professional associations, university presses, research organizations, and publishers who specialize in a particular field
Language	Language easy to understand No jargon or specialized terms	Specialized vocabulary and style of writing familiar to scholarly readers in the field (professors, researchers or students)
Documentation	Few, if any, cited references or bibliographies	Includes cited references
Advertisements	Contains advertisements	Usually none, but minimal if included
Evaluations	Rely on the publication's reputation among readers and its marketing success	Articles and books are usually peer reviewed, i.e., reviewed by a person or persons of similar or equal expertise to that of the author
Examples	*Time*; *US News and World Report*; *Sports Illustrated*; *PC Magazine*; *Rolling Stone*; *The World Almanac and Book of Facts 2006*; *If Life Is a Bowl of Cherries, What Am I Doing in the Pits?* (Book) by Erma Bombeck	*Psychological Bulletin*; *JAMA: The Journal of the American Medical Association*; *American Historical Review*; *Mental Measurements Yearbook*; *Modern Fiction Studies*; *The Impossibility of Religious Freedom* (book) by Winnifred F. Sullivan (Princeton University Press)

- Use the sources listed in Figure 11.3 to help you select keywords.

- Include words that have narrower or broader meanings than your original terms.

EXAMPLE

Broad term—television
Narrow term—television advertising
Narrower term—television advertising and children

ANALYZING INFORMATION NEEDS

Analyzing your information needs is best done by focusing on a set of questions that will help you determine the aspects of the topic you wish to explore.

- **TREATMENT OF TOPIC** Do you need facts? Opinions? Background Information? Statistics? Analysis? Do you need an in-depth treatment of the topic? Do you need an account of an event as it happened? *Primary* sources allow you to get as close to an event or an account as possible. Do you need analyses or interpretations? *Secondary* sources based on primary sources will provide these. For a research paper, a good rule of thumb is to choose both primary and secondary sources.

- **TIMELINESS** Is timeliness an issue? Do you need current information? Do you need a historical perspective? If your topic is scientific, you will probably need recent information. For example, research on avian flu will require the most recent information available. Research in the humanities is not usually dependent on current information. For example, a paper on the genre of science fiction literature does not require current publications.

- **FOCUS** Do you need a specific subject area or discipline such as humanities, social science, or science? For example, if you are researching the causes of eating disorders among teenagers, would you look for information in the medical field or would you look in the social and behavioral sciences?

- **LEVEL OF SCHOLARSHIP** Do you need brief facts, not backed by research? Do you need a description of an event? If so, you should use *popular* sources. If you need a more in-depth treatment of a topic, you should consult *scholarly* sources.

LOCATING INFORMATION SOURCES

You are now ready to locate the information sources that you will use in writing your research paper. Some of the materials you use will be located in the library in various formats such as paper, microform, CD-ROM and DVD. Others will be on the Internet. Figure 11.8 provides a basic guide to selecting appropriate materials. Later chapters of this book provide more detailed descriptions of the major sources to consult in the research process.

ASKING FOR HELP

Reference librarians can provide valuable assistance with research questions if they know what you are looking for. The key to getting assistance is asking the right questions.

FIGURE 11.8

Selecting appropriate sources

Guide to Selecting Sources		
Information	**Sources to Consult**	**Finding Aids**
Preliminary Ideas	Library of Congress Subject Headings magazine and journal articles	consult reference staff browse current periodicals Internet
Overview of Topic	general encyclopedias books periodicals	consult reference staff library catalog indexes and abstracts
Definitions	dictionaries	library catalog
Primary Sources	newspapers research reports manuscripts (archives) government publications	library catalog databases (e.g., LexisNexis Academic) Internet
Secondary Sources	books magazine and journal articles subject encyclopedias	library catalogs indexes and abstracts databases
Facts	almanacs and yearbooks statistics government publications	library catalogs statistical indexes Internet
Current Information	newspapers magazines and journals	indexes and abstracts databases (e.g., InfoTrac)
Historical Information	books encyclopedias and reference books periodicals	library catalog browse reference shelves indexes and abstracts
Evaluative Sources	book reviews biographies	indexes to book reviews Internet

GUIDELINES

Obtaining maximum help from the librarian

- Explain the purpose of the research.

- Give the assignment specifications—for example, length of paper, number of sources needed, and due date.

- Explain the level of difficulty of information you need—scholarly, technical, popular, easy-to-understand.

- Give the time framework—current, historical.

- Describe the kinds of sources needed—primary, secondary, or both.

- Ask for assistance for finding specific information that may be difficult to locate—statistics, dates, little-known facts.

EVALUATING SOURCES

Evaluate each source that you locate for its suitability and reliability.

ASK YOURSELF

- Is the information relevant to your thesis and the points covered in your outline (argumentative) . . . or is it relevant to the proposed research (objective/ analytical)?

- Is the information sufficiently up-to-date?

- Is there a later edition of the work?

- Is the source reliable?

- Does the work reflect a particular bias or prejudice?

TAKE AND DOCUMENT NOTES FROM SOURCES

In addition to what Chapter 4 provides, consider what Bolner, et al, suggest for helping you to document sources.

TAKING NOTES

As you examine each source, you should take notes on all the important information and sources you might want to use in your paper. The best way to take notes is to use separate note cards or uniform sheets of paper for each topic that you locate. (If you are using a word processor, you need only create a separate document for each topic.) Each note card or note document should contain a heading that is keyed to a heading in your outline. As you take notes, it is best to paraphrase or summarize the words of the author, although sometimes direct quotations are needed for emphasis or for authoritativeness. In either case it is important to retain the author's intended meaning. Note the page or pages on which you found the information. Include all the essential bibliographic information: author or editor's name, title of the work, series (if any), publisher, date, and place of publication. It is helpful to include the call numbers of books and periodicals and the URL (Internet address) of materials found on the Web in case you need to go back to these.

In academic research papers and in any other writing that includes ideas and facts gathered from other sources, the sources of the information must be clearly documented. To *document* a research paper means to acknowledge, or cite, the sources used or consulted. Failure to do so constitutes plagiarism. Another pitfall associated with research is the violation of *copyright laws*.

COMPOSE ANNOTATED BIBLIOGRAPHY

After the extensive research you do, you will need to hone in on the most useful and appropriate sources and begin actively reading and annotating them. Once you have identified the "for-sure" sources, you will need to complete an "Annotated Bibliography." This kind of writing requires that you provide the citation information for each source you are going to use, an abstract of what the source is about, and a statement that explains what the source is contributing to your overall project.

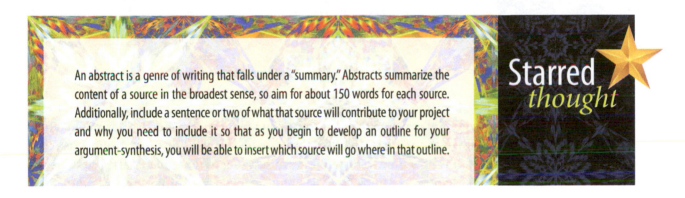

An abstract is a genre of writing that falls under a "summary." Abstracts summarize the content of a source in the broadest sense, so aim for about 150 words for each source. Additionally, include a sentence or two of what that source will contribute to your project and why you need to include it so that as you begin to develop an outline for your argument-synthesis, you will be able to insert which source will go where in that outline.

Starred *thought*

REVISE CONTROLLING IDEA AND OUTLINE

Just as with other genres you wrote, the writing process is always about revising. What happens when you research is the revision of your ideas: what you thought was important and what you now know is important. Thus, you will revise your initial thinking and focus to match your new thinking on the subject matter. The kaleidoscope has shifted and a new image appears. Take that as a sign of intellectual growth. You are shaping what you think as you write and discovering new ideas. This is the key point in research: your view changes and your thinking changes.

Consider what Bolner, et al, suggest for helping you to begin writing.

WRITING THE PAPER

Once you are satisfied that sufficient information has been gathered to support all the points in your outline (argumentative) or found previous, relevant research (objective/analytical), you can begin to write a first draft of the thesis paper or research proposal. Sort the notes so that they are grouped under topics that fit the headings in the outline. Allow yourself sufficient time for the actual writing. It may take several drafts to achieve the well-written paper or the logical research proposal. As you compose your paper, pay careful attention to all the elements of good writing: effective phrasing of ideas, good paragraph development, and logical flow of the paragraphs into a unified paper or research report.

Notice how research shapes how we view other texts. This is exactly what an argument-synthesis allows to happen. In academia, writers are meant to discover new connections that will lead to new ideas and new perspectives on a subject. The act of juxtaposing seemingly different texts allows for a turn of the kaleidoscope, and this allows writers and their readers to consider new possibilities!

WRITING THE FORMAL DRAFT

Once the large part of the research stage is complete, you will need to turn to the writing. You may find that you are missing some information, so you might return briefly to the research to fill-in that gap, but for the most part, your research is done. It is now time to turn to the synthesizing of those materials. Use strategies from Chapter 3, or implement new strategies you have discovered over the course of studying this textbook, to develop your first, working, rough draft.

To integrate texts into your writing, remember to QuAC! This is a tool for you to work actively with source material.

Writer: _____ Reader: _____

PEER-REVIEW OF ARGUMENT-SYNTHESIS DRAFT 1

1. Rate the strength of this paper's controlling idea.

5	4	3	2	1
Wow! Very insightful				*Boo! Lacks a controlling idea.*

2. What part of the argument-synthesis is the strongest? Why?

3. What part of the argument-synthesis is the weakest? Why?

4. At which point did you feel most interested in this argument-synthesis? Why?

5. At which point did you feel least interested? Explain.

6. Rate this paper's overall depth of analysis.

5	4	3	2	1
20,000 leagues deep!				*Shallow, surface.*

7. Where does the synthesis of texts fall short? Suggest what can be done.

8. What questions are you left with that need answered? Explain why.

9. How clearly do I express my ideas?

5	4	3	2	1
Crystal Clear.				*Muddy.*

Name: _____ Date: _____

REFLECTIONS: ARGUMENT-SYNTHESIS WRITING

Describe your writing process for this argument-synthesis. What strategies did you use? Why?

What did you find to be the hardest part about writing an argument-synthesis?

What did you find to be the easiest part about writing an argument-synthesis?

Describe how your process for writing this essay was different from or similar to writing a literary analysis.

Why might that be the case?

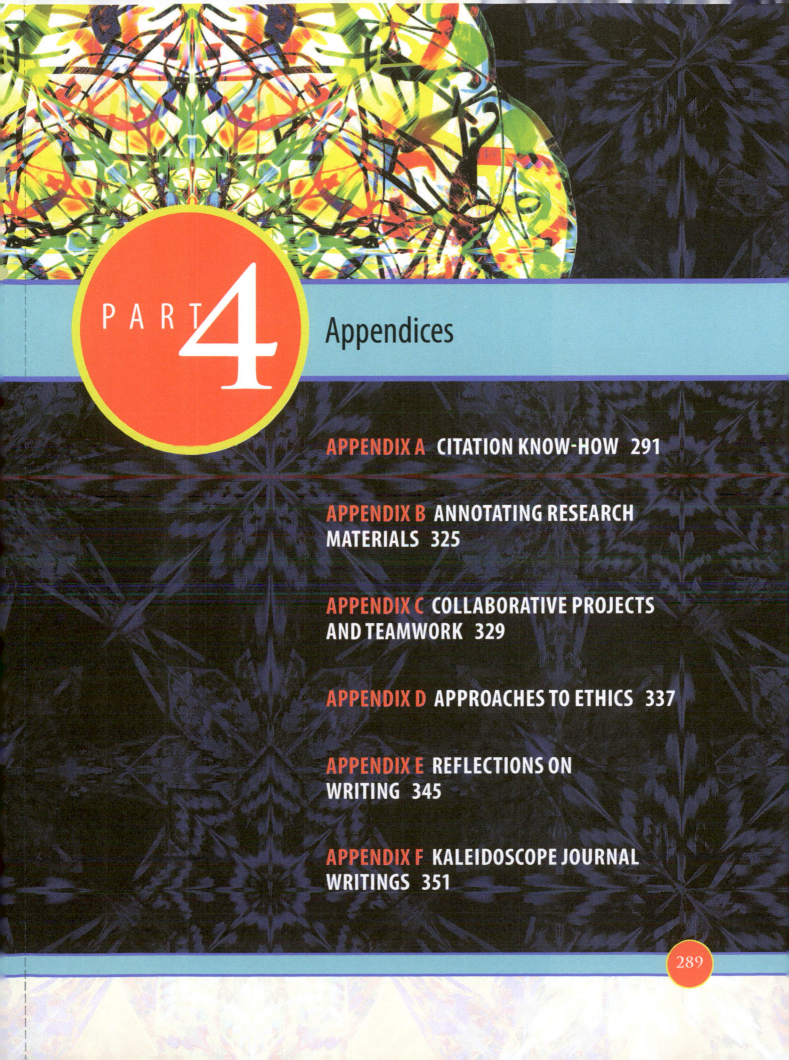

PART 4 Appendices

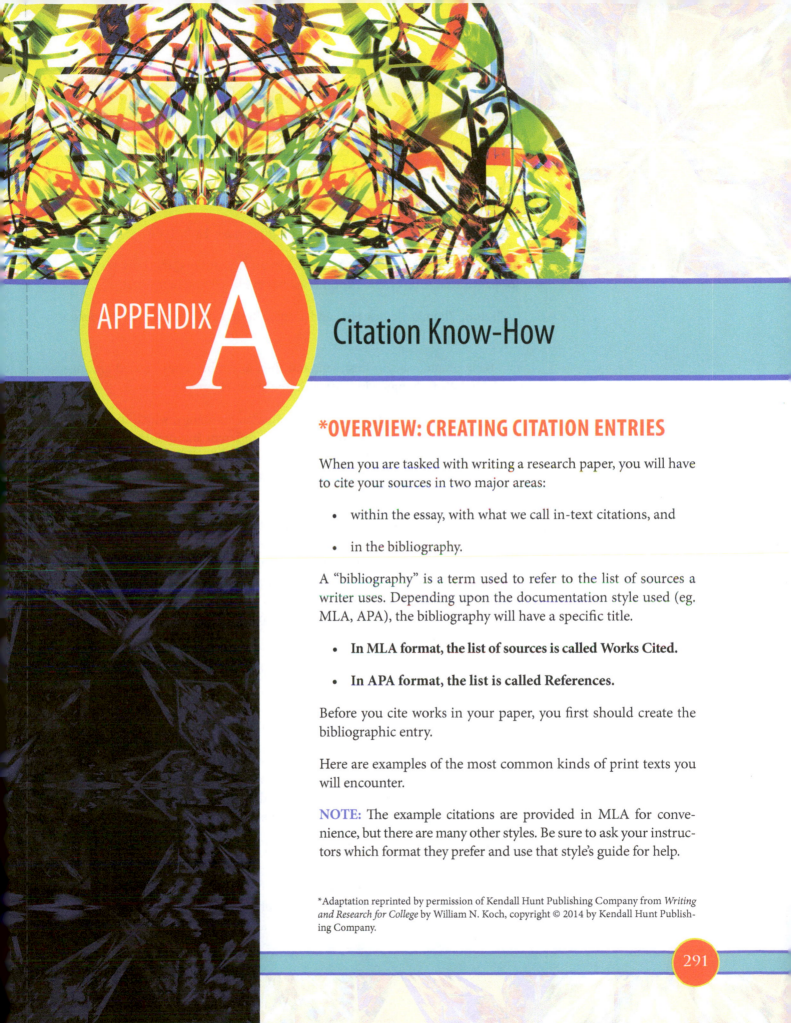

Citation Know-How

*OVERVIEW: CREATING CITATION ENTRIES

When you are tasked with writing a research paper, you will have to cite your sources in two major areas:

- within the essay, with what we call in-text citations, and

- in the bibliography.

A "bibliography" is a term used to refer to the list of sources a writer uses. Depending upon the documentation style used (eg. MLA, APA), the bibliography will have a specific title.

- **In MLA format, the list of sources is called Works Cited.**

- **In APA format, the list is called References.**

Before you cite works in your paper, you first should create the bibliographic entry.

Here are examples of the most common kinds of print texts you will encounter.

NOTE: The example citations are provided in MLA for convenience, but there are many other styles. Be sure to ask your instructors which format they prefer and use that style's guide for help.

*Adaptation reprinted by permission of Kendall Hunt Publishing Company from *Writing and Research for College* by William N. Koch, copyright © 2014 by Kendall Hunt Publishing Company.

ONE-AUTHOR BOOKS: The format for a single-author book is probably the one students know (and even Web site formats try to follow this format as closely as possible). The bibliography begins with the author's last name, then first name, followed by the book title. Then comes the name of publisher and the copyright year.

NOTE: Book titles are italicized; book chapters are put into quotation marks.

> Merton, Thomas. *Conjectures of a Guilty Bystander*. Holt, 1966.

BOOK WITH TWO OR THREE AUTHORS: List all the authors, but only the first author has the name reversed. The other names are listed first name first.

> Merton, Thomas, James Fox, and Daniel Berg. *Conjectures of Bystanders*. Trappist Press, 1988.

NOTE: Bibliographies begin flush left, and then any other lines needed are indented (also called a hanging indent), as in the above example.

BOOK BY AN EDITOR: The edited book is often an anthology, which the editor put together by selecting essays from a variety of different authors. The editor arranged the essays in a certain order and may have written an introduction. To cite the **anthology**, the first element is the editor's name, then the book title, name of publisher, and copyright year.

> Koch, Bill, editor. *The Ways of the World*. Holmstead, 2010.

A WORK FROM AN EDITED WORK (AN ANTHOLOGY): When you take one chapter or essay out of an anthology, you begin the entry with the name of the author of the essay, and you then give the name of the essay or chapter in the anthology, then the title of the anthology. The editor's name is placed after the book title. Then, you have publication information.

> Merton, Thomas. "The Bystander of Conjectures." *The Ways of the World*. Ed. Bill Koch. Holmstead, 2010.

NOTE: Chapter titles or article titles are NOT underlined or italicized. You put them in quotation marks.

BOOK WITH A TRANSLATOR: When you have a book written by a non-English writer that has been translated, you will need to cite the translator, but the bibliography entry begins with the writer's name.

> Watson, Bill. *The World and Its Ways*. Fred Wynn. House Steady, 2002.

TWO OR MORE BOOKS BY THE SAME AUTHOR: The first entry will give the author's name, with the rest of the bibliographical material, and then for the second and subsequent books, instead of writing the author's name, you supply three dashes and a period. List the books alphabetically by book title.

> Merton, Thomas. *The Seven Storey Mountain*. Giroux, 1948.

> ___. *Zen and Zen Masters*. Giroux, 1978.

BOOK OTHER THAN FIRST EDITION: You do not need to cite the edition of the book when it is the first edition, but for all editions after the first, mention the edition after the book title.

> Watson, Bill. *The World and Its Ways*. 4th ed., translated by Fred Wynn, House Steady, 2002.

THE FOLLOWING IS AN IMPORTANT CONVENTION TO APPLY TO ANTHOLOGIES: When you have **two or more articles from the same anthology**, you will need to make a bibliography for each article, as each article is by a different author. This means you will have to make at least three different entries, but there will be no repetition of information. Here is what you will need:

First, an entry for the edited anthology itself:

> Koch, Bill, editor. *Writers on the World's Way*. Nighttime Press, 2006.

Second, you will need a bibliography for each of the articles (chapters) that you used from that anthology, BUT each entry begins with the name of the author of that chapter, and then you include the chapter title in quotation marks. After the chapter title, you put only the last name of the editor and then the page numbers of that chapter. You DO NOT include the publisher information again.

> Sisson, Edward. "Teaching the Laws in Darwinism." Koch, pp. 89-99.

> Gudski, James. "Accept No Imitations: The Rivalries in Natural Law." Koch, pp. 100-125.

You would then list each entry alphabetically, by the first word of the bibliographic entry (which is ordinarily—as in this case—the last name of the author or editor). For example:

WORKS CITED

> A
> B
> C
> …………..

Gudski, James. "Accept No Imitations: The Rivalries in Natural Law." Koch, pp. 100-125.

H

I

J

Koch, Bill, ed. *Writers on the World's Way*. Nighttime Press, 2006.

L

M

N

…………..

Sisson, Edward. "Teaching the Laws in Darwinism." Koch, pp. 89-99.

T

U

V

…………..

To repeat, when citing TWO OR MORE works from an anthology,

- make an entry for each chapter author, and

- an entry for the anthology.

REMEMBER: Only the anthology entry has all the bibliographical information.

PERIODICALS

Here are some other common print texts known as periodicals. Periodicals include journals, magazines, and newspapers. What follows are *print* version examples formatted to MLA style.

There are several distinctions that you will need to make, the first being among the most important: determining the type of periodical you are citing.

DETERMINING THE KIND OF PERIODICAL YOU HAVE:

*Here's how to write a bibliographic entry for **popular magazines**:*

For POPULAR magazines the bibliography entry ALWAYS needs the DATE.

Example of WEEKLY popular periodical:

Lapham, Lewis. "Prairie Skies over Urban Smog." *Time* 12 Mar. 2005, pp. 2-3.

If a popular magazine is a MONTHLY periodical, you just use (of course) the month.

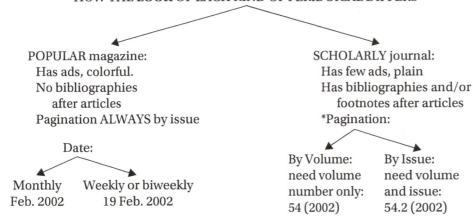

HOW THE **LOOK** OF EACH KIND OF PERIDOICAL DIFFERS

POPULAR magazine:
Has ads, colorful.
No bibliographies
after articles
Pagination ALWAYS by issue

Date:

Monthly
Feb. 2002

Weekly or biweekly
19 Feb. 2002

SCHOLARLY journal:
Has few ads, plain
Has bibliographies and/or
footnotes after articles
*Pagination:

By Volume:
need volume
number only:
54 (2002)

By Issue:
need volume
and issue:
54.2 (2002)

Example of a MONTHLY popular periodical:

> Buchanan, Pat. "Republicans and Demos." *Harper's* Feb. 2005, p. 53.

Note: Months are abbreviated except May, June, and July.

Some names of popular magazines are: *Time, The New Republic, Harper's.*

Here's how to write a bibliographic entry for **scholarly journals***:*

Note: The distinction you must make is whether the journal is PAGINATED by issue or by volume.

If a journal is **paginated by volume**, the bibliography **does not need an** *issue* **number**. Why? Because there is only one page 10 or page 50 in the volume.

This means that when you go to, say, the 1990 volume of *Journal of Television*, you will see that the late pages have high page numbers. That's because each issue's first page begins with the number where the last issue left off.

Example of bibliographical entry for journal paginated by VOLUME:

> Ryan, Katy. "Revolutionary Schlock." *Journal of Television*, vol. 34, 1990, pp. 451-55.

If a scholarly journal is **paginated by issue,** the bibliography **MUST include the issue number**. Why? Because now you will find "page 10" 12 times in the volume. That is, each issue begins with page 1.

Example of bibliographical entry for a journal paginated by ISSUE:

> Ryan, Katy. "Schlock for the Scholar." *Journal of Scholars* 44:3, vol. 44, no.3, 2000, pp. 44-66.

Some names of SCHOLARLY periodicals: *Journal of Popular Culture, American Quarterly.*

OVERVIEW: IN-TEXT CITATIONS:
HOW TO CITE SOURCES WITHIN THE ESSAY

Now that you have your bibliographic *entry*, you are ready to cite sources in your paper.

*BASIC RULES

Whether you summarize, paraphrase, or quote a source, you must cite sources. To repeat: Even when you summarize or paraphrase sources, you must cite the source of that information. That is, you must identify your author by name and give a page number (when the source is a paper product).

Two elements are required in a sentence that has information from your source:

- The first word that begins a bibliography entry in the Works Cited list (most often an author's last name).

- The page number which is put in parenthesis.

Note: In APA, for example, you will also need the publication year.

Here are three different ways to cite a source **in-text**.

1. In your writing, provide the author's name first as part of a summary or paraphrase, as in this example:

   Allan Bloom suggests that rock's roots are in Plato's philosophy (24).

2. Or, in your writing, in connection with a quotation, as in this example:

   The professor of political philosophy, Allan Bloom, contends, "Rock music has its roots in Greek thought" (24).

3. Or, in your writing, provide the author's last name in parentheses, as in this example:

   Rock music seemed to emerge from Plato (Bloom 24).

NOTE: If you mention the sources name in your sentence, you DON'T need to repeat the name in parentheses.

In all cases, the reader understands that the Works Cited page will contain—under the Bs—"Bloom" as the first word in the bibliography.

Provide the first *and* last name of the author first before you use only the last name. After you use the full name, only *last* names are needed. If you use more than one source, be sure it is clear which author are are using *each time*.

Starred *thought*

PUNCTUATION CONCERNS FOR SOURCES CITED WITHIN YOUR PARAGRAPHS:

1. No matter how you present information from you source in a paragraph, when the sentence ends with a parenthetical citation, there is a period after the parenthetical cite, and NEVER before it.

    The period always goes after the parentheses, even with a direct quotation:

    a. "Rock music was born out of classical ashes" (Bloom 24).

    b. "Rock music," Bloom feels, "was born out of classical ashes" (24).

    c. The music of the 60s seems to be linked to classical music (Bloom 24).

    d. "Rock music was born out of classical ashes," observes Bloom (24).

    e. Music of today, what our kids like, seems to have been "born out of the ashes of classical music" (Bloom 24).

2. Question marks and exclamation points are retained within quotes, but still a period follows the parentheses:

    a. "Rock music was born out of classical ashes?" (Bloom 24).

    b. "Rock music was born out of classical ashes!" (Bloom 24).

NOTE ON THE USE OF COMMAS WITHIN PARENTHESES:

1. In MLA, you do not put a comma between the author name and the page number when both are in parentheses. In APA, you do use commas between the bits of information.

2. However, when your Works Cited list has more than one work by a writer, you can cite the book title—in abbreviated form—in parentheses.

3. Then you do use a comma between the author's last name and the book title—but NO comma between book title and page number:

a. The music of the 60s seems to be linked to classical music (Bloom, *Closing* 24).

4. Another option: You could mention the book title in your sentence:

a. In his book *The Closing of the American Mind*, Allan Bloom claims that rock music has roots in classical music (24).

THE USE OF *THAT* BEFORE A QUOTE:

1. Sometimes it is logical to not use a tagline before a quote but let the grammar of the quote complete the grammar that you began in your sentence.

2. When that occurs, you will likely precede the quote with the word *that* and no comma and so construct this kind of sentence:

Example: Koch believes that Frye was correct when he wrote **that** "before too long, all adults will get a CLEW" (23).

If there is a tagline verb just before *that*, then drop *that* and preserve the comma and capitalized first word of the quote.

Example: Koch believes that Frye was correct when he wrote, "Before too long, all adults will get a CLEW" (23).

THE USE OF COLON BEFORE A QUOTE:

1. When you precede a quotation with several words and the words are an independent clause, use a colon instead of a comma:

a. Frye's overall viewpoint expresses several key features: "The university functions to produce intellects that possess a universality of knowledge, combined with astute analytical skills and humane but tempered affections" (33).

*Adaptation reprinted by permission of Kendall Hunt Publishing Company from *Writing and Research for College* by William N. Koch, copyright © 2014 by Kendall Hunt Publishing Company.

FRAMING SOURCES

What follows are options for framing sources in your writing. Experiment with them with the goal of developing your own style for writing. Keep in mind, too, that how you write in one context may require a different style than in another.

INTRODUCTORY PHRASES

Academic writing is often marked by phrases that are typical of academics. For example, here are some *typical* introductions to quotes in writing:

- According to "author's name," "Insert quoted materials and citation."

- In "title of work," the author writes that "insert quotes materials and citation."

- "Author's name" creates an interesting point when he argues, "insert quoted materials and citation."

> All disciplines require that you properly and accurately credit source materials, but the documentation style will differ. Additionally, there are a number of variations for framing sources, and these variations are what define a writer's style. In some disciplines, such as English, a *great* variety in style and sentence structure is valued; however, most disciplines welcome *some* variety.
>
> **Starred** *thought*

I. To introduce direct quotes, using quotation marks followed by the appropriate in-text citation and style, try:

According to X, " "
X writes that " "
In X's essay, s/he writes that " "
In the essay, *title of essay in quotation marks*, X maintains that " "
X complicates matters further when s/he writes, " "
As the literary critic X puts it, " "
Most important to X's argument is " "
Many readers should find X's point interesting: " "
X agrees/disagrees when she writes, " "

II. To explain what the quotes mean, try:

What X is saying is _____
In other words, _____
In making this comment, X argues that _____
X's point is that _____
X is insisting that _____
The essence of X's argument is that _____

> Remember, you are including these statements in your own prose, so you will have to make the appropriate choices based upon what you are writing about and what you are trying to do with the information you have. You will also modify the citation based upon the documentation style you are using.
>
> **Starred** *thought*

III. Instead of using "writes" or "says," you may want to use some of the following options:

Verbs for making claims/argument points or creating neutral meanings:
argue, articulate, assert, believe, claim, depict, describe, elaborate, emphasize, expand, explain, express, identify, insist, itemize, observe, outline, promulgate, remind us, report, state, suggest

Verbs for expressing agreement:
acknowledge, admire, agree, celebrate the fact that, concede, corroborate, do not deny, endorse, extol, praise, reaffirm, support, verify

Verbs for disagreeing or questioning or to create negative meaning:
complain, complicate, contend, contradict, debate, deny, deplore the tendency to, disavow, negate, nullify, question, refuse, refute, reject, renounce, repudiate

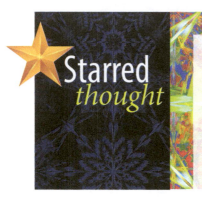

Starred *thought*

Word choice is very important because words have meaning. If a writer simply "states" a point, then she may not necessarily "contradict" anything. It is also unethical to say that a source "refuses" to acknowledge an idea when the source is simply "itemizing" the ideas. Choose words carefully so that you provide some variety yet remain honest and ethical to what the text is actually doing. This is also part of writing ethics. You must allow other writers to hold the views they do; you can disagree, argue with, or discredit them, but you first have to present them and their ideas truthfully and accurately.

*VARIATIONS WITH THE USAGE OF SIGNAL PHRASES (ALSO CALLED TAGLINES)

PLACEMENT OF SIGNAL PHRASES USING AUTHOR'S NAME

Always introduce a quotation with a signal phrase, but vary the placement of that signal phrase.

SIGNAL PHRASE BEFORE A QUOTATION:

Allan Bloom admits, "When it comes down to it, I liked some of that early rock music, like ol' Bill Haley and the Comets" (22).

SIGNAL PHRASE WITHIN A QUOTATION:

"I liked to imagine, " admits Allan Bloom, " that some of that early rock music, like ol' Bill Haley and the Comets will live on forever" (22).

*Adaptation reprinted by permission of Kendall Hunt Publishing Company from *Writing and Research for College* by William N. Koch, copyright © 2014 by Kendall Hunt Publishing Company.

NOTE: Put the signal phrase early in a quote, after a few words. **Avoid putting the tagline between sentences that you are quoting.**

NO: "I like rock and roll because of the beat," notes Bloom. "It tends to lift my spirits" (44).

YES: "I like rock and roll," notes Bloom, "because of the beat. It tends to lift my spirits" (44).

SIGNAL PHRASE AFTER A QUOTATION:

> "I liked some of that early rock music, like ol' Bill Haley and the Comets," Allan Bloom admits (22).

In addition to those three basic signal phrase placements, try to use the following variations.

PLACEMENT OF SIGNAL PHRASES USING AUTHOR'S NAME AND CREDENTIALS

Signal phrase at **beginning** of sentence, mentioning the author's credentials:

> Martha Bayles, who writes on cultural issues, explained, "For my title, I borrow[ed] the name from a song written by Johnny Green and most famously recorded by Coleman Hawkins in 1939" (59).

Signal phrase **within a** quotation, mentioning the author's credentials:

> "For my title," the cultural critic Martha Bayles explained, "I borrowed the name from a song written by Johnny Green and most famously recorded by Coleman Hawkins in 1939" (59).

Signal phrase at the **end** of a quotation that mentions her credentials and deletes part of the quotation, using ellipses:

> "For my title, I borrow the name from . . . Coleman Hawkins," wrote Martha Bayles, a critic of American culture (59).

SIGNAL PHRASES FOR PARAPHRASES AND SUMMARIES

When you paraphrase or summarize material from a source, you can mention the author's name in your writing:

> Hacker suggests that you put the signal phrase in different places within the quotation and that you use different terms in referring to the source (582).

When you paraphrase or summarize material, you can put the author's name in parentheses:

> Resist the urge to use a lot of long quotations linked together by a few of your own words because that style doesn't make for smooth writing (Hacker 582).

You will find that often you will structure the quotation so no comma is needed before the quotation:

> Hacker suggests that you don't want to use a lot of quotations using "your own words only for connecting passages" (582).

YOUR SENTENCE STRUCTURES HAVE TO BE DIFFERENT?

Yes! Remember that reader expectations inform your writing choices, so you should vary the structure of sentences. Here are some revision options:

- If a sentence is in active voice, make it passive voice.

- If a sentence is in passive voice, make it active voice.

- Reverse the sequence of information.

- Change verbs into nominalizations.

- Change nominalizations, participles, gerunds, and infinitives into verbs.

As you can see, there are many ways to create variation in sentence structure, and this is essential when you are paraphrasing. When you paraphrase, remember:

- Every sentence should be rephrased and reworded.

- Rephrased sentences can be longer or shorter than the original sentences.

- Sentences you create must have different structures than the original sentence structures, not just different words.

NOTE ON APA FORMAT

The social sciences ordinarily follow the citation format of the American Psychological Association called APA style. This format highlights the year that a piece is published because with the sciences, it is important to stay current with the latest research, just in case some long-held tenet is overthrown. (Such concerns are not as prominent in the humanities, where some insights into life seem to have already withstood the "test" of time.)

For in-text citations in APA style, keep the following in mind:

1. Usually just the last name is cited with even the first reference to a source.

2. Then the year of publication is placed right after the source's last name, in parentheses.

   a. **Example:** Benjamin (1982) offered an explanation based on a series of tests he ran in 1981.

3. When you have a quotation, the page number is often given and "p." is used in parentheses.

   a. **Example:** Benjamin (1982) concluded, "Adults can get through the period of transition if they detach their beliefs from their understanding of them" (p. 182).

For bibliographies:

1. The list of sources in APA format is called "References."

2. There are differences between APA and MLA.

   a. The year is placed right after the author's name.

   b. Only the first word of the title is capitalized and the first word that follows a colon in a subtitle.

   c. The author's first name is always abbreviated with initials.

   Example: Benjamin, A. (1982). *Liberal education is adult education.* New York: Bantam.

QUACING

When using outside research materials, whether they are newspapers, interviews, lyrics, scenes from a film, or passages from a journal article, it is important that writers use that material not to replace their own ideas but to supplement them, to enrich their own ideas, or maybe even to change or revise their own ideas. Another way to think about using sources is to see what others have written or said about a topic and then have a conversation with them by integrating or synthesizing their ideas into our own writing. There are many reasons why writers incorporate others' ideas, and here are just a few of them:

- to support an idea they are making or to provide a counterargument

- to provide important information from an expert in the field of inquiry

- to acknowledge an interesting, useful, or opposing view on a topic or an issue

- to establish a context for how their own ideas fit into the conversation already in progress

To incorporate outside sources successfully into your own writing and prevent the dreaded "dropped-in" quote, you need to work actively and critically with the source material. One way to do this is by directly quoting a passage and then writing *something significant* about it. An easy way to remember how to do this is to "**QuAC**": **Qu**ote the text, **A**nalyze its meaning, and **C**onnect it to your overall point.

Starred *thought*

This acronym provides a sort of checklist for working with sourced materials. Use it in your writing to help you work with a source actively and honestly!

DIRECTIONS:

1. **QUOTE:** Choose a source that you are using for your essay. From that source, choose a passage, no longer than five sentences (otherwise, you will have too much to work with at one time), and type it word for word, following MLA guidelines.

   Note: When you type the passage into your Word document, count how many lines you end up with. If the passage is *four or fewer* typed lines, then simply use quotation marks around the quote, and transition into the quote by introducing the author or by using some other introductory phrase, following MLA guidelines. If the quote is *more than four* typed lines, then you need to use "block quote" format.

2. **ANALYZE, LEVEL 1:** Look at the passage in and of itself. What important words or phrases stand out for you? Does the author have a peculiar understanding of the words/phrases? How does the author use them in the passage you are quoting?

   ANALYZE, LEVEL 2: Look at how the passage fits into the author's overall essay. What seems to be the purpose of this passage? (Does it highlight an important point? Does it provide an interesting perspective or a valid point on the issue at hand? Does it include a vivid example as support? Does it provide thoughtful insight into the issue?)

3. **CONNECT:** Finally, what are you learning from the author's passage? OR How does this passage help you to understand your own thinking on the issue at hand? OR Why is it important enough for you to include in your own writing?

When you **QuAC**, you are not answering all of these questions. These are merely guiding questions to help you think about what is significant and to help you analyze the significance of it so that it has a meaning and purpose in your own writing.

Although an incomplete essay, what follows is an excerpt from a larger essay that uses MLA document design and documentation style to demonstrate these strategies.

Student's Name

Professor's Name

Course

Date

Martin Frobisher's Quest for the "Other" Language of Power

Perhaps Martin Frobisher is known more for seeking a northwest passage to China than for having notoriously kidnapped several Eskimos during his voyages to the Arctic. In his multiple voyages to find fame and fortune, he—among many of his contemporaneous explorers—encountered many new world peoples whom explorers then textually inscribed and contained in official travel journals. In an excerpt from a 1578 entry, Frobisher described his encounter with the Arctic landscape where, "not seeing anything [there] worth further discovery, the country seeming barren and full of ragged mountains, and in most parts covered with snow[,]" he and his men began their colonial conquest, "ma[king] a column or cross of stones heaped up of a good height together in good sort, and solemnly sounded a trumpet, and said certain prayers kneeling about the ensign" (891). This transplantation of a miniature European-Christian community upon foreign soil foreshadows the more ominous cultural domination into the New World and onto its peoples.

As Frobisher's crew encountered "certain of the country people on the top of Mount Warwick," they exchange certain items between the two groups:

Our men gave them pins and points and such trifles as they had. And they likewise bestowed on our men two bow cases and such things as they had. They earnestly desired our men to go up into their country, and our men offered them like kindness aboard our ships, but neither part (as it seemed) admitted or trusted the other's courtesy. (Frobisher 891)

Here, Frobisher described an apparently friendly exchange between strangers, which seemed to be a neutral, cultural exchange—the offering of each culture's idea of "gifts," an attempt to negotiate cultural understanding. However, as the narrative continues, this negotiation lacked the sincerity of simple, benign sharing of cultural customs. Amused by the explorers' appearance, the "savages," as Frobisher described them, gestured for the travelers to stay a while longer, which prompts the general and the captain "forcibly to bring them aboard" their ship with the feigned acts of friendship, pretending to "bestow certain toys and apparel upon the one, and so to dismiss him with all arguments of courtesy, and retain the other for an interpreter" (Frobisher 892). Frobisher and his men's inability to access the Arctic language—hence, an inability to understand fully the habits of the Arctic people, their strengths as well as their weaknesses, navigation of the land, or the climatic norms—prompts their abrupt violence to gain access to this culture through its language, a powerful tool in controlling and manipulating information.

Work Cited

Frobisher, Martin. "From *A true discourse of the late voyages of discovery, for the finding of a passage to Cathay by the Northwest, under the conduct of Martin Frobisher.*" *The Norton Anthology of English Literature*, editors M. H. Abrams and Stephen Greenblatt, 7th ed. Norton, 2000, pp. 890-4.

…

Yellow: Quoted material
Green: Citation requirements
Blue: Setting up quoted material; contextualizing
Grey: Analysis and connecting to overall point

*MLA AND APA CITATIONS

HOW TO FORMAT IN-TEXT CITATIONS

GENERAL RULES

For citing sources within your text, write a citation within parentheses:

> MLA: (**Jones 12**)
> last name plus page number—no comma
> **APA: (Jones, 2011)**
> **last name plus year of publication—use comma**
> **(Jones, 2011, p. 12) or (Jones, 2011, para. 13)**
> **for quotations or specific references, add page or paragraph**

For referring to sources, use present-tense signal phrases for MLA; use past-tense or present-perfect signal phrases with APA.

> MLA: Ortiz **claims** that
> (keep signal phrase in **present** tense)

*Adaptation reprinted by permission of Kendall Hunt Publishing Company from *The Less Is More Handbook* by Larry Edgerton, copyright © 2012 by Kendall Hunt Publishing Company.

APA: Ortiz ==claimed== that

Ortiz *has claimed* that

(keep signal phrase in ==past tense== or *present perfect*)

GUIDE TO FORMATTING IN-TEXT CITATIONS

SPECIFIC RULES

All your in-text citations won't be a simple author and page (MLA) or author and year (APA). Complexities develop putting together various combinations–one author, more than one author, unknown author, etc.–with various kinds of publications–book, anthology, the Bible, e-mail, etc.

Look for this critical difference:

A. The author's name is *not* stated in the text

or

B. The author's name *is* stated in the text

MLA AND APA

A. The Author's Name Is *Not* Stated in the Text

1. One Author Not Stated in-text
2. Two or More Sources by Same Author Not Stated in-text
3. Two or Three Authors Not Stated in-text (MLA)
4. Two Authors Not Stated in-text (APA)
5. Four or More Authors Not Stated in-text (MLA)
6. Three to Five Authors Not Stated in-text (APA)
7. Six or More Authors Not Stated in-text (APA)
8. An Organization as Group Author Not Stated in-text
9. Two or More Separate Sources Not Stated in-text
10. Nonprint (Web, etc.) Author Not Stated in-text
11. Lecture or Public Presentation Author Not Stated in-text
12. Personal Interview, Telephone Interview, or E-mail Author Not Stated in-text
13. Republished Author Not Stated in-text
14. Author of Multivolume Work Not Stated in-text
15. Author in Anthology Not Stated in-text
16. Unknown Author Not Stated in-text
17. A Religious Work (Bible, Qur'an, etc.): Unknown Author Not Stated in-text
18. An Indirect Source: Author Not Stated in-text
19. Encyclopedia or Other Reference Book: Author Not Stated in-text
20. A Long Quotation: Author Not Stated in-text

B. The Author's Name *Is* Stated in the Text

21. One Author Stated in-text
22. Two or More Sources by Same Author Stated in-text
23. Two or Three Authors Stated in-text (MLA)
24. Two Authors Stated in-text (APA)
25. Four or More Authors Stated in-text (MLA)
26. Three to Five Authors Stated in-text (APA)
27. Six or More Authors Stated in-text (APA)
28. An Organization as Group Author Stated in-text
29. Two or More Separate Sources Stated in-text
30. Nonprint (Web, etc.) Author Stated in-text
31. Lecture or Public Presentation Author Stated in-text
32. Personal Interview, Telephone Interview, or E-mail Author Stated in-text
33. Republished Author Stated in-text
34. Author of Multivolume Work Stated in-text
35. Author in Anthology Stated in-text
36. Unknown Author Stated in-text
37. A Religious Work (Bible, Qur'an, etc.): Unknown Author Stated in-text
38. An Indirect Source: Author Stated in-text
39. Encyclopedia or Other Reference Book: Author Stated in-text
40. A Long Quotation: Author Stated in-text

A. The Author's Name Is *Not* Stated in the Text

1. One Author Not Stated in-text

    MLA: The rising whooping crane population has encountered several "life-threatening setbacks" (Elliott 47).

    For APA, use *p.* plus page number for quoted words but also specific (but unquoted) references to a text.

    APA: The rising whooping crane population has encountered several "life-threatening setbacks" (Elliott, 2012, p. 47).

2. Two or More Sources by Same Author Not Stated in-text

    For MLA, use a short version of title in citation to distinguish source from author's other works.

    MLA: The newest models will be "accessible from your cell phone" (Dvorsky, "Appliances" 26).

    For APA, if more than one publication by author in the same year, letter the sources in the citation and in References.

APA: The newest models will be "accessible from your cell phone" (Dvorsky, 2012a, p. 26).

3. **Two or Three Authors Not Stated in Text (MLA)**

MLA: Nineteenth-century artist William Daniell undertook a series of sketching voyages around the coast of Great Britain to gain admittance to the Royal Academy (Harkins and Stafford 18).

4. **Two Authors Not Stated in Text (APA)**

Use the & to replace *and* in citation.

APA: Nineteenth-century artist William Daniell undertook a series of sketching voyages around the coast of Great Britain to gain admittance to the Royal Academy (Harkins & Stafford, 1997).

5. **Three or More Authors Not Stated in Text (MLA)**

Use the first author plus *et al.* (without italics).

MLA: Passing a single-payer system will cause a dramatic fall in insurance costs (Bobbs et al. 184-86).

6. **Three to Five Authors Not Stated in Text (APA)**

List all authors in first citation; in later citations, use first author plus *et al.* (without italics). Use & to replace *and* in citation.

APA: Passing a single-payer system will cause a dramatic fall in insurance costs (Bobbs, Fitch, Gunderman, & Hernandez, 2005).

7. **Six or More Authors Not Stated in Text (APA)**

APA: An investigation of Milwaukee's redlining has revealed a sordid history of racial intolerance (Henshaw et al., 2010).

8. **An Organization as Group Author Not Stated in Text**

MLA: Malnutrition has ravaged the sub-Saharan continent (World Health Organization 43).

For APA, in first citation, spell out group author with bracketed abbreviation [WHO]; in later citations, abbreviate: (WHO, 2008).

APA: Malnutrition has ravaged the sub-Saharan continent (==World Health Organization [WHO], 2008==).

9. **Two or More Separate Sources Not Stated in Text**

For both MLA and APA, separate with semicolon. Alphabetize sources.

MLA: Two simultaneous studies both point out that Ned Rorem made "major creative breakthroughs" while living in Africa (==Claussen 313; McBride and Peters 128==).

For APA, in parenthetical citation, use *&* instead of *and* when referring to paired authors.

APA: Two simultaneous studies both point out that Ned Rorem made "major creative breakthroughs" while living in Africa (==Claussen, 2011, p. 313; McBride & Peters, 2011, p. 128==).

10. **Nonprint (Web, etc.) Author Not Stated in Text**

Cite page number if using a PDF format; otherwise, identify according to available identifiers:

For MLA, author or title and/or section (*sec.* or *secs.*) or paragraph number (*par.* or *pars.*) following a heading.

MLA: Monopoly is no doubt Parker Brothers' most famous game from the 1930s (=="Great Depression Games," Parker Brothers heading, par. 6==).

For APA, author or title and/or section (*section* or *sections*) or paragraph number (*para.* or *paras.*) following a heading.

APA: Monopoly is no doubt Parker Brothers' most famous game from the 1930s (=="Great Depression Games," 2012, Parker Brothers heading, para. 6==).

11. **Lecture or Public Presentation Author Not Stated in Text**

For both MLA and APA, use name of lecturer or presenter. If more than one lecture or presentation, use identifying date.

MLA: Istanbul as a source of romantic imagery has made its way into a number of spy novels (==Baldridge, 9 Sept. 2012==).

APA: Istanbul as a source of romantic imagery has made its way into a number of spy novels (==Baldridge, 2012, September 9==).

12. **Personal Interview, Telephone Interview, or E-mail Author Not Stated in Text**

For MLA, use author's last name. If more than one communication from same source, use identifying date.

MLA: Significant advances have been made in treating macular degeneration with blood-vessel inhibitors (Stanton-Crosby, 24 June 2009).

For APA, any nonretrievable source like e-mail or personal interview is cited within the text but not included in References. Use author's initials and don't invert name. Identify as *personal communication* (no italics) with date.

APA: Significant advances have been made in treating macular degeneration with blood-vessel inhibitors (C. K. Stanton-Crosby, personal communication, June 24, 2009).

13. **Republished Author Not Stated in Text**

For MLA and APA, with a text that has gone through many editions, give the page number of the text consulted but also a chapter, part, or line number.

MLA: In *Gulliver's Travels*, Gulliver says of a farmer whom he encounters, "[He] by this time was convinced I must be a rationale Creature" (Swift 87; pt. 2, ch. 1).

For APA, with a text that has gone through many editions, also give first publication date as well as date of text consulted. (Abbreviate *Part* but not *Chapter*.)

APA: In *Gulliver's Travels*, Gulliver says of a farmer whom he encounters, "[He] by this time was convinced I must be a rationale Creature" (Swift 1735/1976, Pt. 2, Chapter 1, p. 87).

14. **Author of Multivolume Work Not Stated in Text**

For MLA, give both volume and page number (don't write *volume* or *page*).

MLA: We are told, "Among our Egyptians there was one called Ali Effendi, a captain, who complained of heart disease" (Stanley 2: 226).

For APA, give both volume and page number (but write *Vol.* and *p.*).

APA: We are told, "Among our Egyptians there was one called Ali Effendi, a captain, who complained of heart disease" (Stanley, 1890, Vol. 2, p. 226).

15. **Author in Anthology Not Stated in Text**

For both MLA and APA, use the author of the piece consulted, not the editor of the anthology; use the page number from the anthology.

MLA: "Swamp Search" is typical of the crime stories published in *The Black Lizard Anthology of Crime* for pulp lines like "She had me all clobbered, but I wanted her worse than ever" (Whittington 33).

For APA, with a text that has gone through many editions, also give first publication date as well as date of text consulted.

APA: "Swamp Search" is typical of the crime stories published in *The Black Lizard Anthology of Crime* for pulp lines like "She had me all clobbered, but I wanted her worse than ever" (Whittington, 1957/1987, p. 33).

16. **Unknown Author Not Stated in Text**

For MLA, use full or short form of a title.

MLA: The nursing home industry often escapes "rigorous oversight" ("Nursing Home Laws Needed" 2).

For APA, shorten a title to two or three words, leaving out *The*, *A*, and *An*. Use quotation marks or italics as appropriate; capitalize key words for parenthetical citation but not for References.

APA: The nursing home industry often escapes "rigorous oversight" ("Nursing Home Laws," 2009, p. 2).

17. **A Religious Work (Bible, Qur'an, etc.): Unknown Author Not Stated in Text**

For MLA and APA, use the edition/translation plus book, chapter, and verse. Spell out names in text, but in citation, abbreviate books with long names.

MLA: The reader is given yet another metaphor: "Our skin is as hot as an oven with the burning heat of famine" (*The Holy Bible, New Revised Standard Version*, Lam. 5.10).

For APA, cite classical work like the Bible in the text but not in References; no page numbers required because such texts are normally numbered; don't italicize.

APA: The reader is given yet another metaphor: "Our skin is as hot as an oven with the burning heat of famine"(The Holy Bible, New Revised Standard Version, Lam. 5:10).

18. **An Indirect Source: Author Not Stated in Text**

For MLA, use *qtd. in* ("quoted in") to show that your source is quoting or paraphrasing another source.

MLA: Hamwell often insists that, in the words of the famous Irish playwright, "I can resist everything except temptation" (qtd. in Murray 334).

For APA, use *as cited in* to show that your source is quoting or paraphrasing another source.

APA: Hamwell often insists that, in the words of the famous Irish playwright, "I can resist everything except temptation" (as cited in Murray, 1982, p. 334).

19. **Encyclopedia or Other Reference Book: Author Not Stated in Text**

For both MLA and APA, if the reference book doesn't provide the author of an entry, put the entry title in quotations (and alphabetize by title in Works Cited or References). Don't use page numbers for reference books that list entries alphabetically.

MLA: The history note on the etymology of the word reveals the tree's origins in the Middle East ("Lemon").

APA: The history note on the etymology of the word reveals the tree's origins in the Middle East ("Lemon," 1992).

20. **A Long Quotation: Author Not Stated in Text**

For MLA, set off quotations longer than four typed lines:

- indent *one-half inch* from flush left
- double-space
- don't use quotation marks unless the passage quotes a quotation
- don't indent the first line unless (1) the passage is longer than one paragraph and (2) the first paragraph in the original is indented
- indent each new paragraph *one-fourth inch*
- place a period at the end of the quotation and then one space after, type the parenthetical citation: author and page number (no period follows)

> It may turn out that historians will credit Algeria for the recent unrest in the Middle East:
>
> > On January 5, young protestors in Algiers, Oran, and other major cities blocked roads, attacked police stations and burned stores in demonstrations against soaring food prices. Other concerns–high unemployment, pervasive corruption, lack of housing–also aroused their ire, but food costs provided the original impulse. As the epicenter of youthful protest moved elsewhere . . . the food price issue was subordinated . . . but it never disappeared. (Klare 7-8)

For APA, set off quotations forty words or more:

- indent *one-half inch* from flush left
- double-space

- don't use quotation marks unless the passage quotes a quotation
- indent each new paragraph one more *one-half inch*
- place a period at the end of the quotation and then the parenthetical citation: author, date, and page number (no period follows)

> It may turn out that historians will credit Algeria for the recent unrest in the Middle East:
>
> > On January 5, young protestors in Algiers, Oran, and other major cities blocked roads, attacked police stations and burned stores in demonstrations against soaring food prices. Other concerns–high unemployment, pervasive corruption, lack of housing–also aroused their ire, but food costs provided the original impulse. As the epicenter of youthful protest moved elsewhere . . . the food price issue was subordinated . . . but it never disappeared. (Klare, 2011, pp. 7-8)

B. The Author's Name *Is* Stated in the Text

21. One Author Stated in Text

MLA: According to Elliott, the rising whooping crane population has encountered several "life-threatening setbacks" (47).

For APA, use *p.* plus page number for quoted words but also specific but unquoted references to a text.

APA: Elliott (2012) shows that the rising whooping crane population has encountered several "life-threatening setbacks" (p. 47).

22. Two or More Sources by Same Author Stated in Text

For MLA, use a short version of title in citation to distinguish source from author's other works.

MLA: The newest models, argues Dvorsky, will be "accessible from your cell phone" ("Appliances" 26).

For APA, if more than one publication by author in the same year, letter the sources in the citation and in References.

APA: A current projection (Dvorsky, 2012a) claims that the newest models will be "accessible from your cell phone" (p. 26).

23. Two Authors Stated in Text (MLA)

MLA: A pioneering study by Harkins and Stafford explores how nineteenth-century artist William Daniell undertook a series of sketching voyages around the coast of Great Britain to gain admittance to the Royal Academy (18).

24. **Two Authors Stated in Text (APA)**

Use *and* and not *&* in-text.

APA: A pioneering study by <mark>Harkins and Stafford (1997)</mark> explores how nineteenth-century artist William Daniell undertook a series of sketching voyages around the coast of Great Britain to gain admittance to the Royal Academy.

25. **Three or More Authors Stated in Text (MLA)**

Use the first author plus *et al.* (without italics).

MLA: <mark>Bobbs et al.</mark> claim that passing a single-payer system will cause a dramatic fall in insurance costs (<mark>184-86</mark>).

26. **Three to Five Authors Stated in Text (APA)**

List all authors in first citation; in later citations, use first author plus *et al.* (without italics).

APA: <mark>Bobbs, Fitch, Gunderman, and Hernandez (2005)</mark> claim that passing a single-payer system will cause a dramatic fall in insurance costs.

and

APA: According to the study by <mark>Bobbs et al. (2005)</mark>, the single-payer system has been successfully instituted in Massachusetts.

27. **Six or More Authors Stated in Text (APA)**

APA: An investigation by <mark>Henshaw et al. (2010)</mark> of Milwaukee's redlining has revealed a sordid history of racial intolerance.

28. **An Organization as Group Author Stated in Text**

MLA: The <mark>World Health Organization</mark> has published a study demonstrating that malnutrition has ravaged the sub-Saharan continent (<mark>43</mark>).

For APA, in first citation, spell out group author with parenthetical abbreviation (WHO); in later citations, abbreviate: WHO (2008).

APA: The <mark>World Health Organization</mark> (WHO) has published a study (<mark>2008</mark>) demonstrating that malnutrition has ravaged the sub-Saharan continent.

29. **Two or More Separate Sources Stated in Text**

For both MLA and APA, separate with semicolon.

MLA: <mark>The dissertation by Claussen and the book by McBride and Peters</mark> simultaneously point out that Ned Rorem made "major creative breakthroughs" while living in Africa (<mark>313; 128</mark>).

For APA, in parenthetical citation, use *&* instead of *and* when referring to paired authors.

APA: <mark>The dissertation by Claussen (2011) and the book by McBride and Peters (2011)</mark> simultaneously point out that Ned Rorem made "major creative breakthroughs" while living in Africa (<mark>p. 313; p. 128</mark>).

30. **Nonprint (Web, etc.) Author Stated in Text**

    Cite page number if using a PDF format; otherwise, identify according to available identifiers:

    For MLA, author or title and/or section (*sec.* or *secs.*) or paragraph number (*par.* or *pars.*) following a heading.

    MLA: <mark>"Great Depression Games"</mark> reminds us that Monopoly is no doubt Parker Brothers' most famous game from the 1930s (<mark>Parker Brothers heading, par. 6</mark>).

    For APA, author or title and/or section (*section* or *sections*) or paragraph number (*para.* or *paras.*) following a heading.

    APA: <mark>"Great Depression Games" (2012)</mark> reminds us that Monopoly is no doubt Parker Brothers' most famous game from the 1930s (<mark>Parker Brothers heading, para. 6</mark>).

31. **Lecture or Public Presentation Author Stated in Text**

    For both MLA and APA, if more than one lecture or presentation, use identifying date.

    MLA: <mark>Dr. Baldridge</mark> claims that Istanbul as a source of romantic imagery has made its way into a number of spy novels (<mark>9 Sept. 2012</mark>).

    APA: <mark>Dr. Baldridge</mark> (<mark>lecture, 2012, September 9</mark>) claims that Istanbul as a source of romantic imagery has made its way into a number of spy novels.

32. **Personal Interview, Telephone Interview, or E-mail Author Stated in Text**

    For MLA, if more than one communication from same source, use identifying date.

    MLA: To summarize <mark>Stanton-Crosby</mark>, significant advances have been made in treating macular degeneration with blood-vessel inhibitors (<mark>24 June 2009</mark>).

For APA, any nonretrievable source like e-mail or personal interview is cited within the text but not included in References. Identify as *personal communication* (no italics) with date.

APA: To summarize C.K. Stanton-Crosby (personal communication, June 24, 2009), significant advances have been made in treating macular degeneration with blood-vessel inhibitors.

33. **Republished Author Stated in Text**

For MLA and APA, with a text that has gone through many editions, give the page number of the text consulted but also a chapter, part, or line number.

MLA: In *Gulliver's Travels*, Swift tells how Gulliver says of a farmer whom he encounters, "[He] by this time was convinced I must be a rationale Creature" (87; pt. 2, ch. 1).

For APA, with a text that has gone through many editions, also give first publication date as well as date of text consulted. (Abbreviate *Part* but not *Chapter*.)

APA: In *Gulliver's Travels*, Swift (1735/1976) tells how Gulliver says of a farmer whom he encounters, "[He] by this time was convinced I must be a rationale Creature" (Pt. 2, Chapter 1, p. 87).

34. **Author of Multivolume Work Stated in Text**

For MLA, give both volume and page number (don't write *volume* or *page*).

MLA: We are told by Stanley, "Among our Egyptians there was one called Ali Effendi, a captain, who complained of heart disease" (2: 226).

For APA, give both volume and page number (but write *Vol.* and *p.*).

APA: We are told by Stanley (1890), "Among our Egyptians there was one called Ali Effendi, a captain, who complained of heart disease" (Vol. 2, p. 226).

35. **Author in Anthology Stated in Text**

MLA: Whittington's "Swamp Search" is typical of the crime stories published in *The Black Lizard Anthology of Crime* for pulp lines like "She had me all clobbered, but I wanted her worse than ever" (33).

For APA, with a text that has gone through many editions, also give first publication date as well as date of text consulted.

APA: Whittington's "Swamp Search" (1957/1987) is typical of the crime stories published in *The Black Lizard Anthology of Crime* for pulp lines like "She had me all clobbered, but I wanted her worse than ever"(p. 33).

36. **Unknown Author Stated in Text**

   MLA: "Nursing Home Laws Needed" blows the whistle on how the nursing home industry often escapes "rigorous oversight" (2).

   APA: "Nursing Home Laws Needed" (2009) blows the whistle on how the nursing home industry often escapes "rigorous oversight" (p. 2).

37. **A Religious Work (Bible, Qur'an, etc.): Unknown Author Stated in Text**

   For MLA and APA, use the edition/translation. Spell out names in text.

   MLA: Lamentations 5.10 gives the reader yet another metaphor: "Our skin is as hot as an oven with the burning heat of famine"(*The Holy Bible, New Revised Standard Version*).

   For APA, cite classical work like the Bible in the text but not in References; don't italicize.

   APA: Lamentations 5:10 (The Holy Bible, New Revised Standard Version) gives the reader yet another metaphor: "Our skin is as hot as an oven with the burning heat of famine."

38. **An Indirect Source: Author Stated in Text**

   For MLA and APA, give page number in parentheses. Do not abbreviate *quoted.*

   MLA: As quoted in Murray, Hamwell often insists that, in the words of the famous Irish playwright, "I can resist everything except temptation" (334).

   APA: As cited in Murray (1982), Hamwell often insists that, in the words of the famous Irish playwright, "I can resist everything except temptation" (p. 334).

39. **Encyclopedia or Other Reference Book: Author Stated in Text**

   For both MLA and APA, if the reference book doesn't provide the author of an entry, use entry title ("Lemon").

   MLA: The history note on "Lemon" on the etymology of the word reveals the tree's origins in the Middle East.

   APA: The history note on "Lemon" (1992) on the etymology of the word reveals the tree's origins in the Middle East.

40. A Long Quotation: Author Stated in Text

For MLA, set off quotations longer than four typed lines:

- indent *one-half inch* from flush left
- double-space
- don't use quotation marks unless the passage quotes a quotation
- don't indent the first line unless (1) the passage is longer than one paragraph and (2) the first paragraph in the original is indented
- indent each new paragraph *one-fourth inch*
- place a period at the end of the quotation, and then one space after, type the parenthetical citation: page number (no period follows)

> Klare notes that historians will credit Algeria for the recent unrest in the Middle East:
>
> > On January 5, young protestors in Algiers, Oran, and other major cities blocked roads, attacked police stations and burned stores in demonstrations against soaring food prices. Other concerns–high unemployment, pervasive corruption, lack of housing–also aroused their ire, but food costs provided the original impulse. As the epicenter of youthful protest moved elsewhere . . . the food price issue was subordinated . . . but it never disappeared. (7-8)

For APA, set off quotations forty words or more:

- indent *one-half inch* from flush left
- double-space
- don't use quotation marks unless the passage quotes a quotation
- indent each new paragraph one more *one-half inch*
- place a period at the end of the quotation, and then one space after, type the parenthetical citation: page number (no period follows)

> Klare (2011) notes that historians will credit Algeria for the recent unrest in the Middle East:
>
> > On January 5, young protestors in Algiers, Oran, and other major cities blocked roads, attacked police stations and burned stores in demonstrations against soaring food prices. Other concerns–high unemployment, pervasive corruption, lack of housing–also aroused their ire, but food costs provided the original impulse. As the epicenter of youthful protest moved elsewhere . . . the food price issue was subordinated . . . but it never disappeared. (pp. 7-8)

HOW TO FORMAT THE BIBLIOGRAPHY: WORKS CITED (MLA) AND REFERENCES (APA)

PAGE FORMAT

MLA

1. Start the bibliography section (*Works Cited*) on a new page one inch from the top.

2. Center the words *Works Cited* (don't italicize or underline; use normal capitalization; don't put a period after it). If you have only one source, then use the singular form: *Work Cited*.

3. Double-space throughout.

4. Use a hanging indent: for each entry, type the first line flush left; indent each succeeding line one-half inch.

5. Alphabetize each entry by last name; if no author, by first word of title (excluding *A*, *An*, *The*).

APA

1. Start the bibliography section (*References*) on a new page one inch from the top.

2. Center the word *References* (don't italicize or underline; use normal capitalization; don't put a period after it). If you have only one source, then use the singular form: *Reference*.

3. Double-space throughout.

4. Use a hanging indent: for each entry, type the first line flush left; indent each succeeding line one-half inch.

5. Alphabetize each entry by last name; if no author, by first word of title (excluding *A*, *An*, *The*).

WARNING: MLA and APA format each entry in very different ways. Do not mix styles.

ENTRY FORMAT

MLA

One author
Last name, First name, Middle initial. (*Use middle initial if stated.*)
Smith, John J.

Two authors

Last name, First name, Middle initial, and First name Middle initial Last name.

Smith, John J., and Mary R. Smith. (*Use comma.*)

Three or more authors

Last name, First name, et al. (*Use* et al. *or list all names.*)

Titles: Books, journals, magazines, newspapers, Web sites (*Capitalize the first letter of all words except the following unless they start or conclude a title:* **the, a, an**; *prepositions:* **at, by, between**, *etc.; these conjunctions:* **for, and, nor, but, or, yet, so**; *and* **to** *in infinitives* [**The Way to Win**].)

Book title: Subtitle (*Italicize.*)

The Warming of the Planet: A Guide to Climate Change

Titles: Book chapters, articles, Web pages (*Capitalize the first letter of all words except the following unless they start or conclude a title:* **the, a, an**; *prepositions:* **at, by, between**, *etc.; these conjunctions:* **for, and, nor, but, or, yet, so**; *and* **to** *in infinitives.*)

Article title: Subtitle (*Use quotation marks.*)

"The Slow Death of the Planet: And Then What?"

Publisher

Use short form of publisher: *UP* **for university presses and first word of multiple names.**

Farrar *(Farrar, Straus and Giroux, Inc.)*

Gale *(Gale Research, Inc.)*

Knopf *(Alfred A. Knopf, Inc.)*

CAL *(Center for Applied Linguistics)*

UP of Mississippi *(University Press of Mississippi)*

U of Chicago P *(University of Chicago Press)*

Scribner's *(Charles Scribner's Sons)*

Norton *(W. W. Norton and Co., Inc.)*

APA

One author
Last name, First initial., Middle initial. (*Use middle initial if stated.*)
Smith, J. J.

Two to seven authors
Last name, First initial., Middle initial., and Last name, First initial., Middle initial.
Smith, J. J., & Smith, M. (*Use comma and ampersand [&].*)
Smith, J. J., Smith, M., & Jones, P.

Eight or more authors
Smith, J. J., Smith, M., Smith, R. J., Smith, P., Smith, A. C., Smith, B. T., . . . Jones, B. (*List first six authors, ellipsis, last author.*)

Group author
World Health Organization

Titles: Books, book chapters, articles, Web articles, Web pages (*Capitalize only the first word and proper nouns in titles and subtitles; capitalize book volume numbers.*)
Book title: Subtitle (*Italicize.*)
The warming of the planet: A guide to climate change (Vol. 1)
Article title: Subtitle (*Don't italicize or use quotation marks.*)
The slow death of the planet: And then what?

Titles: Journals, magazines, newspapers; Web sites, online journals, online newspapers, reference databases (*Capitalize the first letter of all words except the following unless they start or conclude a title:* **the, a, an,** *prepositions, and these conjunctions:* **for, and, nor, but, or, yet, so.**)
Journal Title (*Italicize.*)
The Journal of Social Media

Place of publication
For nonperiodicals, use first city stated on title page, comma, state postal abbreviation. (*Follow with a colon.*)
Boston, MA: Harvard University Press
Omit state with a university press that uses a state name.
Columbia: University of South Carolina Press
If publisher is located outside the United States, give country. (*Follow with a colon.*)
Dublin, Ireland: University College Dublin Press

Publisher

Use short form of publisher (leave out *Inc.*, *Co.*, etc.) but write out *Books* and
Press.

WARNING: MLA omits a digit in consecutive page numbering: 213-15; 789-91. APA retains the digit: 213-215; 789-791.

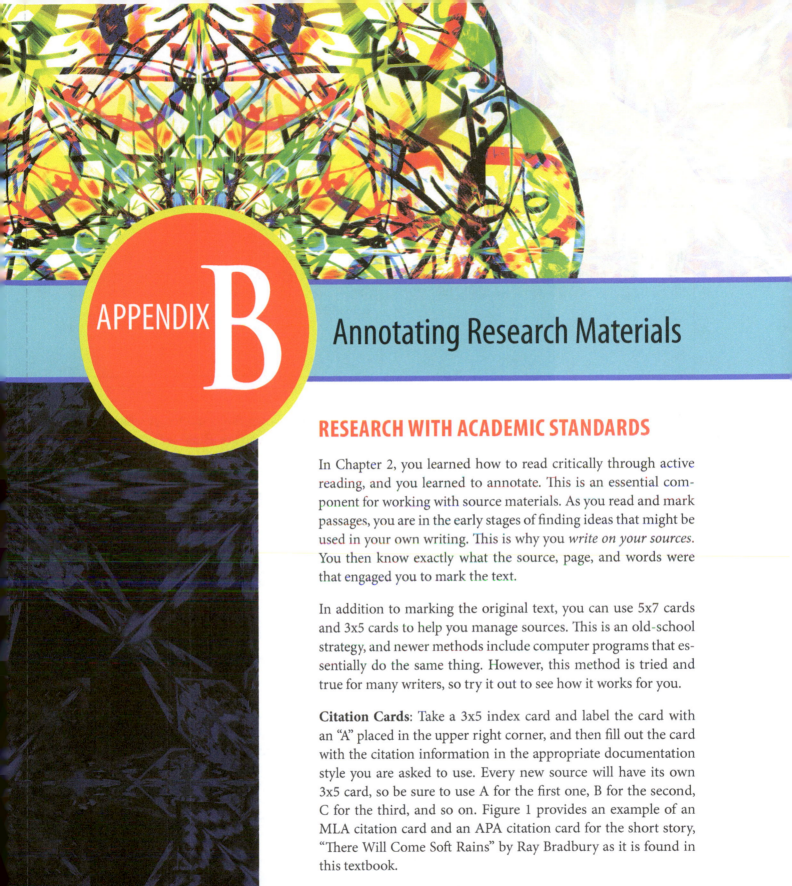

RESEARCH WITH ACADEMIC STANDARDS

In Chapter 2, you learned how to read critically through active reading, and you learned to annotate. This is an essential component for working with source materials. As you read and mark passages, you are in the early stages of finding ideas that might be used in your own writing. This is why you *write on your sources*. You then know exactly what the source, page, and words were that engaged you to mark the text.

In addition to marking the original text, you can use 5x7 cards and 3x5 cards to help you manage sources. This is an old-school strategy, and newer methods include computer programs that essentially do the same thing. However, this method is tried and true for many writers, so try it out to see how it works for you.

Citation Cards: Take a 3x5 index card and label the card with an "A" placed in the upper right corner, and then fill out the card with the citation information in the appropriate documentation style you are asked to use. Every new source will have its own 3x5 card, so be sure to use A for the first one, B for the second, C for the third, and so on. Figure 1 provides an example of an MLA citation card and an APA citation card for the short story, "There Will Come Soft Rains" by Ray Bradbury as it is found in this textbook.

Example of a 3x5 citation card.

MLA	APA
A	A

Bradbury, Ray. "There Will Come Soft Rains." *Kaleidoscope: Shaping Language, Shaping Identity,* edited by Deborah M. Scaggs, Kendall Hunt, 2019. 165–170.

Bradbury, R. (2019). There will come soft rains. In D. M. Scaggs (Ed.), *Kaleidoscope: Shaping language, shaping identity* (pp. 165–170). Dubuque, IA: Kendall Hunt.

NOTECARDS: Use a 5x7 index card to write down direct quotes, paraphrases, or summaries that you are getting from the source you are using. In the upper right-hand corner, place the letter from the 3x5 card that corresponds with the source you are using. Place the page number(s) in the lower right-hand corner. Figure 2 provides an example of a "direct quote" and a "paraphrase."

Examples of 5x7 notecards.

Direct Quote	Paraphrase
A	A

"The five spots of paint—the man, the woman, the children, the ball—remained. The rest was a thin charcoaled layer."

p. 166

After the nuclear explosion, all that is left of humanity are these painted remnants, showing the ultimate destructive power of technology.

p. 166

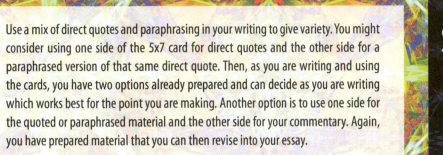

Use a mix of direct quotes and paraphrasing in your writing to give variety. You might consider using one side of the 5x7 card for direct quotes and the other side for a paraphrased version of that same direct quote. Then, as you are writing and using the cards, you have two options already prepared and can decide as you are writing which works best for the point you are making. Another option is to use one side for the quoted or paraphrased material and the other side for your commentary. Again, you have prepared material that you can then revise into your essay.

This tells you which source you will need to cite in your essay. As you build up your sources and develop a set of quotes, ideas, concepts from your sources, you will begin to have a stack of 5x7 cards. You can rearrange the order of these cards to fit into or help you revise your preliminary outline, which will help you to structure what you want to cite, when, and how.

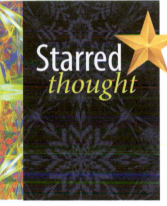

If you have six sources (A, B, C, D, E, and F), you might have a stack of 5x7 cards that start with a quote from source C on top, followed by any combination of sources. You might have two direct quotes from C, one concept from B, one paraphrase from C, another direct quote from F, and so on. As you insert quotes into your writing, you will look at the upper right-hand corner to recall the source. After quote from C, you insert the in-text citation information from the 3x5 card labeled C. Continue to do this as you write with all of your source material. This is an easy, inexpensive method for keeping your research straight, accurate, and ethical!

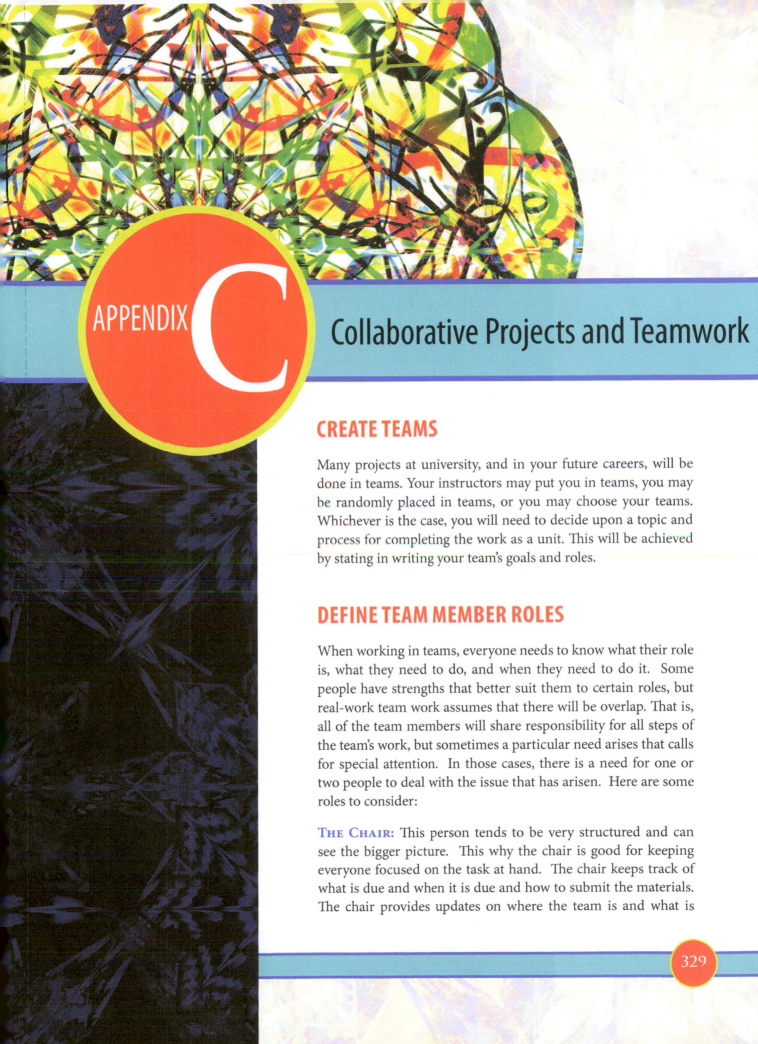

APPENDIX **C**

Collaborative Projects and Teamwork

CREATE TEAMS

Many projects at university, and in your future careers, will be done in teams. Your instructors may put you in teams, you may be randomly placed in teams, or you may choose your teams. Whichever is the case, you will need to decide upon a topic and process for completing the work as a unit. This will be achieved by stating in writing your team's goals and roles.

DEFINE TEAM MEMBER ROLES

When working in teams, everyone needs to know what their role is, what they need to do, and when they need to do it. Some people have strengths that better suit them to certain roles, but real-work team work assumes that there will be overlap. That is, all of the team members will share responsibility for all steps of the team's work, but sometimes a particular need arises that calls for special attention. In those cases, there is a need for one or two people to deal with the issue that has arisen. Here are some roles to consider:

THE CHAIR: This person tends to be very structured and can see the bigger picture. This why the chair is good for keeping everyone focused on the task at hand. The chair keeps track of what is due and when it is due and how to submit the materials. The chair provides updates on where the team is and what is

329

coming up next. The chair participates in all stages of the process, but when someone has a question about the process and schedule, the chair is the "go-to" person.

THE NOTE-TAKER: The note-taker participates in team discussions, but because s/he is good at capturing what others are saying while they say it, s/he is ideal for jotting down the notes and sharing them with the team. During team discussions, the note-taker literally writes down the ideas and questions the team has so that they can be reviewed later. The note-taker allows the speakers not to worry about remembering what was said or trying to think, speak, and write at the same time.

THE EDITOR: All team member contribute their portion of the writing, but the one who is the strongest at catching mistakes and errors is good at final editing. This does not mean that the other members do not participate in the editing process. Rather, what it does mean is that the editor's strength is catching the nitty-gritty details, and the editor likes to do it! The editor helps the team to polish and finalize the project's final product.

THE TECHY: The person who usually takes the reins here is the one who is strongest at figuring out how to insert images into a Word document, manipulate or modify charts, or incorporate digital files (in composing a multi-media text). They are tech-savvy and know how to use technology to the team's benefit.

THE RESEARCHER: All members of the team will contribute their part of the research. This role, however, is specifically reserved for when all the research seems to be done, but then there suddenly arises a gap in the final product that needs to be closed. (This could happen during the drafting stage when peer-reviewers notice there is a missing element in the writing.) The Researcher is then tasked with finding the needed research/sources for the project while the other team members continue with the writing portion. When the research is located and shared, the researcher's task is complete and returns to the normal role of the writer alongside the other team members.

If your team comes up with other roles, be sure to define what that role entails and what is expected from them.

Starred *thought*

Remember that team members are not relegated only to one role. There are times when a specific role is needed for a specific purpose or time-frame. After that need is met or time frame has elapsed, the role recedes into the background until needed again.

DEVELOP A TIMELINE FOR PROJECT

Start from the end. When is the project due? How long will it take to complete the project? Then, build back from there.

Use an actual calendar, electronic or paper, that sets you up for success. Assign due dates for the activities below in light of how long you have to complete the project. Do you have an entire semester or only a few weeks? If you have an entire semester, then the expectation is that you will have a very complex project that will require more sources and more analysis than one that only takes two weeks, so plan accordingly.

DEVELOP A TEAM CONTRACT

A team **contract** is a document that lays out all that the team needs to know in order to function. All members must contribute to its development so that all members know exactly what is expected of them. You will share this document with me and the members of your team. Once teams are established, you will develop a contract that will help to shape the goals you and your team members will accomplish.

1. The Team Members: *Who* are the team members?

   This may sound silly, but how many times have you forgotten your class-mate's name? Also, the projects you will be working on may or may not be familiar to some members, or the project might need some kind of expertise that a member may have and be able to contribute the whole team. Knowing something about the members' background will help the team make de-cisions about how to function. You also need to consider whether or not any of the team members live outside of Laredo. Do they have full-time/part-time jobs? Do they have families? All of these things—and perhaps others—need to be discussed so that both the individual and the team as a whole work out how to get things done.

2. Assigning Roles: What Am I Supposed To Do?

   Your team will need to identify what the roles will be for each team mem-ber, keeping in mind that roles sometimes overlap. Write these down so that everyone has a reference for what is expected.

3. Making Contact, Part I: *How* will you contact each other? (Ex. F2F (face-to-face), e-mail, Skype, chat, etc.)

   All members need to be able to contact each other by some method or a combination of methods. You will need to discuss this and define how you will work together.

4. Making Contact, Part II: *When* will you contact each other? Specify days and times.

Yes, you need a calendar. Using your phone's calendar is fine, but ALL members need to know what the days/times are. The calendar should be used to record the agreed upon meeting dates and method of communication in addition to any deadlines you establish for getting the project done.

Starred *thought*

If you or your team members are taking a class online or someone cannot make a meeting for some legitimate reason, then you may not always be able to meet F2F, so what CAN you do? The members must accommodate the team's needs. It is a back-and-forth negotiation. Once the plan is set, however, it should be carried out as explained in the contract. (The only exception would be if a serious illness or death in the family forces someone to have to renegotiate, and the team needs to inform the instructor of such situations.)

5. Goal Setting: What are we going to do?

The team needs to establish what goals they will have for each project and what the deadlines are for each component of that project. For example, if a project is two weeks long, what should each member have completed by Day 5? Day 10? Day 14?

6. Firing Members: What Do We Do with the Losers, the Wimps, and the Down-Right Lazy?

You will need to brainstorm about what the potential problems might be when working as a team on the give project, list them on the contract, and then explain what the penalty should be for each. Consider just as an example that if the team agrees to meeting F2F on Sundays from 1-3, and one team member shows up at 2, the penalty might be that s/he should lose 1 or 2 points off the final project grade.

Starred *thought*

A team can not simply fire or kick-off a member from the team. Only the instructor will be able to do this. For this to happen, both sides would need to provide documentation for why the group is dysfunctional and has been unable to resolve the conflict. After reviewing the case, the instructor will make the final call.

SUBMIT THE CONTRACT

Once you have made initial contact and have set-up a time and method of continued communication, you will then work on the contract and submit it to your instructor for the record. Your team has full rights to design the contract, yet the team should keep in mind that this is a formal document.

TEAMWORK GROUP LOG

Here is a log for you and your team members to keep track of several aspects of group work: number of times the team met, when, who participated, what work was identified as the meeting's goal, and what actually was accomplished. This chart is intended to help you manage your time and complete activities needed for team projects. Use or add as many rows as you deem necessary for the given project.

Teamwork Group Log

Team Name: _____   Course/Section: _____

Meeting #	Date/Time	Attendees	Goal for the Meeting	Completed Tasks
1				
2				
3				
4				
5				
6				

Meeting #	Date/ Time	Attendees	Goal for the Meeting	Completed Tasks
7				
8				
9				
10				
11				
12				

APPENDIX D

Approaches to Ethics

ETHICAL APPROACHES TO ETHICAL DILEMMAS

When examining ethics, there are many formal approaches housed in the discipline of Philosophy. The *Stanford Encyclopedia of Philosophy* or *Internet Encyclopedia of Philosophy* (IEP) websites offer excellent information about the multitude of various approaches to ethics or moral philosophy. Kurt Mosser offers an introduction to ethics and some of the more common approaches.

*HOW SHOULD ONE ACT?

Ethics, or moral philosophy, investigates how we can evaluate our behavior in terms of right and wrong, good and bad—in short, how we determine what we should do, what we should not do, and how to tell the difference. After looking at the three classical ethical views philosophers have presented, and some of the problems with each of those theories, we will look at some alternative approaches to those traditional views.

*From *Introduction to Philosophy* by Kurt Mosser. Copyright © 2010 by BridgePoint Education, Inc. Reprinted by permission.

UTILITARIANISM

You and five of your friends are hanging out one night and decide to order a pizza. You are all equally hungry, and decide to order two pizzas, each of which has six slices. Thus, when the pizzas are delivered, it is pretty easy to determine how to divide the pizzas in a way that is the fairest: Everyone gets two slices of pizza. Someone may have wanted a third slice, of course, and is not entirely satisfied; someone may have not wanted a second slice, and may think the solution is not the most efficient. But without knowing anything else, we see that the greatest number of people here will be made the best off if we decide that everyone gets two slices of pizza, instead of any other arrangement.

This simple example is the basic notion at the heart of the ethical doctrine of **utilitarianism.** Often associated with the philosophers Jeremy Bentham (1748–1822) and John Stuart Mill (1806–1873), utilitarianism, at least at first, offers a very straightforward and direct way to evaluate behavior. If given a choice between two acts, and one of them creates greater happiness for the greatest number of people, then that is the act that should be chosen. Philosophers, and economists, often use the term **utility** to express this idea (which is, of course, why this view is called utilitarianism). One's utility is the satisfaction one gets from something: For instance, you may like chocolate ice cream more than vanilla ice cream, so we can say that chocolate ice cream has a higher utility for you, relative to vanilla ice cream. In theory, at least, a person can rank all of his or her choices, and thus has a scale of things that show which things he or she prefers, relative to others. Some philosophers, such as Bentham, even attempted to put numbers on these preferences: So, for instance, if one likes chocolate ice cream five times as much as vanilla ice cream, that person would, presumably, be willing to accept five vanilla ice cream cones as a substitute for one chocolate ice cream cone.

Because utilitarianism considers the consequences of an act in figuring out whether it is a moral thing to do, utilitarianism is also regarded as a **consequentialist** theory. The basic idea, again, is to look at the choices one confronts: If the consequences of one act produces the greatest good—or the highest utility—for the greatest number of people, that is the act one should carry out. Many people find this to be rather obvious as an ethical viewpoint; clearly if we had decided to give all the slices of pizza to just three people and no pizza to the other three, this would seem to be a rather unfair solution! It should also be clear that utilitarianism offers an approach to things other than pizza and ice cream. Imagine Mary really loves to go dancing, and she doesn't get to go dancing very often. Mary has three children, with whom she enjoys spending time and who enjoy spending time with her. One night she is given the option of staying home and spending time with her children or going dancing; what should she do? The utilitarian might well argue that the pleasure Mary gets from dancing is greater in this case than staying with her children, but that if one also factors in the pleasure her children will receive if she does not go dancing, then the "utility calculation" becomes clear. The total happiness of Mary and her three children will be higher if she stays home, although Mary's individual happiness might be a bit lower. This calculation then suggests that what Mary should do, given these two choices, is to stay home; that way, she is fairly happy, and her children are fairly happy, and this consequence produces the greatest good for the greatest number.

DEONTOLOGY

Deontological ethics—"deontology" comes from the Greek word for "obligation" (or "duty")—is usually associated with the philosopher Immanuel Kant. In contrast to consequentialist theories, Kant, and more generally the deontologist, ignores the consequences of an act in evaluating whether it is a good act, a bad act, or a morally neutral act. It is important to remember that deontologists do not deny that acts have consequences; their point is that those consequences should not play a role in evaluating the morality of the act. Rather, deontological ethics focuses on the will of the person carrying out the act in question, his or her intention in carrying it out, and, particularly, the rule according to which the act is carried out. Deontology, then, focuses on the duties and obligations one has in carrying out those actions (rather than on the consequences of those actions).

Kant claimed that certain kinds of rules established what he called a **categorical imperative** (Kant, 1997). This is a requirement, or demand (which is why it is an imperative), and it has no exceptions (which is why he calls it "categorical"). We might contrast this kind of imperative with what Kant calls a "hypothetical imperative." For instance, if you are hungry, you decide to eat something: In that case, the action (eating) is designed to achieve a goal (making you less hungry). But there is no obligation or demand that you eat; it is just what you do in this specific situation. The categorical imperative, on the other hand, has no exceptions, is something one must do, and never depends on the details of the situation. Kant assumes, as do most moral philosophers, that being a moral person is something that is good to do; we don't, that is, really regard it as a goal one might or might not adopt.

These rules can seem pretty abstract, but a very famous and very old rule—the Golden Rule—captures much of what deontology is all about. The Golden Rule is quite ancient, and can be found in many different civilizations beginning with the ancient Egyptians and the ancient Greeks, as well as in many religions, including Buddhism, Christianity, Judaism, and Islam. What is probably the best-known version comes from the Christian Bible: "Do unto others as you would have them do unto you." In other words, if you don't like being stolen from, you shouldn't steal from others; if you don't like being a victim of violence, don't act violently toward others. You don't want to be treated by others as simply some kind of "thing," so you yourself shouldn't treat others that way. This last claim is, more or less, what Kant provides as the second version of the categorical imperative we just saw.

VIRTUE ETHICS

"Virtue ethics" is a term philosophers use to refer to a particular approach to moral and ethical questions that focuses on the character of the person. Some discussions of the idea can be found in Plato, as well as in such Chinese philosophers as Confucius; however, the classic conception of virtue ethics in Western philosophy is attributed to Aristotle. The virtuous person, or the person of virtuous character, is, for Aristotle, that person who has the appropriate virtues and has them in a way that is balanced and harmonious. Thus, a person who is virtuous will have many of the characteristics we admire, while keeping them in balance. This person won't have too little or too much of any one virtue, and they will all be appropriately related to each other.

Some of these are traditional characteristics that we still use to describe a good or moral or virtuous person. Aristotle's list includes courage, generosity, and friendliness. For Aristotle, all such virtues have their excesses in two different directions: One may, for instance, have too little courage, which we would call cowardice. Another person may have too much courage and also act badly by being too rash. A soldier who runs from the field of battle when first confronting the enemy might not have enough courage, whereas the soldier who runs straight into machine-gun fire may have too much. Aristotle insists that the virtuous person will have the right amount of courage, not too little, not too much, and will aim at what he calls the **Golden Mean** between having too little and having too much of any of the virtues. So one may be moderately generous, and thus virtuous, whereas one who has too little generosity may be regarded as a cheapskate or stingy, and one who has too much generosity might be regarded as being a spendthrift or wasteful.

ETHICAL EGOISM

"Ego" comes from the Greek word for "I." We probably know someone about whom it is said "he has a big ego": that is, a person who has an exaggerated sense of just how great he is. Egoism, then, is the idea that the focus is on one's self. Hence, **ethical egoism** is the idea that one's conception of right and wrong, good and evil, and other moral terms, is to be determined by one's own sense of value. To return to utility, a notion we saw earlier, we could describe this as the position that one should do what maximizes one's own utility. In short, I should do what is in my self-interest. This is a theory that is, in the most literal sense, "selfish." But unlike other, more traditional moral theories, selfishness is not seen as wrong, or immoral, but how one should in fact act—out of self-interest.

To return to the example we've used before: A group of children are playing in a sandbox, and have access to only one toy. Cherita, the ethical egoist—who we will just call the egoist from now on—determines that what makes her happiest, or maximizes her utility, is to have the toy to herself. Thus, it is in Cherita's self-interest to get the toy, keep the toy, and play with the toy all by herself. This isn't, however, the only result possible. It may be that she decides that she would get more out of it if everyone shared, or, for that matter, if only one other person got to play with the toy. If she concludes that some other option is in her self-interest, then she should adopt that choice. So we can see that the crucial thing in this case isn't that Cherita gets the toy to herself; it is that what she perceives as making her best off will be what she should do.

We also had an example earlier that will provide a contrast to the ethical egoist and the utilitarian. We saw Mary trying to decide whether to go dancing or stay home with her three children. Factoring in the happiness of Mary and the three children, the utilitarian argued that everyone would be best off—producing the greatest good for the greatest number—if Mary stayed home. The egoist might conclude otherwise: If Mary sees her greatest happiness achieved by going out dancing, then she should go out dancing. Again, Mary may conclude that it would make her happiest to stay home. The egoist's position is that what Mary should do is whatever Mary sees as in her self-interest.

CONCEPT REVIEW: THEORIES AND THEORISTS

Ethical Theory	Key Figure	Basic Idea
Utilitarianism	J.S. Mill	An act (or rule) is good or right if it produces the greatest good for the greatest number.
Deontology	Immanuel Kant	An act is good or right if it is done because it is the right thing to do, in accordance with a justified moral rule or rules.
Virtue ethics	Aristotle	Morality is determined on the basis of specific virtues, exemplified by a person of noble or virtuous character.
Ethical Egoism		What is ethical is determined by what is the best interest of the self.

After studying the basic ethical approaches, read the following articles so that you can see what kinds of ethics are at work. There may be more than one approach, too.

IS HUMILIATION AN ETHICALLY APPROPRIATE RESPONSE TO PLAGIARISM?

by Loye Young

I'm a business owner in Laredo, Texas. I had never taught a college course before, and I never asked to teach. The department asked me to teach this course. I accepted because of my commitment to Laredo's future.

Copyright © 2008 by Loye Young. Reprinted by permission.

I worked hard on the syllabus, and everything in the syllabus was deliberate. Specifically, the language about dishonesty was based on moral and pedagogical principles. The department chairman, Dr. Balaji Janamanchi, reviewed the syllabus with me line-by-line, and I made a few changes in response to his comments.

I was surprised by how common and blatant plagiarism turned out to be. Six students in one class is an extraordinarily high number. I thought and prayed about what to do for about a week before following through on my promise. I decided I had only one moral choice. I am certain it was right.

My decision was guided by two factors: What is good for the students themselves? and What is good for other students?

What is good for the students themselves?

I am cognizant of extraordinary moral difficulty involved when deciding what is in another's best interests. Nonetheless, I am convinced that public disclosure, including the concomitant humiliation, is in the interests of the student because it is the best way to teach the student about the consequences of dishonesty and discourage the student from plagiarizing again. Humiliation is inextricably part of a well-formed conscience.

The Vice President-elect, Senator Joseph Biden, is perhaps the most well-known plagiarizer in recent history. Biden was caught plagiarizing while at Syracuse Law School. The school gave him an F, required him to retake the course, and subsequently treated the incident as confidential.

Unfortunately, Biden didn't learn his lesson at law school. He continued to plagiarize for another 20 years. During the 1988 presidential campaign, Senator Biden's career of plagiarizing came to light, and he was forced to end his presidential bid.

It is my belief that the Syracuse incident left a subtle and subliminal message in Biden's mind: plagiarism is not a deal breaker. Consequently, he continued to plagiarize. Unfortunately for the Senator, the facts came to public light at the worst possible time: when he was running for President.

I believe that had the Syracuse incident been available publicly, Mr. Biden would have actually learned his lesson and would not have plagiarized later. Twenty years later, if the incident had come up at all, the Senator would have plausibly and convincingly maintained that the incident was a youthful mistake.

There is yet another reason for publicity in such cases: unjustly accused students are protected, for two reasons. One, a professor will be more careful before blowing the whistle. I myself knew that posting the students' names would be appropriately subject to intense public scrutiny. Therefore, I construed every ambiguity in the students' favor. Two, public disclosure ensures that subsequent determinations by the I university are founded on evidence and dispensed fairly.

What is good for other students?

On the second question, four reasons convince me: deterrents, fairness, predictability, and preparedness for life.

Deterrents—Only if everyone knows that violations of plagiarism will be exposed and punished will the penalties for plagiarism be an effective deterrent. (As a lawyer once told me after hearing of another lawyer's disbarment, "I'm damn sure not going to do THAT again!") In fact, one of the six students had not plagiarized (to my knowledge) until the week before I announced my findings. Had I announced the plagiarism earlier, it is possible that student would not have plagiarized at all.

Fairness—Honest students should have, in fairness, the knowledge that their legitimate work is valued more than a plagiarizer's illegitimate work. In my course, the students were required to post their essays on a public website for all to see. Thus, anyone in the world could have detected the plagiarism. Had another student noticed the plagiarism but saw no action, the honest student would reasonably believe that the process is unfair.

Predictability—By failing publicly to follow through on ubiquitous warnings about plagiarism, universities have convinced students that the purported indignation against deceit is itself deceitful and that the entire process is capricious. TAMIU's actions in this case have confirmed my suspicions that such a perception is entirely justified.

Preparedness for life—In the real world, deceitful actions have consequences, and those consequences are often public. Borrowers lose credit ratings, employees get fired, spouses divorce, businesses fail, political careers end, and professionals go to jail. Acts of moral turpitude rightly carry public and humiliating consequences in real life, and students need to be prepared.

In closing, I submit that education died when educators came to believe that greater self-esteem leads to greater learning. In fact, the causality is backwards: self-esteem is the result of learning, not the cause.

CREDITS. Current URL is: http://www.adjunctnation.com/2008/11/01/64-is-humiliation-an-ethically-appropriate-response-to-plagiarism/

QUESTIONS TO CONSIDER:

What ethical dilemma(s) does Young's article raise?

Why are these considered "ethical dilemmas"?

Which of Mosser's approaches to ethics seems the most useful here in understanding the dilemma? Explain.

What alternative consequences might exist?

Are these more or less "ethical"? Explain.

Reflections on Writing

Name: _____ Course: _____ Date: _____

REFLECTIONS: MY WRITING PROCESS

How would you describe your overall writing process now compared to what you started with?

What old habits have you given up? Why?

What old habits have you kept? Why?

What new habits have you developed? How do they help you?

If you were to give a future student-writer some advice, what would you offer? Why?

Name: _____ Course: _____ Date: _____

POST-SURVEY

How much do you agree to the following statements? Circle the appropriate number following each statement.

5	4	3	2	1
Strongly Agree	Agree	Not sure	Disagree	Strongly Disagree

1	I am able to express my ideas clearly.	5	4	3	2	1
2	When I write, I am able to identify my purpose for writing.	5	4	3	2	1
3	When I write, I am able to identify the needs of my audience.	5	4	3	2	1
4	I am an active reader.	5	4	3	2	1
5	I can identify and use appropriate sources.	5	4	3	2	1
6	I give good, effective feedback to my peers.	5	4	3	2	1
7	I am a more confident writer now than when I entered this course.	5	4	3	2	1
8	I understand the concept of genre.	5	4	3	2	1
9	I want to write.	5	4	3	2	1
10	"Writing is a process" is concept that I appreciate.	5	4	3	2	1
11	Writing is easier for me now than when I started this course.	5	4	3	2	1
12	I am able to help my peers with their writing.	5	4	3	2	1
13	I can apply the rhetorical triangle to any writing situation.	5	4	3	2	1
14	I understand the "features of the form" concept.	5	4	3	2	1
15	I am a writer.	5	4	3	2	1
16	I use active reading strategies often.	5	4	3	2	1
17	I know how to do academic research.	5	4	3	2	1
18	I can identify errors in my writing.	5	4	3	2	1
19	I can correct errors in my writing.	5	4	3	2	1
20	I have adopted several new writing strategies.	5	4	3	2	1

APPENDIX **F**

Kaleidoscope Journal Writings

KALEIDOSCOPE JOURNAL # _11_ three images

Name: _____ Date: _____

KALEIDOSCOPE JOURNAL # _____

Name: _____ Date: _____

KALEIDOSCOPE JOURNAL # _____

Name: _____ Date: _____

KALEIDOSCOPE JOURNAL # _____

Name: _____ Date: _____

KALEIDOSCOPE JOURNAL # _____

Name: _____ Date: _____

KALEIDOSCOPE JOURNAL # _____

Name: _____ Date: _____

KALEIDOSCOPE JOURNAL # _____

Name: _____ Date: _____